BAUDRILLARD LIVE

This book collects together many interviews which have been published in very different locations and publications into a coherent work, which with new interviews and an introduction makes available the conversational thought of one of the leading French intellectuals associated with postmodernism. The scope of the interviews is enormous, from the experience of visiting the cinema, on film and photography, through to the Gulf War and the new world order. These interviews provide a peerless supplement to Baudrillard's often difficult sociological and theoretical writing and illuminate many points of contention in his work, particularly those relating to postmodernism.

But the book is far more than a supplement. It is in its own right a contribution of the highest importance to the analysis of modern society, and it raises many disturbing issues and problems. The collection is edited by a leading authority on Baudrillard's work. It will appeal not only to those interested in French intellectual life but also to those interested in the debate on modernity and postmodernity. It is an essential document for the understanding of one of the most creative and important French thinkers alive today.

Mike Gane is Senior Lecturer in Sociology at Loughborough University.

BAUDRILLARD LIVE

Selected interviews

Edited by Mike Gane

London and New York

First published in 1993
by Routledge
11 New Fetter Lane, London EC4P 4EE

Simultaneously published in the USA and Canada
by Routledge
29 West 35th Street, New York, NY 10001

© 1993 selection and editorial matter, Mike Gane

Phototypeset in 10pt Times by
Mews Photosetting, Beckenham, Kent
Printed in Great Britain by
T.J. Press (Padstow) Ltd, Padstow, Cornwall

British Library Cataloguing in Publication Data
A catalogue record for this book is available from the British Library.

Library of Congress Cataloging in Publication Data
Baudrillard, Jean.
Baudrillard live: selected interviews / [edited by] Mike Gane.
p. cm.
Includes bibliographical references and index.
1. Baudrillard, Jean – Interviews. 2. Sociologists – France –
Interviews. 3. Postmodernism. 4. France – Intellectual life.
I. Gane, Mike. II. Title.
HM22.F82B383 1993
301'.092–dc20   92-26081
CIP

ISBN 0–415–07037–6 (hbk)
0–415–07038–4 (pbk)

CONTENTS

CONTENTS

Part IV Radicalism has passed into events . . .

Part V When reality merges with the idea . . .

ACKNOWLEDGEMENTS

I would like to acknowledge the generous support of Chris Rojek, George Salemohamed and Nicholas Zurbrugg in this project. I also owe a debt to Monique Arnaud who helped at every stage of the process of preparing this book and who gave invaluable assistance with translations. Of course the book would not have been possible without the cooperation and participation of Jean Baudrillard.

Mike Gane

INTRODUCTION

Mike Gane

Jean Baudrillard is one of France's leading intellectuals, with a growing world reputation. In 1989 the Paris weekly *L'Evénement du Jeudi* organized a 'referendum' of some 700 representatives of intellectual society – journalists, writers, university teachers, artists. The question required its recipients to list five personalities in order of their significance as representing '*le pouvoir intellectuel*' – intellectual power. Jean Baudrillard was eighth in the ranking, equal in fact with figures such as Georges Duby, Gilles Deleuze and François Wahl, and above Pierre Bourdieu, the rival sociologist. Certainly Baudrillard has managed to break out of the purely academic world and its confines into a wide audience interested in cultural analysis.

But who is Jean Baudrillard? He comes from the Ardennes, Champagne, region of France. He was born in Reims in 1929 into a family plainly in transition from peasant farming to urban life. If Baudrillard succeeded at his studies in the Lycée he did not find it easy to get access into university teaching and in this respect his career is very different from that, say, of Michel Foucault, born only three years earlier in 1926.[1] Foucault was already in the Chair of Philosophy at the University of Clermont-Ferrand in May 1962, in 1968 in the Chair of Philosophy at Vincennes, and in 1970 was at the Collège de France. Baudrillard, by contrast, was an outsider, a late arrival on the scene. He had taught German in a Lycée before taking up sociology, becoming an assistant in September 1966 at Nanterre (University of Paris X), and then maître-assistant in 1970. Unlike Foucault once more, Baudrillard's early writings of 1968–70 were not translated into English, and thus his thought played no significant part in the debate on the affluent society in English until the emergence of postmodernism in the 1980s. However, in France itself, Baudrillard's celebrated but notorious critique (1977) of Foucault in 'Forget Foucault' almost certainly led to Baudrillard's exclusion, rather like that of Derrida's, from those sectors of academic influence under the increasing patronage of the Professor at the Collège de France. The text of the piece was originally a book review for the journal *Critique* but was sent to Foucault himself for possible response. After a long delay Baudrillard published it with Galilee. Foucault was not amused and is reported to have said, 'I would

1

have more problems remembering ... Baudrillard' (in Eribon 1991: 275). Certainly, Baudrillard's critique was written at a major turning point in his career, at a point when his writing was moving decisively away from academic sociological forms of work – opening up a considerable rift between the orthodox sociologists and Baudrillard. Baudrillard retired from university teaching at the first available opportunity.

Baudrillard was politically radicalized under the influence of Sartre and the opposition to the Algerian War at the end of the 1950s and early 1960s. He was interested in literature, poetry and political analysis. His first publications were in Sartre's journal, *Les Temps Modernes*, in 1962–3; they were pieces of literary criticism for works by Calvino, Styron and Uwe Johnson. Clear in these reviews is not only the influence of Sartrean Marxism but also his reading of Dostoyevsky and Nietzsche. But most of Baudrillard's publications in the following years were translations from German into French. These included many works by Peter Weiss – *Pointe de Fuite* (1964), *Marat/Sade* (1965), *L'Instruction* (1966), *Discours sur la genèse et le déroulement de la très longue guerre de libération du Vietnam* (1968) – as well as pieces by Brecht (1965), and Muhlmann (1968). Baudrillard completed his thesis in sociology (*troisième cycle en sociologie*) in March 1966. At this time he was closely associated with Henri Lefebvre (very much an anti-structuralist thinker) and then by 1968 with Roland Barthes (very much the high structuralist at that moment). Teaching at Nanterre from September 1966, he found himself at the centre of the brewing storm of the student revolt of 1968. He cooperated with a typical journal of the time, *Utopie*, evidently influenced by the bizarre cocktail of anarcho-situationism, structural Marxism and media theory, in which he published a number of theoretical articles on the ambience of capitalist affluence, and the critique of technology. His encounter with Marshall McLuhan and media theory, as well as the publication of his first book, *The Object System*, which clearly complemented Barthes' own *The Fashion System*, also took place in 1968.

Although the dominant line of enquiry was certainly a new form of cultural analysis influenced by structuralist techniques, Baudrillard's use of these always displayed an ironic edge. Nevertheless, the theoretical underpinning was a growing application of Freud and Marx to the analysis of consumer society itself, in an enquiry which developed an impressive epistemological critique of the concept of 'need' as an explanatory notion; this was subordinate to the determinations of class logic and social fetishism, he argued in two important essays of 1969 (contained in Baudrillard 1981b). The arguments were developed in full in *Consumer Society* in 1970, where it became clear that Baudrillard rejected most of the conclusions of more orthodox Marxists such as the Althusserians by defining consumption as the dominant form and mechanism of class domination and integration in advanced capitalist societies. In this he was much closer to Barthes and Marcuse than he was to Marxists adhering to the French Communist Party. Nevertheless, the basic framework

2

of the argument was still Marxist in the sense that it was the economic mode of production which in the last resort determined consumption as dominant:

> Abundance and consumption are not the realised Utopia. They are a new objective situation, governed by the same fundamental processes, but overdetermined by a new ideology (morale) – the whole corresponding to a *new* sphere of the productive forces on the way to a controlled reintegration in the *same* but enlarged system.
>
> (Baudrillard 1970: 116)

At the same time Baudrillard's thought also contained the seeds of a problematic which was quite different from that of structural Marxism, and this derived from the influence of Mauss and Bataille. In these early essays of Baudrillard, the influence is clear in the idea of the gift as forming part of a system of exchange which rested on completely different principles from that of commodity exchange. These initial formulations in 1968–69 were to have enormous repercussions when Baudrillard began to elaborate the opposition between the symbolic order of the gift and that of commodity exchange in the collection of essays published in 1972 as *For a Critique of the Political Economy of the Sign*. Baudrillard began to take up a position against Marx's contrast of use value and human need against exchange value and commodity form. The fundamental opposition, he argued, must be between the symbolic order and the capitalist culture of exchange value. Marx himself had simply been trapped into a theoretical collusion with capitalist forms by assuming that needs and uses were themselves outside the order established by capital. This is perhaps the key point of Baudrillard's intellectual trajectory, for what follows is an attempt to work out all the implications of the contradictions between symbolic exchange and commodity exchange. The immediate outcome of this move was Baudrillard's direct attack on the way that structural Marxists had sought to demolish and domesticate the symbolic cultures by reducing them to primitive modes of production (in his book *The Mirror of Production*, 1973). Against the trend Baudrillard argued that it was fundamentally only from the position of the symbolic order that the most radical critique of contemporary capitalist developments could be made. Analyses on the basis of the principle of production, and which took capitalist production as a model, were compromised as critical weapons.

By 1976 Baudrillard had worked out a full set of analyses of the opposition between the symbolic and commodity exchange and had recast his general theory into a new vocabulary, published in his most impressive work, *Symbolic Exchange and Death*. This work contained long sections on 'the end of production', 'the order of simulacres', 'fashion', 'the body', 'political economy and death' and 'the extermination of the name of God'. Each of these analyses was built up on the contrast between symbolic exchange and its disenchanted equivalent: production *versus* gift exchange, simulation *versus* symbol, fashion cycles *versus* reversibility, the body in a sign system *against* the body in symbolic order, death in the crisis of linear accumulative time *against* death in the eternal return, accumulative prose *against* sacrificial poetry. Probably dominant in these studies was the growing contrast not between gift and commodity exchange, but a deepening theoretical vocabulary and shift of emphasis. Commodity exchange was to be understood as one aspect of a larger code system that was to become predominant in Western culture from the Renaissance, in a process parallel to that outlined by Nietzsche and then Weber as the disenchantment of symbolic cultures under the impact of a process of rationalization, secularization, bureaucratization and modernization. Thus Baudrillard now talked of the opposition between symbol and sign, between the symbolic order and structural law of exchange defined in relation to sexuality as the 'phallic exchange standard'. Poetry is symbolic, sacrificial, anagrammatic, enchanted, as against the reductive semiotic order of the sign (signifier, signified in relation to a 'real world').

Of course, implicit in the new theory was a new anti-epistemology, a new attack on Western rationalism and its notion of the difference between superstition and the real knowledge. Baudrillard following Nietzsche began to outline the stages of disenchantment as stages of the evolution of the notion of 'reality' in Western cultures, ending with his famous evocation of the stage of 'hyperreality' and 'virtual' reality. In the process of radicalization of basic concepts, Baudrillard was now proposing that so-called primitive societies were not primitive and not even societies in the sense understood by Western sociologists. Fundamentally, the notion of reality itself, along with all the notions of production and technical practicality, could not be found in them and could only be applied to them in the violent process of misunderstanding them. More than this, all the cherished ideals of human progress associated with the bourgeois revolution had created the necessary mystification of primitive and backward societies as morally corrupt, as unjust, unequal, poor, nasty. Ironically, says Baudrillard, following Nietzsche closely here, it is modern societies which have brought these ideologies into existence as self-justifications. It is from this point that Baudrillard very clearly moves against the progressives – the socialists, ecologists, feminists, anti-racists, etc. – for these too have become part of the modern consensus against the symbolic order. In 1977 he published a short, but devastating, critique of the new Pompidou arts centre in Paris (known as the Beaubourg) in which he launched the same kind of attack: this building is part of the semiotic system of modern architecture, an architecture of cultural disenchantment. Where is the secret, the charm, the ritual, the meaning of this building, he asked; it looks more like a petrol refinery. In 1978 he published what amounted to a Nietzschean defence of the right of the 'silent' masses to remain outside the orbit of the socialists or the educators or improvers in general attempts to impose either the 'social' or 'culture' on them – the masses, he argued, always reject these modern forms of *ressentiment* and are always more interested in the fatal, the spectacle. Their lack of enthusiasm in culture is itself a silent strategy of abstention, a form of struggle. Baudrillard wrote a number of directly political essays critical of the left . . . .

His next major project altered the terms of the opposition between production and gift 'exchange' to a more radical one between production and seduction (*Seduction* 1979), wanting in fact to move away from the term 'exchange' itself as still inflected with mistaken presuppositions. Elements of his published poetry (*L'Ange de Stuc* 1978) are interwoven into an account of the emergence of *trompe-l'oeil* in the Renaissance. Baudrillard goes much further than Weber here who simply talked of the importance of perspective in the process of cultural rationalization. Baudrillard refers to the 'studiolos' of the Duke of Urbino – 'tiny sanctuaries entirely in *trompe-l'oeil* at the heart of the immense space of the palace . . . cut off from the rest of the structure, without windows, literally without space – *here space is actualised by simulation*'. He continues and draws some dramatic conclusions:

> A complete reversal of the rules of the game is in effect here, allowing us to surmise ironically, by the allegory of the *trompe-l'oeil*, that the external space, that of the palace, and beyond it, the city, that is, the political space, the locus of power, *is itself only an effect of perspective*.
>
> (Baudrillard 1979a/1990a: 65)

Instead of being produced, power is better understood as a form of seduction.

But there are different forms of seduction. There is an evolution, he suggests, from the seduction in its radical sense, that is as duel, as ritual, the play for maximal stakes, to 'seduction in its "soft" sense – the seduction of an "ambience", or the playful eroticization of a universe without stakes' (1990a: 156). This forms a direct continuation with Baudrillard's critique of affluence, but now the terms are centred on seduction rather than consumption, and against the image of economic determination:

> One is speaking of a seduction reviewed and revised by the ideology of desire. A psychologized seduction that results from its vulgarization with the rise in the West of the imaginary figure of desire.
>
> The figure does not belong to the masters, but was historically produced by the oppressed under the sign of their liberation, and has been deepened by the failure of successive revolutions. As a form, desire marks the passage from their status as objects to that of subjects, but this passage is itself only a more refined, interiorized perpetuation of their servitude. Large scale seduction now begins. For if an object can simply be dominated, the subject of desire, by contrast, has to be seduced.
>
> (Baudrillard 1990a: 174–5)

Thus, with the emergence of the mass media, information technology, there arises the specific forms of ludic and soft seduction connected with the transition to a society in which all internal opposition becomes subject to the rigours of the code of exchange, and becomes recycled as fashion.

Persisting in chasing the forms of opposition between the symbolic and the semiotic, Baudrillard's next major study moved from seduction to a theme already touched on but now given a detailed examination: 'fatal strategies' (1983b). The implicit question posed here is: if the world is not ordered by reason, by the technical and scientific determination of purposes, how is it ordained? The question is exactly that posed in the work of Nietzsche and Max Weber. But whereas for Weber the category of the fatal, drawn from Tolstoy, is stated and used in opposition, it is never theorized. Baudrillard not only draws on the notion of fate as expressed in symbolic cultures, he suggests that its power re-emerges in very specific ways in the advanced societies. Given the period of production, polarity, expansion and revolution is over, our society has entered a period of implosion, where the logic of the dialectical movement of history has been superseded. In order to grasp this, he conjectures, it is necessary to abandon all the perspectives developed on the basis of assumptions of human praxis, *homo faber*. What has happened is that the world, the object, not the subject, has been radicalized, has burst through all the constraints and balances inherent in the symbolic order and has become the site of contemporary *ressentiment*. The world is post-modern in the sense that it is post-dialectical, that is, post-historical. As against a world increasingly mastered by science and technology, Baudrillard describes a world which subtly evades control, and takes its revenge on apparent human omnipotence: the revenge of the crystal. But instead of conceiving this form as bland, low in energy, flat, as many theories of consumer society tend to do, Baudrillard imaginatively conceives these forms as an ecstatic paradox.

> Terrorism is the ecstatic form of violence; the state is the ecstatic form of society; pornography is the ecstatic form of sex, the obscene the ecstatic form of the scene, etc. It seems that things, having lost their critical and dialectical determination, can only redouble themselves in their exacerbated and transparent form.
>
> (Baudrillard 1983b/1990i: 41)

The book ends with a consideration of the principle of evil, and perhaps reveals something of the limit of the Nietzschean in Baudrillard. For what Baudrillard picks up is the fact that the way the object resists, as he says, disobeys the will of the subject in all these projects, reveals something about servitude. 'The whole problem of voluntary servitude should be re-examined ... obedience, in effect, is a banal strategy, which doesn't need to be explained, for it secretly contains – all obedience secretly contains – a fatal disobedience to the symbolic order' (1990i: 182). Thus the principle of evil lies in the transparent rape of the symbolic order itself, transparent, that is, not in the subject but in the object. The way out of the problem of voluntary servitude, he argues, is the fatal logic of the escalation of the worst, and it is this escalation of the fatal spiral which in the end protects us from reality itself (1990i: 186).

Baudrillard extended these analyses in his most recent substantial essay, *The Transparence of Evil* (1990b). In an interview in this collection, he describes his difficulty in finding a title for this work, which he would like to have called *The Transparition of Evil*. Here he continues with the theme of the bursting of limits in Western society, which he now calls the formation of the 'transpolitical', the breaking down and intermixing of all the categories and genres in the culture: the transsexual breaks down the boundaries of the male and female, the transaesthetic the boundary between art and non-art, the transeconomic the formation of financial circuits which break the boundaries of the economic and the political. Western culture becomes more and more repressively tolerant so that religion becomes fashion, revolution becomes style in a culture progressively dominated by the effects of the mass media in McLuhan's sense: the cooling of history. But Baudrillard maintains the opposition between the symbolic and the semiotic, and reflects in the last section of the work on the concept of the 'radical alterity' of the symbolic from semiotic 'difference'.

It is clear from an interview that Baudrillard also began to keep a diary from about 1980. These have been published as *America* (1988a), *Cool Memories* (1987b) and *Cool Memories II* (1990d). They seem to have been inspired by Nietzsche, Canetti and the challenge of the aphorism and the fragment. These texts do not attempt to reproduce a linear story of a life. Rather they present impressions, fugitive reflections, paradoxes, poetic play, short accounts of people, encounters, events, and theoretical exploration, experimentation. They record something of Baudrillard's tourist gaze, the traveller on the world scene. In this sense they complement his other writings and it is possible to cross-reference between the two styles: one can find some of the background to *America* from *Cool Memories* , as one can for the visits to Australia, to New York, etc. *Cool Memories* brought Baudrillard considerable fame. The *Guardian* (21.9.88) devoted a whole page to 'Who is Baudrillard?'; Brian Rotman reported that Baudrillard was 'professor of sociology, prophet of apocalypse, hysterical lyricist of panic, obsessive recounter of the centreless desolation of the post-modern scene and currently the hottest property on the New York intellectual circuit'. The first edition of the new weekly newspaper *The European* (11.5.90) presented a digest of Baudrillard aphorisms in a special feature under the title 'What are you doing after the orgy?' as a presentation of what European intellectuals could offer. He made an appearance on French television with the celebrated Bernard Pivot.

The most recent essay by Baudrillard (1991d) was a collection of three articles which first appeared in the French daily *Libération*, under the title 'The Gulf War did not take place' (*La Guerre du Golfe n'a pas eu lieu*). This has given Baudrillard added notoriety, and there has been not a little effort on the part of his critics to make him appear ludicrous. The first of the three pieces was translated for the *Guardian* in January 1991, and it appeared as a straight prediction that there would be no war, only the simulation of a war.

7

Obviously when the war actually broke out, Baudrillard was faced with some important problems. He could have said: the war has broken out, there is something wrong with my theory – in the style of a philosophical falsificationist. That of course would have been something of a triumph, given the fact that there were so many interpretations of the war which could never have reached the point of making such a singular prediction. Indeed, had Saddam Hussein backed down and there had been no Western invasion, this might have been taken as empirical evidence in support of Baudrillard's prediction and no doubt Baudrillard would have enjoyed the irony. Instead Baudrillard took the line that even though there was an invasion, this was not a war. Again he appeared on a television discussion programme, and surprisingly did not find himself in a minority of one. Certainly, it would have been easy to outline the novelty of a war in which computer simulation played such a major part in the technical armoury of both sides. But Baudrillard went considerably further; he pushed Clausewitz's famous dictum to read 'non-war is the absence of politics continued by other means' (1991d: 95). Everything was unreal: the war, the victory, the defeat, and now, as he suggests in the following interviews, the subsequent Israeli–Arab negotiations – the simulation of a war followed by the simulation of negotiations.

The interviews contained in this selection relate to the period of Baudrillard's writings dominated not by the concept of production and scientific analysis, but by seduction and fatal analysis. Yet it seems clear both from his writings and the interviews that Baudrillard's actual practice is highly complex, a combination of critical and fatal modes. Although the movement in modern culture is governed by mechanisms of simulation and not a simple economic commodity mode, the irony is, he argues, that 'the present system . . . succeeds in neutralizing all finalities, all referentials, all meanings' (1988c: 74). This thesis is strikingly like that of Max Weber's evocation of the triumph of rationalism. Baudrillard develops this idea in a way which is far more radical than any of Weber's responses, that rationalization 'does not control the seduction of appearances'. Here Baudrillard's theoretical continuation is audacious:

there is . . . a contemporary strategy of seduction which would counter the surveillance and computer processes, the ever more sophisticated methods of biological and molecular control and retrieval of bodies . . . .
Seduction as an invention of strategy, of the body, as a disguise for survival, as an infinite disperson of lures, as an art of disappearance and absence, as a dissuasion which is stronger yet than that of the system . . . . Seduction remains the enchanted form of the devil's share (la part maudit).

(Baudrillard 1988c: 74–5)

AN INTERVIEW WITH BAUDRILLARD

Clearly, reading or listening to a Baudrillard interview is something altogether different from reading one of his written essays. If it is not worked over and effectively rewritten it is a record of a direct and immediate spoken reply to questions. We know that in Baudrillard's case the interviews, with the rare exception, are not rewritten, not even 'corrected' as such. In a sense this is a risk on Baudrillard's part. First, without checking the transcription and the translation, there may be a series of more or less severe discrepancies between what was said and what appears in print. But this is obviously true of any translation, and there exist translations of Baudrillard's works which contain serious errors. Those interviews which have been undertaken by French journals can, perhaps by and large, be assumed to have grasped Baudrillard's general meaning in the French language. English publications are a different matter. The interviews which are included here have been undertaken by interviewers with a close and detailed knowledge of Baudrillard's work in French. As Baudrillard does not conduct his interviews in English there are here some impressive efforts on the part of English-speaking interviewers to follow Baudrillard into close conversation, and it is clear that some interviewing teams have sought to include native French speakers to deal with problems of interpretation and supplementary questions.

The second risk for Baudrillard is that of meeting an interviewer who might throw up problem questions, or where he himself might appear in working out an answer to begin to contradict himself. Of course, there are occasions where Baudrillard might certainly say, I don't really want to answer that question. And he does just that in the interview included here, on two sets of questions, first that dealing with people he knew or might be working with, second on directly 'political' and 'ideological' questions. The brief answers to these questions do not appear in the published version. But as for the risk involved in facing the difficulty of the question itself, or its apparent novelty, Baudrillard was quite prepared to trust to the situation and to the competence of the interviewers to reproduce the interview accurately. What appears then is the version that is edited by the interviewers.

This has enormous advantages for the reader. Baudrillard's replies are as they were pronounced, they are not rewritten in any way. They are live.

I do not want to suggest that I am aware of the situations under which all the interviews included here were conducted. But I am familiar with at least one. It is clear that a number of people are interested in just how Baudrillard lives with his theories, given their strange post-apocalyptic nature (see the interview with Lotringer). Is Baudrillard morose? Is he malicious? Does he indulge in continuous *schadenfreude*? Is he offhand, or shy? Is he pompous or pretentious? All these questions arise in the expectation of the interview, since it is in the interview situation that one might be able to get behind the formal texts, to begin to see the subject as a living being. There is also the interest in the way the person lives, the interior style of the apartment, especially in the case of a sociologist who has written so much on furniture and interior décor, as well as on art. On this score there was a certain rather protracted series of difficulties in setting up the interview for, although the interview had been arranged for some considerable time, the specific arrangements were very vague. Having booked into a hotel within easy striking distance of Baudrillard's address there still remained the problem of arranging a time and place. Baudrillard's telephone remains permanently on answermachine. Having left a message that we had arrived, we went for a short walk. When we returned, we learnt that a man had called at the hotel, and left his telephone number. We left another message on the answer-machine, asking Baudrillard to leave some instructions about how to proceed. After this he phoned through with some instructions on how to find his apartment (which is in a complex guarded by special codes of entry). We went along carrying a cassette recorder and a sheaf of questions.

It was not as if we were completely unaware of what to expect, since there is an account of an interview with Baudrillard in *Face* magazine (4 January 1989: 61–2). Here the interviewers report:

> In person, Baudrillard doesn't quite look the part. From his books you expect maybe a witty, seductive rake. He actually looks a little like a union boss. He's thickset, wears mostly brown, and rolls his own. He doesn't gaze at the world through a haze of Gauloise smoke. He also doesn't speak English (or doesn't want to). This caused a few problems at his recent sell-out lecture at London's Institute of Contemporary Art as the translator reduced three-minute French monologues into a couple of English sentences. 'Um . . . what Jean is saying is that we're trapped by an escalating hyper . . . er, hyper . . . um . . . sorry, hyper what?' Baudrillard doesn't seem to try too hard to make himself accessible to his disciples.
>
> (*Face* 1989: 62)

I had already sent a number of queries in preparation for two books on Baudrillard. I received the replies in January 1990. The letter had been returned with the replies written in the margin or across the question itself. Typical was this, for example: Is your background protestant, catholic, communist, trotskyist, anarchist? Baudrillard had put a line through each of these, and had added simply 'no background'. A further question said: A commentator suggests that you have simply surrendered to the mass media by appearing on television to 'promote' your book *Cool Memories*. Baudrillard wrote in the margin: 'fool'. Finally I asked: I have noticed that some of your poems have found their way into your prose works. Do you envisage a kind of fusion between poetry and prose in your work? Baudrillard wrote: 'Sure it is the same game, in other ways. But poetry as such is now impossible. I hope it can be displayed and dispersed through the theoretical assomption [sic], or fiction-theory (especially in the last books). But it can never be "envisaged", it occurs or not. *Excusez mon anglais*!'

Baudrillard lives in central Paris, in a quarter alive with restaurants, cinemas, small shops. We entered his apartment block and, in the absence of a lift, climbed some wide circular stairs. At the entrance, we paused for breath, rang the bell. It was immediately apparent that we were not in the presence of a morose, dull, conceited and pretentious French intellectual, but a genial, witty character. We were offered coffee and then wine. The apartment is unpretentious, well used, with little evidence of wealth or luxury. Rather plain drapes had been thrown across the furniture, black and white photos (his own perhaps) on the walls, a large mirror above the fireplace, a large television, a video recorder, a CD player and a pile of discs. We were seated at a table placed against one of the walls. Here we talked for over an hour before the interview began. Certainly he was rather like a union boss, thickset, and indeed rolled his own. Tobacco tended to fall onto the table-cloth and he periodically swept this up with his hands. The discussion ranged from the problems of his second home in the Languedoc, his political and intellectual relations with a number of leading intellectuals, and thoughts on recent books. He was on good form.

Baudrillard left the room. The cassette was prepared. The interview started with Baudrillard's reappearance. The questions were in French as was the entire interview, in a French spoken with great rapidity, accompanied by gesticulations, cigarette rolling and smoking, drinking of beaujolais nouveau. There was a considerable amount of laughing, chuckling. After about forty minutes, Baudrillard retired to make a phone call, the tape was changed, and we resumed for another half an hour. By then it was time to stop, even though we had not finished all the questions. He quickly agreed to try to tape answers to them, or to write. Of course, for the interviewers the real practical problems start to become obvious. Had the recording been a success? Were there to be difficulties in transcribing and translating? Should one try to transcribe everything, every repetition, every redundant phrase? Once back in England the tapes were copied and transcribed. It immediately became clear why Baudrillard is a celebrated interviewee: the rapidity and range of detail of the responses to unseen questions was just as appeared to be the case in the interview situation, and from the evidence of his published interviews.

But what should be the strategy of an interview in these circumstances? In this case it was decided that it was essential to try to cover a certain amount of ground, and this naturally limits the possibility of a conversational form of interview. This type is clearly exemplified in Baudrillard's interview with Sylvere Lotringer. Here Lotringer seems to play the role of colleague, politico-cultural accomplice. But Lotringer is above all concerned to probe all the implications of Baudrillard's position, not to subject it to criticism. The polar opposite is the interview which appeared in *Marxism Today* in January 1989 (Interview 14). Here there is an underlying tone of criticism and opposition.

In another interview of a rather aggressive type, Interview 13, Baudrillard seems forced into positions which he admits sound a little stupid. Having seen him in interview on French television, it seemed that Baudrillard was not dogmatic in argument and could be bullied by an aggressive interviewer (like Bernard Pivot, for example).

I have argued elsewhere (in *Baudrillard – Critical and Fatal Theory*) that there are two Baudrillards: one who is 'less assured and will often appear to be pushed into a position he really does not accept, even to the point of putting his own position into question. But a more confident Baudrillard appears in the written texts, when the writing is pushed to the limit . . .' (1991: 3). (After we returned to England, we received a written conclusion of the interview, and Baudrillard commented: 'Perhaps we will have the opportunity of picking this all up again. I hope to discuss all this in person (but as you are so right in saying, it's in the written form that I express most radically what I think).' See this volume, *Amor Fati*, p. 209.)

This could mean of course that Baudrillard live is the conservative Baudrillard. Could the outcome of an interview vary with the interviewer and the situation of the interview? This seems more than just a possibility. What does an interviewer want to achieve in any case? Information? A victory? An exchange of opinions? If the interviewer is on the offensive, what happens in the exchange? The interviewee tightens up, looks for a way out. Evidently Baudrillard himself does not mind allowing into print a situation where he admits his position may sound stupid; he allows the interviewer an easy victory, or so it seems. Such an interview is really a failure, for we suspect something interesting is missed, and in effect Baudrillard is saying: If you want to hear your own voice, stage manage the situation, well and good.

Other interviews establish the possibility of a conversation. The interview conducted in Paris for this collection (Interviews 1 and 20) followed on from a long conversation, and in the interview there was a sharp change of modality; there are few interruptions of Baudrillard's flow of thought. None of the apparent inconsistencies or extreme formulations are picked up with objections. In this sense the interview was very relaxed, allowing Baudrillard to begin to question himself, to alter his opinion during a response, to play with inconsistencies, to display his current repertoire of theoretical concepts and oppositions (which often appear in a quite different light from his published theoretical reflections). At the end of a reply to a question there was a pause rather than an immediate posing of a counter or new question and, on a number of occasions, Baudrillard added supplementary comments which may have added not just balance to an answer but a qualification which altered the whole character of the answer. It was characteristic that Baudrillard was very concerned at the beginning of a new question to make absolutely clear the sense and meaning of the question. At one point, presented with a quotation from his own work, he replied to the effect: I don't remember that, where did I say it? (This also occurs in Interview 15.)

So what was going on in the interview? This could certainly be answered with a reference to the situation itself, for Baudrillard afterwards genuinely tried to sit in front of the tape recorder with a set of questions, and found it impossible to complete the interview: 'I am truly incapable of recording anything in a tête-à-tête with a machine,' he wrote (see p. 208), yet he was able to tape the replies. This provides some sort of evidence that at least the interview is an encounter, and evokes a specific kind of response; the interview responses compared with the written ones are considerably longer, more detailed, slightly rambling, cover more ground, laugh and play with their own form. As a writer Baudrillard finds it easy to compose at the typewriter, yet the letter (*Amor Fati*), which contains his answers to questions for an interview, is almost like a person-to-person letter, although the intention is to publish for a wide audience. The interview could perhaps be said to have the character of a spoken letter, very much sent to an individual or individuals. In the interview there are all kinds of visible and audible responses to the answers as they develop, as if there is a complicity in the very process of performing the response. In this respect Baudrillard remains on guard against the sovereignty of the machine. It appears to alarm him; he wants to remain close to the human after all.

Perhaps in this sense the interview is an ambiguous form for Baudrillard. It retains something of the human and, even when the encounter is mercenary, there is something of the whiff of alienation. But Baudrillard's writing now is not of the world of alienation, it evokes the world of simulation, fractal culture or, in the fragmentary form, the paradox. Take some typical moments from *Cool Memories* where he says:

> It is difficult to find a remedy for our own sadness, because we are implicated in it. It is difficult to find a remedy for other people's sadness because we are prisoners of it.
>
> (Baudrillard 1990c: 150)

or:

> Thought can no longer keep itself in a critical equilibrium. It has to be spread-eagled between violent nostalgia and violent anticipation.
>
> (Baudrillard 1990c: 152)

or:

> If you say, I love you, then you have already fallen in love with language, which is already a form of breakup and infidelity.
>
> (Baudrillard 1990c: 153)

These kinds of utterances are not going to find themselves making an appearance in an interview. They are above all written, even secretive. More pertinent as a basis of comparison, perhaps, are the sections in *Cool Memories II* which deal with Baudrillard's own personal background. Take a short

13

passage: 'Pataphysician at twenty – situationist at thirty – utopian at forty – transversal at fifty – viral and metaleptic at sixty – my complete history' (1990d: 131).

But he also constructs more lengthy fragments:

Generations of peasants worked hard all their lives: we owe it to them to make up for their expenditure by our own idleness.

Grandfather stopped working only when he died, a peasant. Father stopped working well before old age, state employment was an anticipatory retirement (he paid with mortal hypochondria, but perhaps it was necessary). As for me I never even started work, having attained very rapidly a marginal and sabbatical situation: university teacher. As for the children they haven't had children. And thus the chain continues up to the ultimate stage of laziness.

This laziness is, in essence, rural. It is founded on a sentiment of 'natural' merit and equilibrium. One must never do too much. It is a principle of discretion and respect for the equivalence of work and the earth: the peasant gives, but it is up to the earth and to the Gods to give the rest – the essential. A principle of respect for that which does not come from work, and will never come from it.

This principle involves an inclination for the fatal. Laziness is a fatal strategy, and the fatal is a strategy of laziness. It is from it that I draw a vision of the world which is at the same time extreme and lazy. I am not going to change my vision whatever the course of things. I detest buoyant activism in fellow citizens, initiatives, social responsibility, ambition, competition. These are exogenous values, urban, performative, pretentious. They are industrial qualities. Laziness on the other hand, is a natural energy.

(Baudrillard 1990d: 17–18)

These extracts can be compared directly with the answers to questions in the interviews, where Baudrillard says:

My grandparents were peasants. My parents became civil servants. A traditional family development which meant that they left the countryside and settled in a town. I was the first member of the tribe, so to speak, to do some studying, that was the point of rupture, when I broke away and got started. Apart from that I don't have much to say. I was not brought up in an intellectual milieu – there was nothing around me – my parents were what they were, not even petit bourgeois, or perhaps very lowly petit bourgeois. It was not a cultural environment. So I had compensated for this by working extremely hard at the Lycée. That's when an enormous amount of primitive accumulation took place.

(Interview 1)

It is possible to argue that the difference between the written fragment in *Cool*

14

Memories II and the interview extract is very much the difference between textual *jouissance* and textual *plaisir*, between the ecstasy and the pleasure of the text, terms developed by Roland Barthes (1973),[2] a writer who not only became very influential on Baudrillard, but who also wrote a number of texts in the mode of fragments. The fragment in the mode of aphorism seems altogether highly composed and at the same time a precise play on contrast, paradox, condensation, a characteristic recognized even by Francis Bacon in a famous defence (1605)[3] of the aphoristic mode:

> the writing in aphorisms hath many excellent virtues, whereto the writing in Method doth not approach. For first, it trieth the writer, whether he be superficial or solid: for Aphorisms, except they should be ridiculous, cannot be made but of the pith and heart of the sciences; for the discourse of illustration is cut off; recitals of examples are cut off; discourse of connection and order is cut off; descriptions of practice are cut off. So there remaineth nothing to fill the Aphorisms but some good quantity of observation: and therefore no man can suffice, nor in reason will attempt to write Aphorisms, but he that is sound and grounded. Aphorisms, representing a knowledge broken, do invite men to inquire farther; whereas Methods, carrying the show of a total, do secure men, as if they were at farthest.
>
> (1605, Bacon nd: 142)

It is no wonder that the fragment in Schopenhauer, Nietzsche, through to Barthes and Adorno, and Baudrillard, has been regarded as the postmodern form *par excellence*, since it appears to break up and to challenge the claims of method to mastery. But it is not a new form. The interview/ questionnaire is not a new form either, of course (for it obviously has a juridical genealogy), and the similarities with the aphorism perhaps should not be taken too far.

Fundamentally, the interview process involves more than the interviewee: questions arrive from the outside. This means that in the encounter there are opportunities for improvisation, for the unexpected and the unusual. In Interview 2, Baudrillard is asked: Do you sometimes go to sleep in the cinema? It is quite unlikely that we would ever have known Baudrillard's thought on this if this playful question had not been posed. Interview 2 is one of the most successful in the collection, purely because of the idiosyncratic questioning and the mood of hilarity which prevails; it also allows us to see Baudrillard's 'peasant' opposition to 'art high culture'. In Interview 19 with Nicole Czechowski, we read one of the most dramatic interviews in the collection where the interviewer persists with a narrow line of questioning. Baudrillard, at the moment he appears to be cornered, reveals his resort to a form of intellectual terrorism.

But this form of 'terrorism' is not to be considered part of a political strategy as conventionally conceived. In these interviews Baudrillard presents his own position as a form of challenge – one which poses, he admits, considerable problems for himself. His 'one strategy' is no longer dialectical but 'a process of pushing a system or a concept or an argument to the extreme points where one pushes them over, where they tumble over their own logic. . . . So there is a destabilization'. He continues: 'But among all those disciplines that one traverses or ironizes or whatever, no one of them is privileged. That goes for myself too. I don't have any doctrines to defend. I have one strategy, that's all' (pp. 81–2).

Yet Baudrillard does have a privileged modality, that of writing – though not 'writing considered as a sacralized act' (p. 181). 'To write is to be oneself at the heart of the system of this demand for a drive to disappearance and the power to bring it about' (p. 38). For Baudrillard it is 'writing's "fatal strategy" to go to extremes. And that strategy is a happy one, vital. That is my vitality . . .' (p. 180). But there are risks. 'The danger of this indifference is taking delight in it in a sort of perverse contemplation'; but more than this he insists 'the risk I am taking is that of destabilizing myself, of creating a void to set off a chain reaction against the things I want to see fall. It is not a question of positive action of the revolutionary sort. All that I can do is to create this zone of strategic indifference . . . It's a non-militant, non-spectacular sacrifice, the opposite of action as it is usually understood . . .' (pp. 195–6).

NOTES

1 See D. Eribon, *Michel Foucault*, Cambridge, Mass.: Harvard University Press, 1991.
2 Roland Barthes, *Le Plaisir du Texte*, Paris: Seuil, 1973.
3 F. Bacon, *Advancement of Learning*, London: Dent, nd.

Part I

A VIRTUAL STATE
OF RUPTURE ...

1

I DON'T BELONG TO THE CLUB, TO THE SERAGLIO
Interview with Mike Gane and Monique Arnaud

MA *Can you tell us about your youth? What your parents did for a living? Who were your first intellectual influences?*

My grandparents were peasants. My parents became civil servants. A traditional family development which meant that they left the countryside and settled in a town. I was the first member of the tribe, so to speak, to do some studying, that was the point of rupture, when I broke away and got started. Apart from that I don't have much to say. I was not brought up in an intellectual milieu – there was nothing around me – my parents were what they were, not even petit bourgeois, or perhaps very lowly petit bourgeois. It was not a cultural environment. So I had compensated for this by working extremely hard at the Lycée. That's when an enormous amount of primitive accumulation took place. It was a period in my life when I worked really hard at acquiring an enormous amount. After that was the rupture with my parents. This break-up played an important part in my life, because breaking away from my parents established a mode of rupture which then by a process of transposition influenced other things. I have always been in a virtual state of rupture: with the university, even with the political world where I was able to get involved but always only at a distance. So there's a kind of prototype in my childhood, adolescence, etc. I didn't get into the Ecole Normale Supérieure. I took the *agrégation* but I didn't succeed. So I didn't become '*agrégé*' either. I got into the university in the 1960s but by an indirect route. In short, as far as the normal stages of a career are concerned, I've always missed them, including the fact that I was never a professor. I say this without any recrimination, because that is how I wanted it. It was a little game of mine to say that I wanted a degree of freedom. It was also how people sometimes thought at the time, people of my generation. You lived off anything and the energy came from rupture. Whereas today, it is completely different. That is why I was out of phase with the university: even with the students there was a great feeling of complicity about everything, about seduction and all that, which lasted ten to fifteen years, that completely changed and the university became a foreign and tiresome environment; I couldn't at all function

19

in such a world. Nevertheless, I was very lucky that I was able to live at Nanterre in the sixties and seventies, some of the best years. Once these were over, we mourned. We didn't do that well either, we became melancholic. That was that. But afterwards things became dead; they had become funereal, even Nanterre. So I left. I should have left before. But I wasn't such a success carrying it out, and it was even unlikely that I would redeploy myself. I don't think you find too many cases of successful redeployment at that time and among people of that generation. So it's true today ... because those who were there at the time, our mentors, well, they were not really mentors, they were fathers that have since died. It's the whole spirit of an era which has disappeared. I don't want to be nostalgic about all this. On the contrary, looking back, I rather think I was very lucky to have been there at that time in that milieu at Nanterre, in Paris. So I have no complaints. That said, it has all gone.

MG *Your articles in* Les Temps Modernes *and* Utopie *were Marxist. How did you become a Marxist, under what influences?*

I am not quite sure whether they were really Marxist. I haven't read them for a long time. In *Utopie* they certainly weren't. The articles I wrote for *Les Temps Modernes* were literary articles. The influence was less political, more Sartrean. That was the dominating influence of the age. But as far as the first stage of my involvement was concerned, I was much closer to a kind of anarchism and things like that. Then there was the Algerian War which had a vital part to play, a kind of Marxist-type politicization. With regard to thought and analysis, yes, there was a Marxist analysis in my work but very much mediated by many other things. I set about doing some theoretical work. From the start there was semiology and psychoanalysis and things of that sort, all of which went well together.

Then Marxism was already a thing of the past. We were already in something like a post-Marxist age. So I find it difficult to say whether I was really a Marxist. But Marx's analysis was certainly influential on my work. From the beginning, the analysis of it in terms of production was accompanied by analysis in anthropological terms of consumption of the gift and expenditure (*dépense*), so then the analysis of production was left behind. As far as political economy is concerned, I only came to it in order to deconstruct it. In fact from the beginning I subscribed to Marxism but almost immediately began to question it and became ambivalent about it, distancing myself from it more and more as I went along. It's true that Sartre had a great influence, and then came another influence, in the 1960s, that of Barthes. I discovered Barthes and worked with him, and found it straight away more interesting. I'm not saying that he was more important, but more fascinating. Barthes offered a more virgin territory. From that point everything changed.

MG *There appears to be a strong influence of German romanticism on your first books, that is, the influence of Kleist and Hölderlin. Up to what point has the German romantic movement been the basis of your thought?*

German romanticism? No, no. There was Hölderlin, that's all, and to me he wasn't a German romantic. No. It was something much more specific, dazzling in its own way. I know German romanticism very well, I have read a lot of it, but it wasn't for me. In my view Hölderlin wasn't romantic at all. He was mythical. He was rather in the line of Schopenhauer, Nietzsche and writers like that. So it is not German romanticism, this is not what inspired me, it is too subjective, too romantic, too sentimental, so let's not get things mixed up. It's true that I was well into German culture. So I know German culture quite well. I did German, in fact, to read all those texts. So there must be some way in which I've been influenced by it, but I can't tell. In fact I've often been told that my work has an affinity with German thinking. On the other hand, I don't owe my intellectual formation to German philosophy. The texts I've read in German I've already mentioned: Nietzsche, Schopenhauer, and many other works, of course, but they are not philosophical works. In addition I didn't read them systematically as I would have done if I had been to the Ecole Normale. There I would have acquired a solid philosophical culture, soemthing I have never had. I have a good familiarity with it but no training in it in the proper sense. This also means that I have never been a real philosopher and when these days I find people desperately trying to get back to philosophy to resuscitate it, and rediscover Kant, I can't quite understand it. The whole thing leaves me rather cold .... These are cultural peripheries, they are there, but I don't .... If I started anywhere it was with poetical things, Rimbaud, Artaud, etc., Nietzsche, Bataille. It was things like that, they were classical things, not very original, but they were not philosophy. In fact, I've always had a great deal of mistrust for philosophers, so I've developed a kind of allergy which makes me dislike the stereotyped language used in philosophy. Even its most beautiful texts fail to impress me. I've read Heidegger also but very quickly. I can't say much more about what's influenced me. Of course, there are other things as well ... but German romanticism no more than .... Well, German romanticism is much superior to French romanticism, for sure, but it has never had a great impact.

MG *Many people think of you as the high priest of postmodernism. What do you think of this?*

This reference to priesthood is out of place, I think. The first thing to say is that before one can talk about anyone being a high priest, one should ask whether postmodernism, the postmodern, has a meaning. It doesn't as far as I am concerned. It's an expression, a word which people use but which explains nothing. It's not even a concept. It's nothing at all. It's because it's

21

impossible to define what's going on now, grand theories are over and done with, as Lyotard says. That is, there is a sort of void, a vacuum. It's because there is nothing really to express this that an empty term has been chosen to designate what is really empty. So in a sense there is no such thing as postmodernism. If you interpret it this way, it is obvious that I do not represent this emptiness. I am quite happy to be – I don't know what – of a kind of void, to analyse the disappearance of a number of things, to analyse simulation which is also a form of void and where things get dislocated. But this is a form of void which is intense, intensive, and not the emptiness which is simply just what comes out of the residual, say, at the end of a culture, a sort of *bricolage* which consists of the vestiges of that culture. I have nothing to do with that kind of thing, but it would explain why there has been this collage, because postmodernism is made up of montage, collage, etc. . . . but that collage seems to me completely incorrect (*abusif*). It doesn't have anything to do with me, and I am not the only one in this situation. . . .

Everything that has been said about postmodernism was said even before the term existed. Lyotard has obviously done a lot to make the term popular, but he didn't erect it into a doctrine either. There is perhaps a conjunctural postmodernist practice, which is to define that void, what is in my view the non-structure of an epoch. So what to do? To want to disassociate oneself from it, to say that I am not a postmodernist, is still to say too much because it is a contradictory opinion and therefore defensive, and I don't want to go along that road either. . . . So I have nothing to say about this because I say, and I know this from experience, even if I prove that I am not a postmodernist, it won't change anything. People will put that label on you. Once they have done that it sticks. There are ways of getting rid of a problem. People just label it and in my opinion this is not really a process of . . . how shall I say . . . it's not really a fraud . . . let's not exaggerate, but there is something that is not very clear in all this. There are perhaps areas in which the term 'postmodernism' may mean something to the extent that people claim to belong to this, perhaps in architecture. But as soon as it is clear that the term adds nothing new it is best to let go of it. But it'll be around for a while. It has been around for a long time already. In any case, postmodernism would seem to mean that one was 'modernist' and that after modernism there was still something. Thus one is still caught in a linear meaning of things. There is linearity which is after all postmodern. For me postmodernism would be something of a regression, a retroversion of history. There is, rather, a return towards the past. There is no beyond in the sense of the future but rather a curvature towards . . . which is worse in that sense. I can no longer recognize myself in this because my wager has been one of anticipation even if it meant making a leap, going forward beyond the year 2000; what I had proposed was erasing the 1990s and going straight on to the year 2000, to play the game on the other side through excess rather than lack. Postmodernism seems to me to do with being resigned, or even largely to do with regression. This possibility of tinkering about with these forms, through a kind of juxtaposition in complete promiscuity of everything in sight. I don't recognize myself in all this . . . . So there you are. I won't change anything but I shall have said it.

MA *What are your thoughts on photography and film?*

These are two different questions. I have only really been doing photography for four or five years. I am fascinated by it, it's something very intense. It's the form of the object, the form of the appearance of the object, more so than in the cinema, which is more realist. I like photography as something completely empty, 'irreal', as something that preserves the idea of a silent apparition. This fascinated me a lot. The photo and travel, because at one time they went together, the fragment, the notebook and the diary; all these functioned together as one whole, a machine with differential axles. But photography now, I don't know, I don't pursue it any longer as an activity, because what is done today is so beautiful, so perfect, so well done, that photography raises itself to the status of art, technically and otherwise. Once again, I can't do photos like that.

As for the cinema, I am still very much in love with it, but it has reached a despairing state. I am not the only person who finds it in a hopeless state. I have seen three or four films in the last few months. I found them depressing. It is kitsch, it's not cinema. Here, too, huge machines are set up which possess great technical refinement. This is a racket on images, on the imaginary of people. Cinema has become a spectacular demonstration of what one can do with the cinema, with pictures, etc. Everything is possible, it's obvious, and everything is done any old how, there is no magic in it except, well, a mechanical magic. One has a feeling that it's all been done before, there are only superb demonstrations; it's performance, that is all. I don't know, perhaps I have a utopian idea of the cinema, but it used to be something different from what it is now. I have a feeling that the old cinema has completely disappeared. There is a kind of amnesia to do with the cinema. One doesn't know what one has seen, what it's worth, whether it is good or not, what one should think of it. People you know, you trust, have a different view from yours, a totally different conclusion about the film from ours. Everything has lost its credibility in this business. I feel this very sharply. There are things which disappear and do not affect me, but this loss of the cinema of my youth is something of a cruel loss to me, it is something that is really lost. At least photography remains, and one can practise it. It has a sort of autonomy which is able to escape the general production system. There is some hope here, even though photography these days is so hyped up. This is the paradox of the aesthetic. Something is shown to you, you judge it. It is perfect, it's good, but then there's something to criticize about it. There is everything in it, vision, technique and everything, but it doesn't interest you. It leaves you completely cold. I won't have anything to do with it. So everything seems to be crumbling. Cinema, as well as politics – all this deployment and display of things which, deep down, don't mean anything to you. Photography does not leave me cold, but not the photography one finds in the de luxe market. There are naturally exceptions, but that is the general tendency. The field is monopolized by ... I find this very demoralizing.

MG *Let us turn to art itself. Your writings reveal a deep antipathy for European art since the Renaissance. Have you ever thought of writing an aesthetic?*

No. Not at all. I am not against art, so you exaggerate a bit when you use the word 'antipathy'. I am like everyone else. There are things about European art that I admire as much as anyone else. It's not European art, it's the concept of art, of the aesthetic, of the aestheticization of art that raised a problem. But this is a philosophical concept, and I am conscious of always having had, almost from birth, an allergy to culture with a big C, the ideology of the culture of art. This may have something very peasant-like, an old aversion to culture towards which my attitude has always been coloured by an unconditional anarchism. Cultural activities, cultural spectacles, the whole cultural environment, these are things that have always repelled me. So I have an anti-cultural bias and, since today culture is so identified with art, it's true that I am *a priori* very seriously against all forms of art. It doesn't mean that I don't like them, that I don't admire. I do, like other people. But I don't recognize art as such as a practice, don't write commentaries on art and those people who dare think themselves as artists! I cannot even think of myself as an intellectual. In any case as soon as I see three intellectuals together I run away, I can't stand it. It's the same as far as artists are concerned. However that might be, there is a pharisaism about art and culture. I can't stand it. I try to reconcile myself to all this, but it doesn't work. For me, I've always interpreted the aesthetic of art from the point of view of the object; that's what I was obsessed with from the beginning. So I ask myself: what type of object? But from a point of view which is almost anthropological or metaphysical, because the viewpoint which is internal to aesthetics has never been acceptable to me. I've never adopted it. I find it extraordinarily affected, but that doesn't stop me from being able to enjoy or judge things from an aesthetic point of view. But in principle the analysis assumes that one goes through these limits and this self-exaltation of art. ... I can't stand them at all. So I'll not write an aesthetic, because that would be to privilege art as art, it would be to accept the very postulates of art, of a discipline and of the profession, something I can't do, of course. I didn't do it for politics. I didn't do it for philosophy. I try to cut across all that. No, I don't want to do for art what I haven't done for other things.

As far as art is concerned, take music for example. This is something I don't know much about. I am an autodidact, I have no musical culture. As for the fine arts, I have a culture; you get one for yourself but I remain completely the untutored amateur. I don't belong to the club, to the seraglio. I would never want to be, no more than I wanted to be in a clique at the university, or in an intellectual club. There is, of course, a bit of affectation on my part as far as this goes, but I am as I am, I can't be otherwise.

MG *Nevetheless, is there an aesthetic theory that you find attractive?*

What do you mean by that?

MG *Hegel's, for instance?*

Well, yes, Hegel is interesting to the extent that he questions the disappearance of art, etc. This is interesting. In my opinion he laid the foundation of all modern methods of analysing these things. But people have not drawn appropriately from what he did. This said, I tend to be interested in things as they are now, and people like Warhol interest me, but not as artists within the framework of a history of art, but as people outside it, people who are elsewhere and whose stake is no longer even aesthetic, and therefore who are more interesting, and who are a kind of more enigmatic object than those who fulfil a kind of prophecy within the framework of the Hegelian scheme. Beyond art in its Western definition, what does go on? This interests me more. That's why in the beginning what interested me was the object, the object itself, the banal object – precisely that which is not aesthetic. So if I wrote something then it would be a transaesthetic. This is what I did in a minor way in a recent text on Warhol. It is not that I have a total, unconditional admiration for Warhol, but it is he who seems to me to bring simulation into the reckoning, from an aesthetic point of view, but in the original sense of the irruption of simulation. After that the simulationists etc., only repeated what had already been done. It's Warhol in reality who is the focus of all this. Of course, as you know, Warhol repeated himself. But there are moments when he goes through the wall of glass of the aesthetic. ...

This interview is continued in Interview 20 on p. 199.

© 1993 Mike Gane. Interview with M. Arnaud and M. Gane, November 1991. Translated by G. Salemohamed and M. Gane.

Part II

BEYOND
ALIENATION . . .

2

I LIKE THE CINEMA
Interview with C. Charbonnier

CC *Do you go to the cinema, do you get involved in the films?*

Oh, yes, I'm a good cinema-goer. But because in this area my approach is not very well informed, or critical, or analytical, I watch and enjoy films at a very elementary level. And I want to keep it that way. The cinema is really the place where I relax.

CC *Do you go often?*

Very irregularly. In bursts. I have never been a regular or fanantical cinema-goer, I have no real 'cinema culture'. But I like the cinema. Of all the spectacles it's even the only one I do like.

CC *Do you go to the cinema in the daytime?*

In the evening, usually. But it is nice to come out of a dark cinema into bright sunlight. Like in the gambling halls of Las Vegas, or the poker schools hidden away in the middle of the desert, you come out of the shadows into blinding light. This strong physical sensation is what you find, to a lesser degree, with the cinema. Cinema also serves the purpose of allowing you to lose track of the time of day. It's an impression, a little vertiginous, which conveys the little vertigo of the cinema. On the other hand, I could never think of going to the cinema in the morning. In the morning my day has not really begun: it's a hesitant time of day, when I couldn't possibly do anything so important as going to the cinema.

CC *Have you ever left half-way through a film?*

Yes, François Reichenbach's 'Houston, Texas'. It was the first time. There were ideas in that film that I just couldn't countenance. It seemed to be extremely false and deceitful in the way it dealt with the truth of things. And the position taken by the director, that of the one who 'sees', seemed to me to be both obscene and unnecessarily confused. It all went on a bit too long and I left. But really, usually, whatever I'm watching, I stay to the end.

29

CC *Whether the film is good or bad?*

Yes, it's pure fascination, the magic appeal of the image. There is still a very strong make-believe quality about the cinema – at least, there is for me. But I also have the impression that all the films coming out today, even the best, are no longer so interesting, they belong to another wave. Cinema has become hyper-realist, technically sophisticated, effective (*performant*). All the films are 'good' – at least, you could never say they were of poor quality. But they fail to incorporate any element of make-believe (*l'imaginaire*). As if the cinema were basically regressing towards infinity, towards some indefinable perfection, a formal, empty perfection.

CC *Do you sometimes force yourself to go to the cinema?*

Oh, yes, certainly. Because when you start going less and less, you end up not going at all. Because in some circles, but not particularly in mine, people constantly pressurize you to go. And so you've got to take yourself in hand a bit, and that almost amounts to deciding to go. Not quite saying to yourself, 'Tonight, it's now or never. I'm going.' No, but nevertheless you have to force yourself. But how nice to be forced like that! The cinema is a passion. As for my relationship to the cinema: I won't say that I would go and see absolutely any film, but I'll always be happy to take my seat in a cinema. It is, after all, one way of going out for your pleasure instead of letting pleasure come to you like television does.

CC *Do you watch television?*

In a very irregular fashion. I've only had it for the past two or three years. Before, I didn't want the damn thing. I would see it by proxy, at my mother's, or in friends' houses: it wasn't my choice. And then I was asked to do something on television with Raul Ruiz about simulacres. He wanted to do a satire on television documentaries and soap operas, and I said to myself, 'After all, it really would be idiotic never to have seen them! So why not?' And once I had it, I found I liked having it. But I use it in a very random sort of way. I've seen how the peasants handle it – there are peasants in my family – and their attitude is, 'Okay, it's there', but as soon as a neighbour drops in and starts talking about village affairs, they ignore it. What they're interested in have to do with rituals, games, competitions, things as far removed from television as possible. And the things available to them: moral, pedagogical things like documentaries. These don't interest them at all . . . . And anyway, for me, television doesn't even constitute an image. An image isn't only a technical reality: to have an image you need a scene, a myth, the imaginary. Images on television are not blessed with all that. It's there. It's a screen and nothing but a screen, and I think that is how we perceive it as without consequence, no emotion, no passion. People got things mixed up, but I think now they understand: they're going back to the cinema, and that's the proof of it. The cinema is absolutely irreplaceable, it is our own special ceremonial. As for ceremonial of the theatre, I can't bear it any more, simply can't bear it. Even in its most avant-garde forms, it is still bourgeois. The ceremonial of the cinema, on the other hand, that quality of image, of light, that quality of myth, that hasn't gone.

CC   *In everyday life, do you sometimes have the impression of being in a film?*

Yes, particularly in America, to a quite painful degree. If you drive round Los Angeles in a car, or go out into the desert, you are left with an impression that is totally cinematographic, hallucinatory. You are in a film: you are steeped in a substance which is that of the real, of the hyper-real, of the cinema. This is even so with that foreboding of a 'catastrophe': an enormous truck bowling along a freeway, the frequent allusions to the possibility of catastrophic events, but perhaps all that is a scenario I describe to myself. But sometimes you see scenes that begin strangely to resemble scenes in films. And this play, in my opinion, is one element of cinema. The cinema is also made for it and it is a role that has nothing to do with Art or Culture, but which is nevertheless deep: cinema has a profound effect on our perception of people and things, and of time too. But how can you describe all that?

CC   *Do you go to the cinema alone?*

No, not any more. I've nothing against it, but cinema is for sharing, all the same. It is rather symbolic: there should be somebody else involved. To be alone, just you and the film, it's not exactly masturbation, but it's not right alone, it's too exclusive. A film should be allowed to have a bit of free play, in the first place on a group of friends, or a second person, and then subsequently on the audience as a whole. That auditorium, all that space, after all, does have a purpose. But to be a single unit in that space seems to me to go against the collective make-believe (*l'imaginaire*) of the cinema. But I don't want to be dogmatic. Nor do I like those little avant-garde studio cinemas, those exclusive little cinema clubs for voyeuristic little coteries. I don't condemn them, but I prefer cinema for the general public. I like the sort of thing you get in the United States – big productions in big cinemas, with big crowds, Hollywood style.

CC   *Do you think it's important to see a film from the beginning?*

Now, yes, I tend to arrive at the beginning of a film. It's not a discipline, just one of the rules of the game. But I quite like it when the audience is noisy during a film, hurling abuse. Who said it had all to be solemn? I've been in Italian cinemas: it's all bustle and shouting, lively, a total spectacle. And in Los Angeles too, in those big cinemas, I don't think it has changed since the thirties, that sort of excitement, thrills, enthusiasm, and then everyday calm.

CC *Do you go to films dubbed in French?*

It must have happened once or twice, but I avoid them. It annoys me in Italian films because I know the country so well. And in American films the gap is too great, it's like a caricature. With an original version, on the one hand, you have that feeling of the authentic object, and it's quite normal, and on the other the feeling of belonging to a privileged class. It has become an automatic reaction!

CC *When you come away from the cinema, do you talk about what you have just seen?*

I always come away a bit hypnotized, in a state of numbness or ecstasy. Coherent thought comes a bit later. But talking about the film afterwards and continuing to do so is all part of the ritual, of the echo of the film. But now I've almost lost the faculty of judgement in terms of 'it's good, it's bad'. On one hand, I don't know what the criteria are, and on the other, those who do know are no more reliable or credible than the rest. And then, why judge? We have lost the means for judging. So you accept it as it is. In the field of ideas, I know what I'm saying, what I'm judging. But in the field of images, no. It is relatively alien to me. It has the symbolic advantage of its strangeness. And I'd like to keep it that way, with its uncertainty. I'm not at all anxious to classify, to judge. And then I really do think that the judgements we apply to the verbal are not valid when it comes to images. The charm, in the literal sense, of the image has a very strong, immediate mode of apparition, of seduction, and it's better to leave it like that rather than trying to make sense of it. Of course afterwards, if you want, you can impose meaning on it . . . . But while it's happening it is better to submit to the image, to accept it with a certain degree, not of passivity, but of perceptiveness.

CC *Do you close your eyes during the horrific bits?*

I am naive, but I accept an image for what it is. It's a sort of ecstasy, but 'cool' ecstasy. It is not the innate significance of an image that I really receive, it is its charm. So, even if the image is horrific, it is always mitigated by its seductive remoteness.

CC *Do you like black and white?*

I have always liked black and white a lot. I think it really does lie at the very heart of cinematic representation. It lays things bare, it has depth – and perhaps even silent films had it too. The more things you add to make things real, to achieve absolute realistic verisimilitude, perhaps the further you stray from the secret of cinema. But one must beware of this nostalgic yearning for the origins. If today you try to make silent or black-and-white films which are 'even better' than those of that time, complete mental confusion ensues!

Leave them to rest. But there is a grain of truth in the idea that they were more powerful. The myth still resided in their technique: it was the technique that contained mythical power. Afterwards the two became separated and technique took off, but at the expense of myth. Really, there was a dreadful loss. Of course, one must make allowances for the impact of retrospective optical illusion on these origins.

CC *Can you recall the first films that you ever saw?*

It was in Reims, when I was just a boy. A local cinema, the Alhambra, showed two films per programme. There were some Tarzan films, like 'Aloa, Daughter of the Isles' . . . it was wonderful. I even used to go in secret. (Laughter.) Yes, my father would be at the front of the auditorium and at the end I would slip out quickly so that he couldn't see me. And then there were some Jean Gabin films, *'Quai des Brumes'* . . . and of course I adored Michele Morgan like everybody else. I was deeply in love with her. *'La Symphonie Pastorale'*, I must have seen it four or five times in a row. That was the sentimental phase. . . . I think it is good to go through a rather hysterical, a rather sentimental period like that . . . .

CC *Do you find you are moved in the cinema?*

Oh, it doesn't often happen now. I suppose I must have cried watching *'Quand passent les Cigognes'*. But I haven't seen films like 'Love Story', so I don't know to what extent people cry in the cinema nowadays. Today's films are not the 'tear-jerking' sort, they try hard to avoid all that. No, I'm not deeply moved in the cinema any more. Just the same, mine is a rather cool fascination.

CC *Do you ever feel that a film has completely 'taken you over'?*

Yes, as with dreams. It can stay with you the whole day. When I saw 'Reds' it haunted me for the rest of the day. That long story . . . . But it is also extraordinarily pleasurable to sit for three hours in front of something that, well, tells you a story. I don't give a damn about the ideological context of the film. I just sat there, totally absorbed.

CC *Do you normally choose certain kinds of cinemas and certain kinds of films?*

I do have some geographical quirks. I find it very difficult to stray from my own beaten tracks, the Latin Quarter and, to some extent, the Champs-Elysées. And I have other peculiarities in my choice of films: I would rather see a second-rate American film than a French film. I have a sort of inverted chauvinism in my approach to French films. True, they present a picture of everyday French life, but that doesn't excite me much, I know it too well!

And there's too much history in them, too much psychology, too much meaning, perhaps. It's too familiar, you can see through it, you've some idea of what lies behind it. Except Godard's films – now he provides a real sounding-board. He is perhaps the only one who isn't in hock to the mentality of the French petty bourgeoisie. He is irritating sometimes, but what he gives you to look at, you can't help looking at. You can *live* in a Godard film. It is at the same time a different dimension and a way of handling images, which is the only one worth calling modern, to my mind. Finally, there aren't many film-makers who deal with this contemporaneity, even in the United States; Altman and people like that, but perhaps they are very rare.

CC *Are there any films that have left a strong impression on you?*

Really, I haven't made a list. I even find it strangely difficult to remember actors' names and the titles of films. I can, however, situate them but the dates escape me completely. It has a lot to do with that dream-like situation of imaginary transfer. Films swim together in a cloudy confusion, an all-embracing dream. So, what categories can I define particularly? Italian films of a certain period, American films of all periods, westerns; the German expressionist films, certainly, but they have become part of history: you can see them again, but there's no chance of living by them. Wenders' 'L'Ami Américain' I like very much . . . and there are other great films, Coppola's 'Apocalypse Now', Kubrick's 'Barry Lyndon', where one can still find a mythical dimension but in a muted kind of way, and it's my impression that they no longer have a *direct* impact in terms of power of imagination. So, if we're talking about what provides perpetual stimulation in the cinema, that rests with American films. I've always been devoted to American cinema as somewhere one continues to find real passion: go to America and you find this immediate collage, you *are* in a film. In California, particularly, you *live* cinema: you have experienced the desert as cinema, you experience Los Angeles as cinema, the town as a panning shot. I love all that as I love the galleries in Holland and Italy (and only there) because the town around you *is* the gallery. But as far as cinema is concerned only America gives me this impression. It is there that I discover the 'matrix' of the cinema. It is there, after all, that this extraordinary myth was born, and there that it developed like a perpetual celebration, producing its idols, its stars. And so, of course, the myth, the technique and at the same time the reality, I love all that.

CC *Do you sometimes go to sleep in the cinema?*

No, only very rarely. But I did once have a period of insomnia, and whenever I went to the cinema I would fall asleep. It was really quite nice, going to sleep in a cocoon .... . But I prefer to sleep in lectures and seminars; they are really sleep-inducing. In the cinema, on the other hand, I am wide awake, alert. I always have a reason for being there, and I have no wish to be anywhere else. Yes, I feel good, in a favourable anthropological situation. (Laughter.)

3

BAUDRILLARD'S SEDUCTIONS
Interview with Patrice Bollon

PB *Is* Fatal Strategies *your most metaphysical book?*

Certainly. Not that that will stop the metaphysicians laughing at it. I can just hear them: 'Well, after the symbolic, what does he do but rediscover religion?' And that is certainly not what it is about. For me it is not a question of founding a new mysticism – away with radical subjectivity, long live radical objectivity! That sort of flea circus doesn't interest me. It is rather the idea that today there must be a new sort of understanding, a new sort of distance to discover. Critical distance, the whole heritage of the critical subject, seems to me to be over. The scientists, moreover, come back to the idea when they make the hypothesis, common in the social sciences, of the non-separability of the observer and the object of science. Enigmatically, the sun has risen on the object. Things are inflated, insoluble, irreconcilable.

PB *However, when you talk about the fatal, about destiny, that surely has a religious side to it?*

Not at all. It is completely immoral. The fatal is the irony that lies at the bottom of this indifference of the objective processes to the subject's desire for knowledge and power.

PB *You aren't afraid of being accused of paving the way for a new kind of obscurantism of the kind that says: 'Things are only beautiful when they are mute' or, 'We must preserve the secret of appearances', etc.?*

That would be one way of caricaturing my thought. It is true that I talk about the power of illusion, but you will find plenty of that sort of thing in Nietzsche. There is something very much at stake about the secret, but not in the sense that there might be something hidden. There is no interest of that sort as there is in the religious position on the will to knowledge, a sort of 'there are things which must be kept shrouded to preserve their beauty'. In fact, there is nothing that is really hidden: there is simply a game, there are meta-morphoses and effects which are reduplicated and which don't need to be

36

deciphered, and anyway the thing appears to know the rules of the game without seeming to. Without trying to resubjectivize the object, it's a sort of ruse, a laying of false trails and of jamming the waves, which somehow ensures that the secret is preserved.

PB *The first part of your book takes up a point that you have often made before in different forms – the system's total loss of reference and its toppling over into the unreal (*irréel*). Until now it has allowed you to draw up rules of radicality, for combat even, against the social system. But not in this book. So are you rejoicing in this state of ecstasy?*

It is true that I am not denouncing anything – except that when you are writing it is hard to avoid description giving an effect of negation or abjection. Ecstasy consecrates the end of a state, not through sin, guilt, or through some deviation, but through excess. In a way there is no difference between the excess that represents the saturation of a system and that leads it to a final baroque death by overgrowth (*excroissance*) and the excess that stems from the fatal, from destiny. Basically, today, it is impossible to distinguish between good and bad excess. You can no longer find the dividing line. We no longer know when we have reached the point of no return; that is precisely what makes the present situation original and interesting.

PB *The presence of Nietzsche can be felt a little throughout your book. It is felt particularly in your determination to avoid being caught in the Western desire for meaning at any price, for interpretation, for endless commentary.*

That is so. After this tremendous detour that we have all made through ideology, through radical criticism, through Freud and Marx, you will find in my work a return to writers I started with: Nietzsche and Hölderlin. But there is no nostalgia about it. If I go back to them it is not by way of seeking reinforcement, but as the discovery of a fundamental rule.

PB *Which you would define how?*

You have to get rid of all this nervous tension, of all these convulsions that we have got ourselves into in an almost artificial way, which don't represent so much a system running away with itself, but rather a sort of spiral of self-defence which one exercises in a situation which basically has lost all truth and finality. This intellectual, mental, metaphysical situation has through inertia managed to survive beyond its point of relevance. And it is probably from this that we get the stagnation and collapse of thought that we see today. Socialism brings about a sort of decomposition of the intellectual position, but it's deeper than that: we are dragging behind us a whole bundle of ill-digested rationalities, radicalities, that have no support, no enemies, and in which there is nothing at stake. My book no doubt bears traces of that way of thinking, but I haven't tried to expunge from *Fatal Strategies* all vestiges of the old order of things. If you attempt that in a deliberate way you find yourself returning to a will, to *a priori* coherence: you are wide of the mark.

PB *Could we have avoided making that detour?*

You might say that for some of us all that would have been immediately obvious: that is the problem of poetry. I recently read a little piece by Kenneth White, who is always playing around with ideas like these. And he said that for him poetry that tried to be poetry had become frightening in its complacency – nostalgic for the good old days – but that the power, the stuff of the meaning of poetry was to be found nowadays in theoretical tricks that roam all over the place and wander over various fields without ever taking firm hold anywhere. Perhaps that is where we can find poetic power, the poetic function in its primal state, which certainly has nothing to do with metre and rhyme, with melody, or anything you find in modern poetry.

PB *What you say about Kenneth White almost defines your way of writing. In* Fatal Strategies *there are so many things going on at the same time, each of which could form a book in itself.*

That's true. You could almost make each paragraph into a book. But it's not through some merit of mine that I don't succumb to that temptation. To do that would need qualities I haven't got: patience, a sort of will to knowledge, a desire to arrange phenomena around thematics that become more complex. You would then encounter a stock of things. But I want to slim things down, get rid of things, reduce stocks. To escape fullness you have to create voids between spaces so that there can be collisions and short circuits. For the traditional imagination that is not acceptable. It's sacrilege.

PB *That is why you are considered to be a very difficult philosopher to read. But the striking thing on reading your books for the second time is that they do in fact form a very coherent system.*

Yes, my way of thinking is very systematic, and basically very moral. But there is also a sort of counter-game (*contre-jeu*) which destroys things just as they are being constructed. It is not a question of deliberate, 'subversive' will to deconstuct, but an attempt to identify the curvature of things, the mode in which things try to disappear – but not just in any way. They don't want to die, they want to see their disappearance as an effect. Maximal energy is contained in those moments. It's a little like those societies which come to enjoy the violent spectacle of their democratic illusions – or the violent illusion of their sacrifice, of their disappearance. To write is to be oneself at the heart of the system of this demand for a drive to disappearance and the power to bring it about. I'm afraid I don't explain this process very well, but for me it is essential.

PB *One feels that when reading your books. What is more it is sometimes rather frustrating and baffling: just when you think you've grasped the meaning it evaporates, only to reconstruct itself a little further on.*

That's right. Theory for me is a fatal strategy – perhaps even the only one. That's the whole difference between a banal theory and a fatal theory: in the first the subject believes himself to be cleverer than the object; in the second the object is always supposed to be cleverer, more cynical and more inspired than the subject, whom he awaits ironically at the end of the detour. There is nothing more anti-pedagogical, anti-didactic, than my book. Nor is it something I wrote as a therapy. Sometimes I really do wonder who it is written for . . . .

PB *Then why offer it to the public?*

There are some problematics which are quite insoluble today in terms of psychology or sociology – a whole area of contention, growing all the time, and which will never be recycled. That is why we must try to jump over the wall, cross to the side of the object, side with it against the subject. An entire constructivist, structuralist period is coming to an end, but the converse side, of negativity, subversion, radical criticism, is also disappearing. In these troubled times nobody really gets to the bottom of the game any more. Either this situation is enervated – indifferent in the full sense of the term – and becomes nothing more than the area of manoeuvre for banal strategies, or it is an intensely passionate situation. Basically, what is there to do but to go over to the side of this enigma? It is the idea of a 'wager' that I am putting forward; just for a moment let us suppose that things are biased towards the fatal and the enigmatic.

PB *It is a wager which applies first of all to you. I interpreted* Fatal Strategies *as a treatise on your own personal metamorphosis, a sort of 'Confessions of a* fin-de-siècle *intellectual'.*

It is very strange. I had actually thought about publishing at the same time a sort of journal that I have been keeping for about two years. Logically speaking, the two works should be able to mix together. In fact, I could quite well imagine a book with parallel entries where you would have the more theoretical part on one side and the journal on the matching page. It would be a monstrous book, and it would turn out like some gadget that couldn't really work. I got more pleasure out of writing the journal than I did out of writing *Fatal Strategies*, but as soon as I started editing the latter I immediately dropped the journal.

PB *In comparison with your previous books,* Fatal Strategies *had an extra dimension underlying it: as if your life had gone into it a bit. At least, that was my impression.*

That must be true. For a long time I wrote books in a rather offhand manner.

39

There was no vital necessity to do it, and my own life wasn't involved. But from *Seduction* onwards, there was a sort of meeting, a clash between the two. I don't mean I live to write, but everything has got intertwined. There is no longer that sort of distancing, critical and analytical at the same time, that allows you to 'explain' things. The world is an exteriority, as is your own life. You are in a kind of schizophrenia which may be very complex and very rich, but you remain a state of redoubling. Whilst out there, everything is all right: you are not divided. What you write describes what you are. It is true that in Nietzsche's works the intertwining is very striking. At that point, however, a book turns into something else: it is no longer a cultural process, perhaps it becomes rather a rule . . . .

PB *Which brings me to the last question.* Fatal Strategies *seems more like a beginning than an end. It could serve as a sort of platform, even manifesto, for future work.*

It is more nuclear than that. Writing a manifesto would be like mounting a new opera or melocritique. That would need the illusion of rupture. That is what I wanted to avoid. What I was doing previously was more in the nature of a disenchanted, indifferent statement: implosion as an indifferent mass. That remains true. Only now I envisage a sort of energy of implosion which is trying to find itself. Thus there is the possibility of an inverse energy, a departure, but I can't yet see in which direction it leads. Implosion was still a catastrophic system of the subject. To the extent that you manage to pass to the other side, to the object, that opens a new field of possibility.

4

THE 'LOOK' GENERATION – THE MANNERISM OF A WORLD WITHOUT MANNERS

Interview with *Le Nouvel Observateur*

You are one of the very few sociologists – or even poets? – who has understood that our modernity is to be found principally in the play of simulacres and of appearances . . . .

We are no longer in the world of alienation and it is therefore no longer possible to use arguments based on one's own wretchedness, one's own inauthenticity, one's misfortune and bad conscience. It's no longer possible either to hope to come to existence in and through the eye of the other for there is no longer a dialectic of identity. Therefore everyone is henceforth called upon to appear, just appear, without worrying too much about being. Hence the importance of the look . . . .

I don't even know if there is in this a desire to seduce; I don't think there is for this would require that appearances were carefully worked on, stylized, according to a strategy of diverting the other in order to harness his gaze and lead him to his loss. Whereas the 'look' is simply this: I exist, I am here, I am an image, look at me, look, look! It's like Puerto Rican graffiti in New York: my name is so and so, I live in New York, I am brilliant. This is narcissism perhaps, a game of simulacres perhaps, but in any case it is exhibition without inhibition, a kind of ingenious publicity in which each person becomes the impresario of his own appearance, of his own artifice. There is here a new passion, ironic and new, that of beings devoid of all illusion about their own subjectivity. I would say almost without illusion about their own desires, all the more fascinated by their own metamorphosis.

It's in this context that the creation of a look becomes for every individual a task of self-identification whose meaning and importance one would be wrong to underestimate . . . .

The look is a bit like the television in so far as the picture is concerned: a finery with least definition, of minimal definition, like the television picture according to McLuhan. It's the opposite of the ceremonial, an appearance which wanders about, a changeable, ephemeral appearance, a tactile appearance, as McLuhan says in describing the electronic universe, that is to say, one which doesn't even attract attention or admiration – which the mirror of fashion still does – but a pure special effect, lacking any particular meaning. This doesn't even any longer call on the social logic of differentiation (*distinction*), as fashion still does, it no longer plays on a coded difference, it plays at difference without believing in it, it plays at singularity without falling into dandyism or snobbery. It is neither what is chic nor what is distinguished, it is a disenchanted mannerism in a world which no longer knows manners.

What lesson could one draw from the recent history of sartorial appearances, say since the beginning of the sixties?

The miniskirt was perhaps the last episode in the history of fashion that was more than an effect of fashion: it was a sort of event in the history of morals (*moeurs*) to the extent that the rape of appearance came to replace taboo (the anterior fashion). There was in effect a true erotic effect, an irruption of the erotic in the real. Today, with the present erotic look, this is no longer so: it is no more than an irruption of the erotic in appearances, the erotic as special effect at the level of fashion. But there is also a socialist look of the same genre: it is the irruption of all the appearances of socialism in the social world.

In the nineteenth century, Balzac or Barbey d'Aurevilly searched for the truth of their era in the 'physiology' of the dandy or of the bourgeois. Do you think that we need today to relearn how to be curious like them?

We no longer have any great modern incarnations. The last ones were doubtless the proletarians and the cinema idols, that is to say, the two summits constituted by historical revolt and mythical fascination. Today the look of such and such an actress has replaced the glamour of Hollywood stars, the political look of the Communist Party, or the Socialist Party, of such and such a newspaper, of such and such a union boss, has replaced the dialectic of power relations. Hence, in addition, there is no longer any novelistic energy like that of the nineteenth century with Balzac and the others, to recount this mutation. Faced with this task the cinema itself exhausts its energy because it still presupposes an imaginary, whereas the look, this pure extraversion of simulated games, is without an imaginary. Perhaps it would be better as far as the look is concerned to speak of the disappearance of the rhetoric of fashion. The strategies of the beautiful and the useful (including jeans as degree zero fashion) no longer work at the level of the look. Any aesthetic or functional judgement is absent from it. Thus the look escapes from all rhetoric towards a pure combinatory of metamorphosis . . . .

5

THE POWER OF REVERSIBILITY THAT EXISTS IN THE FATAL

Interview with D. Guillemot and D. Soutif

DG/DS *Are you a philosopher, a sociologist, a writer, a poet, none of these or all at the same time?*

I am neither a philosopher nor a sociologist. I haven't followed the appropriate academic path nor worked in the right institutions. I am in sociology at university, but I don't recognize myself in sociology or in philosophizing philosophy. Theorist? I agree. Metaphysician? Perhaps. Moralist? I don't know. My work has never been academic, nor is it getting more literary. It's evolving, it's getting less theoretical, without feeling the need to furnish proof or rely on references.

DG/DS *In* Fatal Strategies *you talk about cancerous society and of a catastrophe that is lying in wait for us. Are we there or moving that way?*

It would be stupid to prophesy an apocalypse in the literal sense of the term. My idea is that the catastrophe has already happened, it's here already. What interests me is precisely beyond the catastrophe, what I would call its hypertelia. Catastrophe is acceleration, precipitation, excess, but not necessarily annihilation. Once I used to analyse things in critical terms, of revolution; now I do it in terms of mutation.

I am not a prophet of doom. I say that in our world there is a logic that is catastrophic in the literal sense, but not in the romantic or sentimental sense of the term. The 'cancerous society' is a metaphor. One has the right to push writing and hypotheses to the very end, to points where, perhaps at the limit, they no longer have any meaning, but that is where they are going. In the literal sense it is true that there is a cancerous form, a metastatic form of the creeping proliferation of things, but I don't want to offer cancer as a concept. I am talking about overgrowth (*excroissance*) instead of growth (*croissance*), and that form can just as easily invade theory as the social fabric or the economy and production. It is obvious in the production of information and communciation, in material goods and sexual contacts: this is overproduction that doesn't any more know what it's for but for the moment finds a sort of logic in its own proliferation.

43

DG/DS *Could not technology make it possible to restore a sense of order? As far as information is concerned, is there not some way that techniques would make it possible to control this process of proliferation?*

Information nevertheless thrives as a force for progress, for balance and enrichment, but I don't think it would be possible to master it. There are perhaps phases in the history of technology. For technology as a whole, we could say what McLuhan says about the mass media: the medium becomes the message. Technology itself becomes the message; it doesn't push things forward or transform the world, it becomes the world. And this substitution of one thing for another might be considered perilous, because it is no longer a question of restoring balance or order.

With information technology, for example, there is an effect of the realization of the world. The world, which from the dawn of time has been myth, fantasy, fable, becomes realized through technology. This materialism seems to me to be a catastrophe in the etymological sense of the term. It is a sort of death, where everything takes on the garb of reality. You can imagine a point where all the thoughts waiting to be thought will be immediately realizable by means of a computer. I am not condemning technology, it's fascinating, it can produce marvellous special effects. But with this faculty of giving reality to the world, then the possible, the imaginary, the illusory all disappear. Now, the illusory is perhaps vital. A world without any illusory effects will be completely obscene, material, exact, perfect.

DG/DS *And where does writing stand now, that old technology that has wrought many changes in its time and that you still use? Doesn't it function in the mode of proliferation?*

Yes, and nobody quite knows how to hold it back. It seems that we have crossed a certain boundary, and that a certain self-regulation that used to come into play, even biologically, in relation to the species, no longer operates. There is now a possibility of limitless proliferation in a world that has lost all sense of perspective, where sight, distance and judgement have been lost. And judgement is no longer needed in a world that is simply there, immanent, realized.

At the limit the effect of something written is nil today. I can choose not to go on writing because I am not caught up in a coercive culture that compels a writer to write, and an intellectual to think. I began to write when I wanted to, and I will stop if it ceases to be worthwhile. I need a challenge myself, there's got to be something at stake. If that is taken away, then I will stop writing. I'm not mad. At a given moment, however, you cause things to exist, not by producing them in the material sense of the term, but by defying them, by confronting them. Then at that moment it's magic. And it's not only writing that functions like that. I don't know if we have a relationship with other people in terms of desire, but we certainly have one in terms of defiance.

We don't exist unless we are subject to a degree of defiance. We need to be desired, caressed, but we also need to be challenged and thus seduced. There is a game, which has nothing to do with the forced realization of the world, a game in which things demand to be solicited, diverted, seduced. You've got to be able to make them appear as well as disappear; to play the whole game. Writing is nothing but that, and theory as well. It is knowing how to conjure up concepts, effects, and knowing how to resolve them. Culture is not just a simple question of producing ideas or differences. It's also a question of knowing how to cast a spell.

We thoroughly understand the rules of production, but not the rules of this particular game. I think we should compare them. On the one hand banality, and on the other hand, this rule of the game whose effects may perhaps be mastered but which belongs to a more secret order: the fated.

It is nevertheless quite possible that we might not today be able to distinguish between fatality and banality. What interests me, therefore, is not fatality in the sense of *fatum*, timeless and transhistorical, but the modern variety of fatality, closely linked with the banal. Banality is the fatality of our modern world.

DG/DS *Could you tell us where you stand with regard to psychoanalysis?*

Psychoanalysis has become useless, a burden. It satisfies a sort of dizziness for explanations, for self-obsession and for reproducing itself. The word was one of the fundamental tools of analysis, then everything began to spin round, and here too there was a delirium of conceptual production, which got more and more sophisticated. Curiously, it has ceased to have any effect. I am not talking about psychoanalysis in its early days. But I do criticize the present-day variety because everything that's at stake must go beyond it and cause it to shatter.

DG/DS *In* Fatal Strategies *we don't know what geographical space you allude to, whether it's a planetary space or not.*

I don't talk about people in the sociological sense. The masses are not locatable in terms of population, they are not the sum of locatable individuals. It's the mass effect, the mass forms that I analyse, and which, somewhere, no longer produces any difference. This something which is there but which doesn't produce any difference is an extraordinary challenge to symbolic order of any kind, be it political, social or whatever.

My analysis, if you put it back into a realistic, geographical frame of reference, is not going to apply more or less well to such and such a model. It is a logical hypothesis of radicality, and it was inspired by the so-called developed countries, particularly the United States. But the Third World is also totally caught up in this explosion of effects, this loss of causality, this proliferation, as in demography for example. It is impossible that one part

45

of the world's population should stick to relatively traditional, logical relationships of production or penury while another part enters another phase. The whole of our world has entered into the same phase; whether one is rich or poor does not perhaps play an important role.

DG/DS *You write that people don't seek collective happiness, but rather ecstasy and the spectacle. What do you mean by that?*

I don't know what people are looking for. They have been taught to look for things like happiness, but deep down that doesn't interest them, any more than producing or being produced. What interests them is rather something that belongs to the realm of fascination, of games, but not in the frivolous sense. The world is a game. Rituals are regaining their importance, and what is a ritual if not a rule of the game, another type of relationship, not of forces, but of metamorphoses? People can sometimes cling passionately to extremely harsh and cruel logics but not for work, retirement, social security.

Ritual didn't exist in savage times only to disappear in our modern age and to be reborn as a revival of some archaic process. It has always been there, and it isn't only against reality that one struggles. That's the whole problem. If the world is reality, then effectively the logic is one of a transformation and a realization of the world, and that's all. But if the world is also illusion, appearance, then that is mastered in another way. There are different logics, different rules, and I believe that nobody has forgotten and nobody has renounced that game. Fashion, for instance, is a continuing collective passion, putting aside any perspective, and you can't say that it is archaic. All transformation of things into spectacle: it is this function of simulation which is perhaps what really makes them work, not their rational and economic mechanisms (*dispositif*).

If Soviet society really functioned in accordance with its system of values, its bureaucracy, its ideology, it would have crumbled a long time ago. This society exists and no doubt will exist for a long time because what works is the game of bureaucracy. Derision is internal to its functioning. It doesn't really run on its bureaucracy, because the people wouldn't survive in that case. Italy also functions on derision for the real state of things, which is a state of political and economic confusion. There is a collective complicity, an agreement that all should continue on a lower plane (*état second*). The real social bond is a pact which is the contrary of the social contract, a symbolic pact of allurement, complicity, derision. That is why socialism is not possible: it wants to bring everything back to the social contract and eliminate this sort of avoidance (*détournement*), this second game, this secret complicity, this pathology of social relationships where all people's imagination and passion is exercised in the double games of the maintenance of fiefdoms and territories.

The socialists are not the only ones to make mistakes. It is simply that they are the only ones who want to make reality transparent, and extirpate all the irrationalities, including all the signs and images which are vehicles for the effects of derision. If they managed to eliminate all that they would put an end to society's survival. But fortunately people work against the grain of any political system which, in appearance, represents the others and makes itself obeyed. In fact, the rule of the game is more secret than that: everything goes on in an ambience of profound derision, and somewhere the murder of that symbolic class is achieved. Everything that has conferred upon it power, status, prestige must be destroyed, killed.

DG/DS *This idea resurfaces in your eulogy of the sexual object.*

The sexual object is not something that plays at being a subject of desire and at liberating itself but one that prefers to be pure object, no longer allowing itself to be judged, watched nor, basically, desired. Exhibition is the perfect form of obscenity. That is what gives it its power.

Nobody has won, nobody has lost. It is quite possible that women have resisted, survived, by the same effect of derision, of the seduction that I was just talking about. When you try to explain that to the feminists, they find it quite unacceptable. There have been dreadful misunderstandings. I've been accused of pushing women back into seduction. 'Women have been stripped of everything; they're left with nothing but their power of seduction', complain the feminists. That is not at all what I meant. Seduction is a subversive power, it makes it possible to have mastery over that rather secret rule of the game, mastery not of power relations but another type of relationship. In that sense, nobody has won and nobody has lost. It would be too easy to say that men have won that age-old struggle. The feminists need the ancestral female woe in order to exist. They have defined themselves as movements in relation to what they claim from society. It is vital for them that their woe has always existed and will always exist. They have shown more detestation for me than they have for the machos. A macho is never anything else but a macho. All you have to do is fight against him. But somebody who comes along and tells you that you have much more sovereignty over men than you think, that throws your mechanism (*dispositif*) into confusion.

The feminists have rejected me definitively. It's a pity. The problematic is completely closed today, and curiously psychoanalysis has thrown no light on the matter. There have been a lot of psychoanalytical studies carried out by women, but it all crystallizes on relations with the mother. Psychoanalysis has put its entire conceptual edifice at the service of that but hasn't thrown any light on the question. In any case they do not want light.

DG/DS *Has sexual liberation failed? Indeed, did it ever happen?*

Whether it has happened or not is a secondary question. You can only find that out from the statistics and they are all indecipherable. I would like to know just what people mean when they recount their behaviour. People

47

are so naive about this. They think that if you ask people about their sexual behaviour they're going to tell you the truth. In fact, it's impossible to know what it is.

DG/DS *There's been talk about trying to liberate us from lots of things, but in the end it turned out not to be that which is interesting.*

The effect of rupture is always interesting. The liberation of productive forces did get people to work. All the revolutions have been liberations in that sense. They shattered the old structures in order to capture people's potential energy with a definite aim in view. The hair-brained liberation that people dreamed about in 1968: in the sense that things would be free to become anything at all, to contain their own purpose, that is the aesthetic vision of liberation. But in reality all liberations have always led to servitude at another level.

DG/DS *You often allude to biology, you talk about cloning and the genetic code. But you seldom allude to neurophysiology, the biology of the brain, which the media are making a big noise about. What do you think about this upsurge of interest in the neuronal?*

I think it's grotesque. I have nothing to do with such truths. It's going in the same direction as everything else, and it's a more subtle, more miniaturized terminal. It doesn't interest me. What I'm interested in is myth. With this proliferation in miniaturization, this pyramidalization of things which renders everything else useless, one can nevertheless ask oneself what a body is. If everything boils down to a definition, either by genetic code or by the brain, the body becomes useless. It's vertiginous! But at least we are still free to consider it an aberration. I am tempted to think this through right to the end; to see what is going to happen at the far limit of these aberrations and of the pathology of the modern world. Is this world irredeemably lost? I don't know. It is so functionalized that everything you might call game, illusion, even language itself, risks remaining caught up in it. However, let's not indulge in complacent catastrophism; things develop by themselves, perhaps, and to apply to them pseudo-moral ideas of humanist deontology – a discourse that has existed ever since there was science and technology – that won't change anything at all.

And then, there will always be a way of playing with the systems, data-processing included. We have the impression that this computer network is all-powerful, and that virtually, in ten years' time, the world will be computer-run (*télématisé*). But it won't happen like that, because things don't operate only at the level of their realistic evolution. Take the exact sciences: the further they advance in hyper-detailed realism, the more the object of study disappears. The more they hunt the object of study into the inner recesses of its real existence, the more it eludes them. That is my only hope.

Analysis in demiurgic manipulative terms, with an ultra-power always on the horizon, we know that that is no longer exactly true and that there are some strange turns of events. Take the example of nuclear weapons. We know that it is the very proliferation of nuclear weapons that stops nuclear war from breaking out, even if nobody wants to admit it. It is fortunate that they have produced a hundred times too much! If ever they manage to find a little theatre well suited to nuclear war, it will start. We are protected by the proliferation, the ecstasy of destruction. We are stuck at a stage of phantasmagoric nuclear destruction that doesn't take place. This fatality, if it is ours, is not interesting. Fatality fascinates me, but not this functionalist, catastrophic fatality. There is another sort. I count on a reversible fatality, on the power of reversibility that exists in the fatal to defy and thwart this process. You can create as many social institutions as you want, there will always be this infra-resistance, this infra-distortion, which will ensure that, fortunately, the social will not function. That is what interests me, and I don't see why it shouldn't be the same where science and technology are concerned.

6

THE REVENGE OF THE CRYSTAL
Interview with Guy Bellavance

GB *Banal strategy and fatal strategy: what is the difference between them?*

Yes, this detour, this opposition is a little facile. As soon as one looks at it it proves to be much more complex. Banality – that of the masses, of silent majorities – all that is our ambience . . . . For me it is however a fatal strategy: something responds of its own accord, something from which it is impossible to escape, but which you cannot decipher either, an immanent type of fatality . . . . It is there at the heart of the system, at a strategic point in the system, at its point of inertia, at its blind spot. That is my definition (there isn't any other) of the fatal. Now, mass behaviour, mass art, Beaubourg, all that . . . that's the extreme point of the banal, the apogee of the banal. I had a good look at all that. Let us say that that is the kind of fatality which comes from systems of simulations and which produces this mass object.

Yet, for me, seduction is also a fatal strategy. It is the first, the most beautiful example, of a sort of fatality . . . . It is something altogether different from, let us say, the banality of sex, it is a stake of another order, of an enchanted order, whereas, obviously, the strategy of the masses is disenchanted. The fatal can in fact embrace the two aspects. Simply, there is a point which they have in common: behind the fatal there is always something like irony. It is not a tragic, sentimental or romanesque fatality, or even a religious fatality. It is ironic . . . but not, once again, a subjective irony . . . there is no subject behind it. The beautiful period of subjective irony, of radical subjectivity, is perhaps for us now over. And this would be the end of an epoch in which all philosophy could effectively express itself (Kierkegaard, the Romantics as well) and marks the beginning of a kind of objective irony.

Behind these strategies, it seems to me, there is an irony of finalities: not a denial of finalities, not a transgression of drama, not the violent destruction of drama, but an ironic detour through the finalities that the subject wanted to impose. So irony, for me, would be almost an anti-definition: this secret, but perhaps the most obvious . . . . Objective irony, isn't it?

50

GB *It is the revenge of the object?*

Yes, that's it. I have called it the 'revenge of the crystal'; and I started out from there in fact. The book, *Fatal Strategies*, crystallized on that theme. When the title came to me the book was very quickly written around it. Of course I already had many of the elements. What is the 'crystal'? It is the object, the pure object, the pure event, something which no longer really has an origin or an end. The object to which the subject has wanted to give an origin and a purpose, even though it has none, is today perhaps starting to recount itself. There is today a possibility that the object will say something to us, but there is also above all the possibility that it will take its revenge! It quite pleased me to see that the object exists in a relatively passionate form, and that there should be passion in objects and not only passion in subjects: passions in the mode of the ruse, irony, indifference, inertias, in opposition, precisely, to those of the subject which are purposeful, stimulate ... desire, for example. Whereas object-passion, that would be indifference. It certainly is a passion in my opinion, an ironic passion. This domain remains to be explored – and it is not done in the book – it could be done by developing certain chapters. I have not done it, but I will perhaps write a theory of object-passions, of the passions of the object, of objective passions.

GB *It is obvious that your relation to the object has been modified considerably since* The Object System *(1968) ....*

Oh yes! It has changed completely! It doesn't even have anything to do with it any longer except with respect to the obsession of the object. It is the same term. And I quite liked that – there is also irony in it – to be thus swamped with objects, to have started from the object, from the obsession I had for them. It was, from the beginning, for sure, a question of something other than the object: to pass across them. But all the same it all started from objects and finished with ... the object! (Laughter.)

The analysis of the system of objects was in any case a detour to approach from behind the problematic of the subject–object dialectic. There is a system here but there is also something else. There is something more than the logics of the alterity of the subject. These are already weakened problematics. To consider therefore objects as a system was already a way to break from traditional approaches. But in the end it has been developed into something different.

GB *The object of which you talk is a quasi-subject. It isn't totally passive. It expresses many things.*

No, it isn't passive and yet it isn't a subject. It isn't a subject in the sense that, unlike the subject, it has no imaginary. It is without imaginary but that is precisely its power, its sovereignty. It is not caught in a system of production,

51

identification, mirror stage . . . desire. The object is without desire, it is that which escapes desire and belongs to the order of destiny. In my opinion, there are only two things: there is desire, or there is destiny!

GB *It is also without negativity.*

It is without negativity, yes, yes.

GB *It is always in the superlative.*

Yes, yes . . . . But that returns even so to many current interests developing elsewhere today, not the search for the positivist position but instead for the positivity of things, the immanence of things. In Deleuze's work, for example, even if we are perhaps a long way from one another, it is a question of the same quest, namely of going beyond all subjectivity, even the most radical, to ask what there is there, what the object has to say, what the world, such as it is, has to say to us. Has it no immanent processes? Is there no emotivity in it? Yet something happens. It's not a passivity. On the contrary it's a game.

GB *This passion for potentialization, for redoubling, which you speak of at the beginning of your book, the more true than the true, the more beautiful than the beautiful . . . this quality which will have absorbed entirely the energy of its opposite, what is it exactly?*

A phantasm . . . I don't know! Some people could say that it is a mysticism. I do not think that because it isn't homogeneous. It remains, despite everything, a game, and there is a rule to the game, and so there is no fusion and homogenization of things. On the contrary, these redoubled effects cut violently into other things, into the order of the mirror, or resemblance, of the image, precisely beyond the imaginary. It is also the hyper-real in this sense: this redoubling is the equivalent of a kind of absolutization. It is at base, in admitting that it is a process (because it can be a situation in movement), something which passes into radical objectivity. Not objectivity in the scientific sense, but radical *objectality* (*objectité*), as one would say.

So that could be a kind of revenge. One has placed the object in the object position: the subject gave it to itself as an object, but with safeguards, etc., and yet the object escapes this kind of trap, this strategy which is that of the subject, and in passing to radical objectivity it escapes the systems of deciphering, interpretation. The problem is to know if that, which greatly interests me, is a detour or a modern vicissitude or if it is at bottom a metaphysical question. I think that it is both: there is a dimension here which is more and more metaphysical, or anti-metaphysical (but that's the same). It is the current modern conjuncture which interests me – not banal fatality, not either the object of metaphysics or of philosophy – I am not at bottom a philosopher, with an interest in argumentation, terminology – it is not that they are outside my concerns but I do not start from that – it is not that I even tried to! I am interested in the way things are. I am interested to start from the nuclear situation at the moment: object-situations, or again strategies of the masses. I don't know if these are modern or postmodern vicissitudes. But they are part of our system. The 'system of objects' was from the start, even so, something which had never been produced as such in other cultures. It is, perhaps, a specific destiny.

GB *In that sense, would you still be a sociologist?*

Oh yes! Sociology was born with modernity, it was born out of an observation on modernity, yes, in that sense.

GB *Do you still situate yourself in the framework of modernity or, as one likes to say, in postmodernity? How do you situate yourself in relation to this play of times?*

I don't know . . . it does not follow 'history' in the generic sense of the term, that is certain, with its sense of continuity, evolution, logic, the search for an origin of causes and of effects. And yet all the same it has a dimension which is not purely anecdotal. It is not for sure a catalogue of modernity. It is something else. It is, perhaps, that modernity I analyse while crossing it . . . or else it's the same thing. It is the same effect of spiral, or of redoubling, that I make of modernity which finally rebounds onto metaphysics. But then it is a question of a metaphysic come from a redoubling of this modernity, rather than a history of a metaphysic, of Western millenarian thought . . .! One must cut out the reference if one wants to describe this modernity in its ruptural effects, its denegation of the past; one must do the same thing in analysis. Cut oneself out of the reference, drop all that. Not by despising it but to find in all that a radical *pathos*, as Nietzsche said, a pure distance. Not the distance of critical observation, not a negative distance, but a kind of pure distance. At that moment, modernity appears in a new way, in a light which is more alive, more violent, more radical. It is then more interesting. That is why I find the USA more interesting than the history of European philosophy. I find the American situation more challenging, exciting. But once this decisive operation is made, there is nothing to predict except that in the vicissitude of modernity, in its turning back on itself, it relaunches a dimension which is no longer sociological at all . . . which is metaphysical. Besides this metaphysic is the outcome of this same thing. It does not come from elsewhere.

GB *When you suggest that one should substitute the mode of disappearance of the object for the mode of production, it seems to me that you play Nietzsche against Marx. It makes me think of the eternal return in Nietzsche. Do you see it in the same way?*

It is certain that there is an echo if not a reference to Nietzsche. I read him passionately, but a long time ago, and since have not reread his work. Anyway, it had somehow quite a decisive effect. Yes, the theme of the eternal return is possibly something quite prodigious in that sense. But I would recover the influence of Nietzsche in terms of *metamorphosis*, for example: possibilities of the entwining of forms without causes or effects . . . or again the possibility on the plane of the disappearance: something which disappears, the traces of which are effaced, origin and end are effaced. So things are not any longer understood in terms of linearity. The passage to the state of disappearance, fundamentally, is the disappearance of the linear order, of the order of cause and effect. Therefore it gives to that which disappears in the horizon of the other the opportunity to reappear. There is evidently a curvature which was not in the antecedent order which implies . . . the *eternal return* in the Nietzschean sense. In the end there is a conjuncture which is very strong and which is linked to the escalation of power. The escalation of power plays on that cycle: it appears precisely when it can transfigure values, that is to say when it has the power to make things disappear, and not simply a power of transformation. It is different, then, yes, there would be an order which truly opposes itself to all other modernity: historical modernity, ideological, etc., and which installs itself after. But it is not a return to that. It would be, besides, perhaps more Hölderlin than Nietzsche.

GB *You oppose, somewhere, the attitude of Baudelaire to that of Benjamin, the attitude of the nineteenth century to that of the nostalgia of the twentieth century.*

It is an opposition not at all to the profit of one or other. Benjamin is someone I admire profoundly. The tonalities of the two universes have also many consonances: the very original *mélange* in Benjamin, in Adorno also, of a type of dialectic . . . and then of presentiment of that which is no longer dialectical: system and its catastrophe. There is at the same time a dialectical nostalgia and a profound melancholy which is something other than dialectical. There is truly a kind of witness as regards the fatality of systems . . . . But I believe that Baudelaire, *vis-à-vis* modernity, saw things a bit like that. But it was not on a point where I thought that curiously Baudelaire was more radical – the question was not posed like that at that moment – but that he saw modernity with a fresher eye than Benjamin . . . and Benjamin saw it again with a fresher eye than we do now! That is to say, the closer one is to the moment of rupture . . . .

GB *Of the beginning* . . .

Yes, the better one sees things. I believe that profoundly. It is always true in practice. When something changes, the response, whether positive or negative, is always strong. Later, it loses definition. Psychologically that is well established. In the analytic realm it also works like that. And in that respect, in the problem of art, modern art, the modernity of art, yes indeed also, this business of 'the absolute commodity', which is practical, which is announced already in Hegel of course . . . art as disappearance, as the magic of disappearance, he had seen that very well.

GB *It is in that sense perhaps that you are interested in art. You say somewhere that art is nothing more today than the magic of its own disappearance.*

Yes, yes . . .

GB *Is it for that reason that you have an interest – I don't know since when – for art?*

Yes, but it is not a leading interest either. I have never been a practising artist . . . . I know many people, I've experienced something there also, and possibly it is true that something aesthetic, in the profound sense of the term, excites me greatly, and that includes the disappearance of the aesthetic dimension of the world. Today it is an enormous stake, even so . . . . Not aesthetic in the artistic sense . . . but a mode of perception: indeed, this art of appearance, this art of making things appear. Not producing them, but making them appear.

It is true that that has always inspired me . . . . But I am not excited by the circumvolutions of modern art, the diverse and overlapping movements . . . . I was very interested at a given moment in pop, then in hyper-realism. But that was rather in analytical terms: it was a field, among others, which well illustrated a number of things. The *trompe-l'oeil* had excited me also, because of seduction. But the history of art itself does not interest me. Art interests me for levelling forms like that . . . . But the aesthetic outcome . . . the term is so annoying, I employ it very little, I believe that I avoid it, because for us it has such a resonance . . . .

GB *. . . aestheticizing . . . .*

Yes, one can't escape it. If only one could render effectively its literal consonance . . . .

GB *Versus ethics perhaps? It becomes more interesting . . . versus morality. One could indeed interpret the negative reactions of the public to your lecture in that sense . . . .*

Yes, I have had some echoes. What did you make of it?

GB *I found indeed that the reaction in the room was a moral one whereas your discourse was an aesthetic one . . . .*

. . . aesthetic certainly, yes. The first question was very pertinent on that level: 'Right then, it disappears, and that is literature!' – because if the analytic disappears, if somewhere, in effect, it searches its own disappearance in trying to conjure an object which would have things to tell us but which would no longer have come from a system of interpretation of the subject . . . and after all what is it that can render that if not the narrative? At that point one enters the aesthetic in the purest sense of the term. I think that the story, the narrative (*récit*), that is where fatality can play, the narrative preserves a fatal character . . . a tale (*une histoire*).

GB *And at the same time you say that the only fatal strategy perhaps would be theory itself.*

Yes, theory, but as narrative (*récit*), as spiral, as concatenation (*enchaînement*). Yes, the concepts that I use are not concepts. I do not claim for myself their conceptual tenor, that would be too demanding. One can make them play one against the other, and that is not frivolous, or fashion; in my opinion it's very serious. It is the only way for power to accommodate itself to the movement of things. Therefore theory, and this is a paradoxical proposition, becomes fatal. It makes itself object.

When I say narrative, one cannot say strictly that one returns to a romanesque form . . . although from time to time I would quite like to . . . . Besides, in the book there are passages . . . .

GB *That is to say, you claim for theory the right not to be true . . . .*

. . . Certainly, the right to play, to be radical. It can become narrative. That is, in two senses in the books I've written, the story as departure. There are always little stories, some little things which start and which have often been the sites of emergence: situations, wit, dreams, *witz* . . . I like the word better in German – '*le trait d'esprit*' is a little too long! In the end '*le trait*', the dash, if one wants: it is not any longer a metalanguage which organizes itself around signs, but a tracking shot which organizes itself around '*les traits*'. Therefore, at that point, there is no continuity in '*les traits*', and in principle things speed and there is no discursivity.

So, it is a mode of narrative, and I think theory can be vindicated as narrative. But indeed it is not literature as such one aims at. The question at the lecture the other day was a good one but, towards the end, a little too tendentious because it drew everything into literature. That is not what I want to do. But there must be other forms to develop this, including philosophy, but on condition that philosophy comes to dismantle itself within its own apparatus of words, concepts, etc. It could be poetry . . . but poeticizing poetry, that neither . . .

GB *It would be as a 'communicative aesthetic' perhaps? In the sense that, in comparison with Habermas who proposes a 'communicative ethic' founded on a rational consensus – you propose rather an aesthetic founded on conflict and on seduction.*

Yes, the challenge and the duel, yes . . . . But I have always had a prejudice against the term 'communication'. It seems to me that it was always situated on a terrain of an exchange, a dialogue, a system, I don't know ... a contact ... with all the linguistic and metalinguistic functions implicated in all that. If that is 'communication' it is not what I have in my sights.

Already in my book, *L'Échange Symbolique et la Mort* (1976), there was something else. But the category of the symbolic is a bit worn, there are too many misunderstandings over the term. Therefore one lets go of it. Or rather that, in my opinion, interesting relations between people do not exist on the mode of human communication. There is something else: a mode of challenge, of seduction, of play, which makes livelier things come into existence. 'Communication' restricts itself to putting things that already exist in contact with each other. It does not make things appear. It then searches for equilibrium ... the message and all that. It seems to me that there is a more exciting mode: that which makes things appear. That is the order of the challenge .... Not exactly communication. I don't know if one can have an 'aesthetic of communication'.

GB *Indeed, that when I say 'communicative aesthetic' it is not aesthetic of communication. It is rather to recover the communicative through the aesthetic in a certain manner ... or rekindle it ... .*

... Yes. The 'communicative' process, it's true, seems to me always a bit functional, a bit functionalist, as if truly things existed only to ...

GB *... to convince ...*

... yes, that's it, always in a relation with either a pedagogic or moral content. I think that the more profound stakes are not at that level, not at the level of communication.

GB *It seems to me, in relation to this, that the question of the 'reversibility of signs' – that you oppose in a way as a strategy to that of the 'transgression of the law' – is quite fundamental. I would like you to explain what you mean by that. It seems to me that it is indeed there that the strongest oppositions are made. One can see there perhaps a lot of perversity ... .*

Yes, perhaps, because there is something immoral in it. There is something in the fact that reversibility proceeds to a superior irony. That theme is very strong in all mythologies, in any case, and that has nothing to do with modernity. We are in systems which do not any more play on reversibility, on metamorphosis. And which have installed themselves, on the contrary, in the irreversibility of time, of production, and things like that. What interests me is indeed something like a fatal strategy behind it somewhere, which dismantles the beautiful order of irreversibility, of the finality of things.

I think what troubles people is the idea of reversibility when given as a kind of law. I do not accept it as law. I take it as a rule of the game, which is quite different. But if one takes it as law, yes, somehow it freezes things. But it is not a law: a law is made to be transgressed. I do not see how reversibility can be transgressed . . . as a result . . . no, there is no transgression. The order of things takes upon itself the task of reversing things. Obviously, a profound ethic, profound moral questioning, resists in certain situations, because one must always be in a situation of having something to do. One cannot admit this kind of irresponsible tone that there would be. . . . One then translates the fatal in bad terms, into the irreversibility of things.

Yes, for me, that theme has become essential. *L'Échange Symbolique et la Mort* was already a theory of reversibility. It is the idea that the subject and object do not oppose one another; that all the distinctive oppositions are not true distinctive oppositions – they do not really function like that – that, in fact, one must find the reversibility of the subject and of the object. Then these terms disappear as such and one must find another mode . . . . I have always preferred the radical antagonism between things – there is something irreconcilable and at that moment the terms are not dialectical: in my last book it was a question of principle of evil in that sense – total irreconcilability and at the same time their total reversibility. There is, all the same, a tension between the two things, where both of them oppose themselves to linearity and dialectic.

There would be thus a radical antagonism on one side, as Freud produced in his principles of Eros and Thanatos: one does not have to try to find a reconciliation. It is not a principle opposed to another principle. That means that one of them takes into account all reconciliation including, eventually, the reconciliation of the two terms, and the other says no, Thanatos says no. Eros will not reconcile the world and one will never be finished with it.

GB *On this subject indeed, what do you think of the contemporary interest in psychoanalysis?*

Yes, I have never directly taken on psychoanalysis. At one moment I truly wanted to write a kind of Mirror of Desire as there had been the Mirror of Production, to do a true critique of all that. I realized that it wouldn't be worth the effort. Things had already changed: lots of things had been written . . . Deleuze, all that. So I no longer wanted to do it. I think that it was too late perhaps . . . of little importance . . . . In reality, this critique passed into my book, *Seduction*. That is to say, *Seduction* was not any longer a critical or negative mode – one exhausts oneself like that in criticizing it and yet reinforces it precisely in doing so – whereas it was just as much a way of passing to the other side of psychoanalysis but, at that moment, in an autonomous fashion. Therefore, psychoanalysis found itself for me marginalized, almost useless in relation to what was interesting. Yet in fact that is the equivalent of providing a radical critique and it has been more and more profound for me.

GB *You reproached it among other things with denying rebirth, initiation.*

I know that seemed a bit simplistic to psychoanalysts. From the start, they resented it as an attack, an aggression, but it was not, and then on a relatively simplistic basis they said, 'Psychoanalysis can do that kind of thing as well.' It is true, relatively. I think indeed that it is a system of interpretation which is relatively enigmatic, which, in its good aspects, has succeeded in saving something of that enigma, of this enigmatic character. But it is also a machine – not desiring at all – a productive, altogether crushing, and terrorist machine. And then, yes, the more that disappears the better it will be. I have been thankful to Lacan for that. I've always liked Lacan: not at all as constructor of psychoanalysis, but as its destroyer, and precisely under the appearance of doing the opposite. Well, that is a very beautiful episode of seduction, of '*détournement*' by excess. I really quite enjoyed that. But psychoanalysts are not so pleased when one makes them view things like that. That does not go down well with them, no, no.

Now, I don't know, because the destiny of psychoanalysis in France – I don't know what it is – in France the word 'psychoanalysis' has very rapidly and strikingly lost its impact. It no longer has at all that authority and omnipotence that it once had.

GB *Like Marxism, and at about the same time. There is a kind of correlation between Marx and Freud. There was at the time a temptation to couple the two types of thought.*

Oh yes. That was the great era of the end of the 1970s. That was the apogee of all that and it was possibly the desperate sign that the two were going under, that it was in their copulation that things could be saved, each one having a child without wanting the other to know. That has not lasted very long, and so one came back to something possibly more interesting because that was truly the ideological apogee of the two traditions.

GB *You have opposed art against obscenity at one time. You presented art as being, in a way, the antithesis of obscenity. You say that the false is resplendent with all the power of the true, that is art; that inversely the true which is resplendent with all the power of the false, that is obscenity. Well, I would like you to talk about obscenity and the game of art in relation to obscenity.*

That would turn, perhaps, around illusion. Well, indeed, at a given moment, one has to take art as an attempt at illusion; not in the sense of its power to fool you, but in its power to put something into play, to create something: scene, space, a game, a rule of the game – to invent, in fact, the modes of appearance of things, and then manage to make a void around them, to abolish all the processes of cause and effect – because they are eminently anti-artistic – and to try to find the point of the interlinking of forms, the point where they interlink of their own accord. That is where art starts, at the very point where forms interweave by themselves according to an internal rule of the game, a rule that one does not know, of which the artist has a presentiment but which, in my opinion, even so, remains secret. From the moment when the rule of the game can become a kind of route, a method, one knows that it is lost. And that comes about very quickly most of the time.

Therefore, it is the power of illusion that seems to me effectively to be a characteristic of art whereas obscenity is a power of disillusion and of objectivity. Obscenity is objectivity in the visible: to show things as they are is a kind of *parti pris* of realism, the possibility to show them off: to manage to cut all their illusory harmonies of play in order to say, 'Here they are, they exist, they are incontestible!' At that moment there is a tendency to the terror of the visible. That is obscenity. Art – the term is a bit vast, but well – it is the only thing which allows one to play. By contrast one is taken into a system, either the social, or, etc., seized by the hopelessness that lies in the fact that most people cannot play, they do not want to, they no longer want to play. Everyone strains themselves reinventing communication.

So, art in my opinion is not communication. It is, evidently, seduction, a provocation .... And that is to say, the aesthetic pleasure is not at all a pleasure of contemplation, it is not a show. Indeed, something is played out, something responds to a challenge, something changes, yet within the immanence of forms. The subject also enters into that play. Yes, art is, even so, illusion; that is to say, that which has the power to unmake the defences, its systems of causality. Suddenly it is resplendent with an energy which is ... I would say which is that of the true, but ... well, in the formulation, there too, one must not ...

GB ... *freeze things?*

That is to say that there is a general rule that art understands, in contrast to processes, let us say 'obscene' processes. It can, besides, be a question of processes which are completely material – of production, interpretation, explanation, etc. When one says it is the false which is resplendent with the power of the true, it means that the true, by having this kind of aura placed on it, can never be found simply by looking for it. The only strategy is the reverse one! You only reach the true, the beautiful – supposing that that is what is wanted – by passing directly to the inverse. (These are ideas which are extremely strong in Eastern philosophy – one does not preoccupy oneself with that, but it remains true.) Indeed, there is a radical contradiction in pretending to find the truth where one is looking for it ... which is our morality. Happily, art does not partake of that self-contradiction. It knows very well that illusion is the sole route to get somewhere if something is to be found – but 'found' without being searched for – that would indeed occur only through the reversible detour of the other thing. It is very fundamental.

I have been looking at that for the social, because there is a terrible self-contradiction in the social as we envisage it – or in *socialism* which proposes indeed the frontal realization of the social, and I would not say without perversion but without any intelligence – that never do things promote themselves like that – in a straight line which would lead from their origin to their end. Happily, things are more subtle than that. That also is the revenge of the object. And art is one of the processes which knows how to find this detour ... when it is successful, of course ... .

GB *Through this question of art and of obscenity you insist particularly on a phenomenon which you identify as being that of disappearance of the 'scene of representation'. What is this precisely?*

There is no mystery here. There is perhaps a secret somewhere, but no mystery. The 'scene' is this very possibility of creating a space where things can transform themselves, to play in another way, and not at all in their objective determination. Everything is involved here: to recreate another space which would be without limit (contrary to the former one) with a rule of play, a caprice (*arbitraire*). Fundamentally, the scene is arbitrary and that does not make sense from the point of view of conventional space. In some cultures this notion of scene does not exist, it cannot be represented. This special, very specific, in my opinion, highly initiatory space is a small miracle. There is a secret in the very existence of the scene. There is an important part here for pleasure which comes from the perfectly capricious division of space. It is the same in play: pleasure comes when one cuts up very arbitrarily a kind of terrain where one permits play in any possible fashion, in another way, where one will be outside the real, outside the stupid realistic constraints of conventional space.

The scene has been an invention. I do not know on what level this invention was made at the beginning. Was it first mental, and then theatrical, and afterwards became the social scene? All the systems of representation have made a secret of their scene, the body has also. And what is being lost at the moment is this possibility of inventing an enchanted space, but a space at a distance also, and the possibility of playing on that distance. With the irruption of obscenity, this scene is lost. Obscenity is not capricious in this sense; on the contrary, everything has its reasons. It produces too many. It destroys distance. It is a monstrous rapprochement of things: there is no longer the distance of the gaze, of play. It doesn't recognize rules any more, it mixes everything together: it is the total promiscuity of things, the confusion of orders. It puts an end to the careful distinction that all rituals, all the systems, have tried to maintain in order to escape the obscenity of things, its total mental confusion, its short circuit between the human and the non-human. But here, also, obscenity is a qualifier more than a concept, a sort of inflection, if it can be called that. More profoundly, however, it corresponds to something which is difficult to analyse other than in terms of loss, the loss of scene. It is true that one has the impression that something here is lost. One must at the same time not go too far down this road. Obscenity is another world. Perhaps one will have to deal with this hyper-visible world, and in that case perhaps there'll be other possibilities of play. And, besides, it was not always played in the same way. One can see this well in art, with Renaissance space, figurative space. When it invented itself as representation, its usage at first was quite delirious and not at all representative, economic, as it was later.

Well, in the end, I don't know. Any change in the rules of the game must produce other possibilities of play, other interstitial ways of play. It would be interesting to see, in the years to come – as the cybernetic and telematic world and all those things settle – what happens in it. Will it be that people cannot find the scene, or fragments of the scene, altogether unexpected possibilities? One must not think that system as fatal in the bad sense of the term: 'There is nothing that can be done,' etc. . . . . It is certain that in this respect one has to deal with the great power which destroys illusion, to bring about a world without illusion in the two senses of the term: that is to say, both melancholic whilst depriving the *'mise en jeu'* of its space. That is to say, the world has lost this kind of secret . . . whereas there was in all religions, cultures, ancient mythologies, even in the traditional order, a power of illusion, the power of the very violent denegation of the real. It was radical even in the first religions. Symbolic culture has always been lived as a denegation of the real, something like a radical distrust: the idea that the essential happens elsewhere than in the real. And that possibly is what is disappearing, little by little, without a pressure from the operation of the world – the idea that the world is real and that all that is required now is to operate in the real. There is not even a utopian world any longer. There is no utopia. There is not even a 'scene' of utopia. And well, now, utopia has gone into the real, we are in it . . . .

GB . . . *It is also for that reason that theory must first be radical rather than true?*

Yes. Of course, radicality is not more true than that which was said before. Radicality is that which displaces. Indeed, radicality is a problem in relation to our old objectives, radicality seen as revolutionary in the subversive sense of the term. That has changed. It no longer means that. Radicality is not necessarily the subversion of a system by negation; it is, perhaps, precisely, in illusion. Radicality is to be found once more the sovereignty of illusion, of distance.

GB *You said in your lecture you have passed from a logic of distinction to one of seduction. Distinction is something associated with Bourdieu, what he's been doing for a long time . . . .*

. . . Yes, that has not changed in fifteen years.

GB *You yourself have done it . . . .*

Yes, I have done it, but yes. I have done that sort of thing. I was a good sociologist, no problem. And at bottom that has always been a useful quality. It allows you to read. But it has become a sort of stereotype, an analysis which is going to produce the obvious for us. So, what is the use of producing the obvious? I found Bourdieu very very strong at a certain moment, but that was a long time ago . . . . And then at a certain point, no! The obvious, conformity, complacency in the truth which one knows where nothing will ever put itself in question, self-verification all the time, a tautology that one finds again in the very discourse of Bourdieu, indeed the form of his discourse. It is true that in that respect I have changed completely, away from that logic of differentiation, of distinction, which had seemed interesting to me but rather at the anthropological level.

GB *And at the level of irony, perhaps? In this type of sociology there is something truly ironic, it seems to me, from the beginning.*

Yes, in relation to Marxism, in relation to everything like that. That has had an impact at the moment of rupture around an ideological stake. Yes, that turned out badly. Suddenly, one talked of culture, of differentiation: 'And well! What about classes! Where has class logic gone?' Well, that was a good intervention (*beau coup*). But that played itself out even before 'sixty-eight. And when Bourdieu brought out his book, *Reproduction*, in 1970 it was almost too late to take that up again. It was an auto-reproduction, reproduction of itself, and what he did was by the same token a severe blow for his own position. We won't pass a judgement on that. What is strange is that all these things are coming back into fashion. They are even taken up in a very serious second form – and in that there is a form of simulation – because they've had their moment of truth, if one can call it that, in the sixties. And then what followed the sixties has largely effaced the stakes of all that. And, lo, after that grand clash, the same things return, without having changed a straw. That kind of *rewriting* no longer interests me: that is sociology, a type of permanent recurrence. And in a phase of depression, intellectual stagnation, or again of the reflux in a historical moment, lo and behold, those thoughts return as . . . lifeboats.

GB *You have a relation to fashion which can appear very ambiguous: it is not a critique, it is not collusive either. At bottom, one does not know very well where you stand.*

That is a general problem. Fashion is a good terrain on which to measure all that because it is at this juncture there was – in radical, leftist analysis, etc. – a denegation – the leftist critiques and denegation of fashion as immorality, as counter-revolution. One has lived a long time in that state of things. At bottom when I was describing objects, there was in a way an almost moralistic denegation from the idea of an alternative ideal. That was widely shared. Today something has changed. It isn't any longer tenable. One feels that in relation to fashion, to advertising, to television, the optic of denegation and of critique does not work any more. It is a very general question, the same which is posed by the existence of a socialist regime. How can one situate oneself in relation to that now? Have we lost all possibility of speaking up against something like that in a credible way? There has been an absorption of things. How can you look at those things without entering into a total collusion, as you say? You would have to evoke a new perception which is not a capitulation of the type: 'Well, yes! Fashion resists, and there must be a reason for that somewhere; everybody watches television, and we watch it also: we exist and put up with it.' Are we to draw a line: we are there!? We are entering that world! And part of the new generation does just that. It goes forward in that spirit. It will manage things and find a new ideology of social action for itself. I do not take that step. I do not want to take it, but at the same time it is true that leftist, moralizing, revolutionary positions of the seventies are finished. At the moment I do not see a new position, one which is original and credible. That is the true problem.

GB *At the political level?*

Precisely. This is for me not prudence, a denegation, a passivity, or a retreat into disappointment. It is the idea that, for the moment, I do not know what type of distance to take. I have lived that through the journals. The journal *Utopie* first: a minor radical review, of a situationist type. There you know what you are doing: the Other, society, power are on the other side. You know that one has somewhere, not a public, but a movement. You speak to someone. There is no problem, things are relatively clear. With a society which evolved towards liberalism with Giscard, in the years 1975–6, it became evident suddenly that those little reviews were going. They did not speak to anyone any more, they no longer had an impact. At that moment, without seeing it clearly at the time, *Traverses* was created, based on a kind of transversality, not any more a transgression, in order to find a negativity of another type, more interstitial, more floating, semi-institutional. *Traverses* significantly is Beaubourg. It is anti-Beaubourg, certainly. It is a culture of another type from that of Beaubourg. At that point there was a game between, on the one side, collusion and something which . . . keeps a sort of scene, a public, etc. Now however, even the position of *Traverses* is no longer credible in my opinion. It is finished as well.

GB *Really, in what sense?*

In the sense that there was a political ultimatum to the journal, via the Beaubourg, to widen its social base, to become a 'social' review, to take account of the requests of the people and not to be intellectual. That has been very hard. It was the socialists themselves who threatened the journal. For the socialists it seemed a good thing to turn the journal into a socialist journal: 'Intelligence and Power in our Midst'. It was an attempt to synergize things, even though things were running smoothly. We tried to make them understand. They did not want to hear. The thing is settled because they had other things to get on with. So we survived, but with the knowledge that we no longer had a margin of autonomy, even liberal.

Therefore, *Utopie* is finished, *Traverses* is virtually finished in my opinion, although it will continue for the time being, of course. What else could there be? What other distance is there in relation to this new society which has absorbed these margins? Which, besides, otherwise couldn't care less about marginal, heretical products? It doesn't want them but it fucks them up all the same. One can no longer find a subversive position. Nothing corresponds to it. It is, therefore, a very general problem. It applies to fashion. What turns up here fascinates, but can no longer be evaluated because there are no longer criteria of evaluation. It's there, it is immanent and it involves a lot of things. It's even a passion. It's not frivolous, it is not insignificant. But analysis no longer has a privileged position in relation to it. Faced with this loss of privilege and of critical gaze, what can be substituted for it? That is the problem.

GB *You have from the start analysed fashion as a differential human system, as a way in which people distinguish each other. And now you would like to envisage in it fatal power, a power of distinction* vis-à-vis *nature, that is to say, in a game with nature, as affirmation of the human capacity to distinguish itself from nature ... to produce its culture?*

Yes, to produce an artifice, a sort of truth ... that is to say, it must take artifice into account. When things confound themselves with nature or the real they are obscene. Everything lies in artifice, in the possibility to become artificial in the Baudelairean, not in the moral or pejorative sense. I want to know that artifice exists. That is the stake, and fashion a very very important mode to make the body exist in a denegation of its sexual, physiological, functional reality. A sublime game of the body fundamentally, without being pornographic: pornography is the absolute antithesis of fashion. As soon as there is a glimpse, the appearance of a lure – I would say of a truth – fashion ceases to exist. If the body appears as a type of obscenity, of a purely sexual demand, it is finished. Fashion must continually play with that, it must never go beyond its own limits. It has the right to be erotic, but never obscene.

This becomes interesting since fashion is extremely ambiguous. It can therefore serve as the motif and illustration of a more general position.

65

Not only does it renew itself in reality, but it also stays an engima. And that becomes extremely interesting.

GB *The interest that you have in fashion indicates perhaps a displacement of the nature of the political towards ... to culture?*

Yes ... it is less concerned with banal scenes. The political and social scenes have become banal. Basically all there is to do is to watch the extension, the adaptation, generalized reconversion of all those things .... It seems that the paralysing apparatus of the political, the revolutionary form, now and in the future, is decisively weakened, eroded, and the centres of interest can slide onto things which will never be in the foreground. Political ideology, be it on the right or on the left, will continue all the same to be in the foreground, although a false foreground – as a system of simulation. Today it is no longer worth doing a critique of politics. Let's go somewhere else, to see what is going on elsewhere.

7

IS AN IMAGE NOT
FUNDAMENTALLY IMMORAL?
Interview with *Cinéma 84*

What place does the cinema occupy in your life? How do you choose your films?

My relationship to the cinema is that of an untutored cinema-goer in a way, and I have always wanted to keep it that way, never wanting to get into the 'analytic' of it. Having said that, I like the cinema very much. It's one of those rare things where I still have a sort of quite intense imaginary. More for instance than in painting, which I know much better. In the cinema I still find a sort of immediate pleasure.

As to how I choose, it's done very simply. I have a preference for the American cinema and a taste for films which are not necessarily the most sophisticated or the most interesting, I suppose. I'm not at all attracted by experimental cinema. In Los Angeles, when I saw big productions like 'Star Wars', in cinemas with 4000 seats and everybody eating popcorn, I caught a very strong whiff of primitive cinema, almost a communal affair but strong, intense. There's one good thing about America: once you're out of the cinema, which is a circumscribed space, the whole country is cinematographic; when you're there, you're in a film. It's the same sort of pleasure you get in a little Italian town; you come out of a museum and find the same thing, an apotheosis of the image. The pleasure is of being in a cinema as in a womb, and you can find it just as easily riding in the American desert as you can in a cinema.

So I've got this quite strong but intermittent relationship with the cinema. It's irregular, arbitrary, completely subjective. I'm not looking for a pre-scribed experience, nor do I seek to control that experience. There is, of course, a contradiction here, because I can't stop being an intellectual, as you say. But for some things I have no desire at all to exercise my analytical faculties. And especially concerning cinema I occasionally cut myself off and disconnect, and go into the cinema as into a dream; there's a dream-like quality about it, dream-like, but the experience of it has a constant impact on daily life; that's what interests me, the telescoping together of life and cinema.

Have you never been tempted to reflect sociologically on the cinema, or even to create a 'sociology of the cinema'?

No, but people have certainly suggested it to me. What interests me about cinema is precisely what goes beyond the bounds of sociology, its prodigious effect and not what causes this effect. The sociology would bore me rather, whereas cinema amuses me; why mix them?

Besides, a true sociology of the cinema would a priori *have to treat all films as equal to one another, evaluate their influence . . . .*

Now here we come up against the problem of sociology itself. Because it concerns itself with more or less impersonal masses it is compelled to operate in terms of statistics, averages, norms, general laws, that is to say in terms of invariables, things that are precisely so invariable and objective that they don't provide any interest; I prefer singularities, exceptional events. Sociology is, I think, a reductive discipline.

What is annoying sometimes, in sociological approaches to cinema, is the way they maintain that certain films, even if they draw very small audiences, are exemplary, landmarks, beacons, or that they are representative of the ideology, the mentality of a group, a country, at a given point in time. It may be true, but how could you justify it sociologically?

I agree. In my experience, in sociology all hypotheses are reversible, or we are asked to grant to sociology a credibility which I personally refuse to grant it. Moreover, I don't consider myself to be deeply sociological. I work more on symbolic effects than on sociological data. I have the impression that cinema is more concerned with the imaginary of a society, the way a society escapes, dispenses itself or bursts asunder, the way in which it disappears rather than the way in which it creates itself, builds itself up. I am suspicious of all academic incursions into this area, and I find it quite revolting the way every discourse tries to exercise a sort of *droit de cuissage* over any other. The different disciplines throw their concepts, usually their worst ones, into the melting pot. What they really exchange is the worst things they've got, never the best.

Indeed, if the purpose of a concept is to define a particular object, it follows that it cannot be exchanged.

Certainly it can't, and it is rather the difference that is interesting, and it is best to go thoroughly into the question, to deepen it. There is something dangerous about present-day cinema, the way it tries to find referential support in all sorts of other things, social questions, psychoanalysis.

In an article you wrote on 'Holocaust' in Cahiers du Cinéma *(1979) you say that television is no longer a vehicle for the imaginary, it is no longer an image. Can you clarify that?*

The television screen seems to me to be a place where images disappear, in the sense that each one of the images is undifferentiated and to the extent that the succession of images becomes total. Contents, emotions, things of great intensity, all take place on a screen that has no depth, a pure surface, while the cinema is also a screen, of course, but has depth, be it fantastic, imaginary or something else. The television is there, it's immanent, and it turns you into a screen. You have a quick, tactile perception of it, little definition. Basically there is no strong image; what it requires of you is a sort of immediate, instantaneous participation, in order to read it, make it exist but not make it signify.

In order to have an image you need to have a scene, a certain distance without which there can be no looking, no play of glances, and it is that play that makes things appear or disappear. It is in this sense that I find television obscene, because there is no stage, no depth, no place for a possible glance and therefore no place either for a possible seduction. The image plays with the real, and play between the imaginary and the real must work. Television does not send us back to the real, it is in the hyper-real, it is the hyper-real world and does not send us to another scene. This dialectic between the real and the imaginary, necessary in order to make an image exist, and necesary to permit the *jouissance* of the image, is not, it seems to me, realized by television.

Remaining with your article on 'Holocaust' we thought we could discern an ironic rejection of the cinema of social criticism, of denunciation, of awareness, what we call social or political cinema.

That is correct. I have no faith at all in the educative or political virtues of the cinema. This may not have been so all the time – there must have been periods when the cinema had a sort of functional polyvalence and might even have had the virtues we have mentioned. But the cinema as we see it today, the cinema that fascinates us, excludes all such possibilities. I think there is a sort of collective self-mystification about educative and moral virtues: and not only where the cinema is concerned either. Is an image not fundamentally immoral? The image takes its place in a register which is not that of judgement, something that takes place in the form of an image, in the cinema or elsewhere, always plays with its own content. We must never make the mistake of thinking that it is a content given to us to see, ingest and digest; otherwise an image would not be an image. The important thing is that it plays with its own meaning.

To talk about a message is ingenuous or else it is the false ingenuousness of all the preachers and politicians, of all those who try to teach the masses how they should live and think. Nevertheless, I don't think that anyone teaches anything at all to anyone in that sense, but the image is certainly the last medium to be used for that purpose, that is why it is so passionate and diabolic. If you want the cinema to be the vector of some message, you are left with nothing except the worst films that have ever been made; those film-makers are endowed either with a superb hypocrisy or with a great candour.

Do you read critics?

Sometimes I do. But I don't read them in order to know what to see and they hardly influence me at all in that respect.

And what in your view would constitute a good press review?

It is very hard to say. It is certain that reviews that confine themselves to recounting, giving a summary and then passing judgement on the scenario, the actors, they don't interest me much. They are articles that I could ... I don't think I could even write stuff like that. (Laughter). I always feel I could do better. What I would doubtless find very interesting would be a way of recounting a film: an article which, in recounting the film, would manage to say everything – but I admit I have rarely come across such articles – and would manage to give to the language exactly the same tone (*tonalité*) as the film, but would not explain everything away in advance and, of course, would not at least make any value judgements; an article that would in some way be a kind of analogue, or equivalent, in discourse, for the movement of the film, for its rhythm ... the precondition would have to be, of course, that the critic had liked the film. I can see it would be a difficult thing to do if you were writing every week. But exceptionally ...

What is the purpose, the function of a critique? What might its role be, if it has one?

I would like to ask you ... among the critics, are there any who end up making films?

Yes, there are a few.

It's not that I think that the critic has a subaltern role, but I think it must be a difficult situation to be in ... to have your eyes glued to the images, and your pen somewhere else ... a schizoid position to be in. And what good does it do? I don't know. Could it be instructive, pedagogic? I suppose it's possible. There was a Golden Age of criticism, in literature, anyway, a time when the critic occupied a fundamental strategic position, and one that could in a way be original, but that time's gone. The criteria for making judgements have become very problematic, very perilous. It is at the moment a very difficult position to maintain, and in fact there aren't really any critiques any longer. One might ask, is there a real demand for criticism? Aside from making things easy, providing 'directions for use', but in that case what we have is a cookbook.

The cinema is threatened more and more by the development of the audio-visual; some people even say that it won't exist at all by the end of the century. What do you think?

I don't think so. I think that the audio-visual is like all technological innovations; at first they drive everything else out, then there is an effect of absorption, of suction. What is more dangerous, perhaps, is that in its internal organization the cinema might turn itself into video, and become television, tha it might adapt from inside. There could be a suicidal complicity on the part of the cinema to be absorbed in this way; that's the real danger, because from the outside it can resist. Cinema is the mode of expression one finds in the street, everywhere; life itself is cinematographic and, what's more, that is what makes it possible to bear it; otherwise the mass daily existence would be unthinkable. This dimension is part and parcel of collective survival. Here is the best safeguard for the cinema, and that is why, in my opinion, it will win through.

What do you think of the introduction of cinema studies at university?

I think it's a good thing. But I'm torn, nevertheless. Would I have wanted to do cinema studies as a student? I would have liked it, most certainly, but perhaps it's better to have cinema delivered to your door from childhood or adolescence onwards, but one can't be sure either. People come to love things by different but parallel routes. It would be possible, I suppose, to set up a standardized type of learning and make it widely available. It's not a bad idea in theory. But if we are going to have real vocations, real passion, these will come through by other means anyway. In the cinema as elsewhere the true things pass across institutions.

© 1984 Jean Baudrillard. Interview, *Cinéma 84*, January. © 1993 Mike Gane and G. Salemohamed this English translation.

8

INTELLECTUALS, COMMITMENT AND POLITICAL POWER
Interview with Maria Shevtsova

MS *You said recently that intellectuals today are unhappy; why do you think this?*

I say this with some irony because intellectuals have chosen unhappiness by wanting to be intellectuals, by taking a kind of relative distance, whether it be one that expresses shame, or torn feelings, or a critical distance. They are always at odds with themselves: this is the condition of being an intellectual. But are they really unhappy? I say they are because it seems to me that their position is less propitious today. There doesn't seem to be any social movement of the kind we had in the sixties and seventies, which also had theoretical inspiration. Around the time of May '68, but also earlier in the sixties, there was a kind of conjuncture which allowed things to solve themselves. We didn't have to pose or solve theoretical/practical problems. There was a kind of theory about, which was autonomous, but which, by being this very thing, connected with a conscious social practice, or an unconscious one, for that matter. It wasn't necessarily a conscious class or mass ideological practice. But movement there was. I think intellectuals felt this energy, and felt it without being affiliated to any group, or being involved in personal terms. For instance, I remember *Utopie*, which was a small review and sold very little. We didn't have any offices or publicity. But we felt we were writing for someone. I am not saying that *we* were happy. We had a favourable critical position, 'favourable' in that its radicalism drew on the energy of revolt that was taking place in one fraction of society. All this slowly came to an end during the seventies. This energy used itself up. It's certainly true in my case.

MS *Could you elaborate on your case?*

I feel this loss of energy through the fact that I do not have relations with the intelligentsia. I am not totally integrated in its networks, cliques and hothouses. Also, I am not fully institutionalized, that is, integrated in the university system. The university was a very warm, effervescent place in the years around '68, but my level of integration in the university wasn't very high. As a result, I find myself in a more detached, more distant, more isolated, more vulnerable position. So I feel this slowing down or this loss of socio-intellectual energy. I probably feel it more acutely than a certain number of other intellectuals, although I think the problem is widespread and has doubtless been also posed for intellectuals who are not well-known. I am sure that people with as much authority and scope as Foucault have felt the same reflux, the same disconnection. This disconnection has been brought out by the Socialists, whose coming to power has entailed their asking intellectuals to participate in social life. This demand was made last summer, and there was no reply. There was an inability to translate an intellectual position into a political act, or into political behaviour. In my opinion, this only deepened the historical disaffection we are experiencing.

Intellectuals are now biding their time because there is no more real dialogue, nor any real discussion. Each person is doing his or her own thing, attached to his or her research or to a group. But the tissue which held together everything underneath is no longer there. There is dispersion and a little confusion about the role that this research could play. Perhaps our problem lies in the fact that we are not faced with a new situation. Our situation is relatively old. The Socialists' coming to power has not really changed the décor. To some extent intellectuals still recognized themselves as such when they were in a semi-political position of opposition, in a society governed by the Right. Paradoxically, intellectuals recognize themselves less well in a society of the so-called Left. Their image escapes them even more, so to speak. Intellectuals of the Third World have the privilege of holding a clear critical position and of having the possibility of struggle, which is also totally clear. Confusion, in their case, is not possible.

MS *In the context of the present French situation, how do you explain the problem of alignment, on the part of intellectuals, with political power, which is indeed the problem raised by the Socialist government's call to intellectuals last summer? For, after all, the Socialist government did ask intellectuals for their political alliance. And it did ask them to play the role of propagators of ideas and to play a very dynamic cultural role all round.*

Yes, indeed. There were two phases. The first phase expressed the Socialists' naive belief that the things you're talking about would happen of their own accord. In other words, since Imagination was in power, intellectuals would find themselves, see themselves, in that seat of power: there would be an osmosis between the two. This was the euphoric, seductive phase. Lots of intellectuals were invited to the Elysée Palace; they were also given specific duties and posts. However, in reality, there was never any adhesion to the Socialist government. There was not, above all, anything like a proper movement. The intellectuals did not come to enrich symbolically the event

73

of Socialism. Nor did they truly participate in it. They took their distance
with respect to it very quickly. And even with respect to Poland and the
Socialists' policy on Poland the intellectuals retreated.

The second phase was marked by an even greater retreat. So the Socialists
came to ask explicitly, 'Yes or no?', 'Where are you?' and 'Why are you
silent?' I don't think they received a reply. There was a kind of debate. I
would have to say it was rather forced, precisely because it had been solicited.
No one replies enthusiastically to solicitation. There was, then, a kind of
confused polemic which didn't change a thing. I wouldn't say there was a
break or a rupture. It was a matter of indeterminacy, of not being able to
define oneself politically with respect to a political class, which itself does
not know how to set out a very sharp, new, political strategy. Then there
is a certain laziness on the part of the intellectuals who feel very, very
comfortable when they are in opposition, but do not know how to define
themselves when they are no longer in opposition and have to participate.
Nor do they know to what extent they are to participate.

MS *Do you think that the intellectuals you are talking about could not
respond to the Socialists because they came from May '68, when they were
not linked to any political party, and therefore had difficulty in seeing
themselves allied with a specific party?*

Yes, this certainly played a role. And yet, there had been that whole theory
of commitment through Sartre in the sixties, which had been more or less
the point of departure for intellectuals. There was the debate with Marxism.
It didn't matter if you were Marxist or not: you were nonetheless in the same
sphere of discussion. Argument was possible. Then all this slowly fell away.
Theory went into different directions and became radicalized in its own sphere
and sometimes just in its own discipline, whether it was structuralist or
semiotic. A kind of detachment took place. There was also the euphoria of
May '68, which affected many more people than the intellectuals.

MS *Do you think that the detachment you mention is tantamount to
depoliticization?*

It's possible. For my part, I took my distance before '68. May '68 was quite
an event, an amazing event. I became involved with it because it was such
an amazing event. Before that we were bogged down in political routine. All
this business of Left and Right was already boring us. Theory during the sixties
was developing in a transpolitical way. It was concerned with other things,
like the question of daily life, for instance. This is a different way of being
critical. It is no longer deliberately ideological. Yet I would say that there
was, in all this, a certain political exigency, as there was behind my analysis
of consumerism. There was a radical politics behind it. Take, for example,
what we managed to do with *Utopie*. These various things culminated

in May '68 and its aftermath. I am excluding those who reconverted into Leftists. After this big special effect that was '68 there was a period of political relaxation, of fatigue and of disaffection, which the Socialists could not break when they came to power.

MS *You spoke of intellectuals in opposition. I wonder whether today, in France, intellectuals don't have a romantic nostalgia for the very idea of 'intellectuals in opposition'? Also, are you suggesting that intellectuals have to be in the opposition, by definition?*

Yes, I think so. Even if this idea is not necessarily clear, it exists just the same at a latent level, at the level of a phantasm. Opposition is the most comfortable position for an intellectual, it's true. But it's also true for a political class. I would probably say that being in the opposition is the most inspiring place to be for a political class. This is perhaps also true for the Socialists. It is perfectly true for the Communists. They are certainly at ease when they are in opposition. They are not at ease anywhere else. This is quite obvious for France. The Communists have just taken back their liberty.[1] They will feel much better for it. Clearly they have done so with relief. In other words, any relationship to power is ambiguous. This does not just apply to intellectuals. It is valid today for the political class. It is assumed that, on principle, the political class ought to want power and want to exercise it. This isn't at all obvious. Indeed, it is far more difficult to be at the heart of organization and management.

MS *So in your view the intellectual is always bound to be marginal?*

Yes, but that is exactly where the intellectual is born. Being on the margin is, in fact, the true position of the intellectual. Intellectuals, in France at least, have inherited a great deal from the artists of the nineteenth century. They have inherited the artist's curse – marginality – which is in any case a curse artists like well enough. After the Second World War, however, intellectuals wanted to become politicized. They wanted to enter the political game, but they wanted to do so from an oppositional basis. A whole class of intellectuals was formed not only by virtue of their being in opposition to the right-wing government, but also because they were in opposition internally to the French Communist Party. Being in opposition may not be a necessity, a destiny. It's probably not an absolute vocation, although people say it is. Let's say that intellectuals are the carriers of negativity.

MS *I was going to ask you whether this was, in fact, your definition of intellectuals. May I ask you now whether intellectuals can be carriers of positivity? When and how can intellectuals assume the role of cultural construction?*

Well, I don't know. Your question implies that inellectuals can create

75

values, that they can nourish the social process. I don't think this is true at all. Values and processes happen somewhere else. Intellectuals are a peculiar problem. Intellectuals cannot create positivity. It's just not possible.

MS *Can't one be critical and also create positivity at the same time?*

Intellectuals who have thought of themselves as creating positive values or as launching positive values have almost always been on the Right. It is necessary to preserve a dialectic between a type of social creativity which occurs among other groups at a mass level and intellectuals, whose marginality is functional in that it, too, has a role to play. The social body must find its energy in this kind of difference, in this kind of separation and distance. Distance must exist.

MS *Well, can't the negativity you are discussing have social effects? You were talking just a few minutes ago about 'special effects'. Can't some of the special effects be social effects? Can we not say that, despite himself or herself, an intellectual ends up by having some sort of cultural, social, institutional or political influence?*

That's difficult to measure because two versions of the thing are possible. We could say that intellectuals lead the show; that they at least propose the discourses and are the holders of reference and representation. This is an absolutely fantastic position to be in. In a case like this, the impact of intellectuals is essential, fundamental. On the other hand, we could say that the writings of intellectuals, and their solidarity, has never changed anything much.

The question was asked *à propos* of Sartre, particularly when he died. It was asked of Sartre's commitment, of his political positions, and so on. We could claim that Sartre's importance was immense. We could claim it was nothing. Both were said. Moreover, I don't see who could give an objective assessment of this. It could well be that the influence in depth of intellectuals is increasingly small.

MS *Why do you say this for a world where the circulation of ideas can go ahead at a phenomenal pace?*

But that's precisely my point. There is an over-circulation of ideas, of the most contradictory ideas, all in the same flux of ideas. What happens is that their specific impact is wiped out. I mean their negativity is wiped out. Mass media, and all that, are not vehicles for negativity. They carry a kind of neutralizing positivity. That's why some intellectuals don't trust the mass media. They want to preserve their purity. We also have the very real fact of how any kind of analysis becomes ready for reception because it has been mediated by the media. But this analysis is too ready for reception. What I mean by that is that it can go anywhere and be accepted anywhere, all over the place. The problem is that in a society of mass media the difference between positivity and negativity is pretty well wiped out by this absolute positivity, which, at that point, is no longer positivity but becomes a media-tape winding forward.

MS *Let's go back, then, to the question of the role of intellectuals. If their influence is very limited, if impact is limited, why do intellectuals speak? Why do they write?*

Ah! But one never knows whether one's impact is limited. That's the whole problem. If intellectuals knew, they would be very strong. I really do believe that, if intellectuals were told they were nothing, they would stop speaking. Just the same, discourse remains terribly important. The organization and management of discourse is a social function. It is fundamental. Why do intellectuals continue to speak? I suppose it's because they do so always in the hope that they will change some people's outlook, or that they will transform the world. After all, what else could it be? As for the intellectuals' credibility, that's another story. It's very difficult to measure the efficacy, even the silent efficacy, of certain ideas. Can this be determined? I don't think so. Intellectual activity is a kind of wager, a defiance. It is a bet on the real situation. An intellectual would be nothing if he didn't lay his bets, if he didn't defy something, at least at the level of discourse. I don't know what is expected of intellectuals. Adhesion? Commentary on things as they are? Discourse must always exist as negativity. The force of negativity lies in the very exercise of discourse. This means that something other than the objective mechanisms, than things, exists. The symbolic, the discursive, the critical, the ironic – *these* exist. *These* are fundamental. Exercising discourse is not a political decision, of course. Political decisions are taken elsewhere. Where an intellectual is put in the position of having to make a political decision, that is, when he is integrated in the mechanisms of power, he is in a totally false position. He risks his originality, without necessarily discovering the art of government. Foucault, for, instance, came across this problem. He would like to have been a kind of political consultant at the highest governmental level. And he was offered this kind of position. If anyone could have done it, it was Foucault. Anyway, when he risked it, he discovered he couldn't do it: it was a failure. So he also withdrew, to some extent. I don't understand what you mean when you ask whether intellectuals can be positive.

MS *But how about Sartre or the intellectuals of the Age of Enlightenment who were extremely critical, yet who proposed, through their critique, a positive vision of how to redress social injustices? In their case criticism also carried the values of construction. I would refer to this in terms of 'positivity'.*

Yes, but these intellectuals were lucky. A whole, enormous, new system of values was there, waiting, about to happen. Do we have the same kind of fortune? I'd say it's unlikely. I don't think anybody would refuse to propose a glorious alternative, a critical and glorious alternative, if such an alternative existed. I don't think I am altogether reactionary, but I don't see any such possibility today.

There are no more alternatives. I don't see anyone elaborating a coherent alternative, even if we were to take the New Philosophers who are more ideological and turn towards a critique of the present. They do not bring a new world with them. They were purely critical. They lived in dissidence. And, in fact, they were rather reactionary.

MS *'Rather reactionary'! I'd have said they were reactionary through and through.*

Well, they explicitly opposed ideas on the Left. The business of the New Philosophers is a complicated business. Are they on the Right? Are they reactionary? You know that I did not defend them, and don't think their critique is really significant. Or rather, it was too opportunistic; it was too well placed at the time given. Then, they used and abused the media. It is more this last aspect which disqualifies them in my eyes. As for saying Left/Right, I don't know. I only want to judge people on new things. The criterion Left/Right leads us into dividing people into good and bad. I can no longer function according to this criterion. If we had new criteria, if we had something else, I would not be averse to taking up some kind of political will. But I would have to have different bases. I refuse to make any pronouncements on these old bases, on this tired political play.

In fact, I am the first victim of this old criterion, of these bases, in France. Nowadays I am taken to be a man of the Right, if not a fascist. Perhaps in objective terms I am on the Right. But I don't give a damn. I would be finished if I began to take this kind of judgement badly. I would stop writing or doing anything at all. So I do not recognize the judgement that I am a fascist, etc. And I can tell you that I have had it heaped on me. I do not recognize the validity of these judgements. People can judge me as they will, but I think it is all a piece with the political poverty I mentioned. People are hasty to judge ideologically before they try to understand what is going on and what is being said.

MS *I would like to relate to the question of the role of intellectuals the question of the responsibility of intellectuals.*

I personally think there is such a thing as the responsibility of intellectuals, only this responsibility cannot be manifested with the same kind of good faith and determination as before. Of course intellectuals are responsible, since they are the ones who use discourse. They are responsible for a fantastic thing. But does this mean that they must take the responsibility for the political sphere? In relation to what are intellectuals responsible? What responds to the intellectuals? I don't know if it's a particular group. Or among students? I don't think so. Individually? I still feel responsibility at an individual level. There's also a problem here because, as you know, after '68 people were saying that nobody could speak for anybody else; expression was not something that could be monopolized. We were asked to leave behind our role of subjects of knowledge, our role of teachers, etc. Speech, it was said, had been sold out. All this was doubtless utopian. It was the utopia of '68, which blurred all the contours. It's extremely difficult, after this, to take up, once again, the position of the intellectual who is conscious of himself. What is an intellectual? How can he claim to speak in someone else's name? Here we have a really radical question. I don't think an intellectual can speak for anything or anyone. Something similar holds for the political class. It is very difficult to believe, today, that political representatives can speak for others. How can they? Who gives them the right or the limits according to which they can decide in the name of others?

MS *Why do you keep using the word 'class' in your 'political class'? Are you suggesting that intellectuals are a 'class'?*

I don't use the term 'class' in a Marxist sense. For me it's something of a metaphor. What I mean isn't too far off the term 'caste'. The same term would hold for intellectuals.

MS *Would you accept the idea that intellectuals appropriate and circulate class values; that they can be allied to the values of a particular class; that they can agree implicitly or explicitly, consciously or unconsciously, with certain social values which can be analysed and called class values, or even class interests?*

Yes, except that I would say that intellectuals cannot make that analysis, or are hardly likely to be able to do it. Bourdieu would have something to say about this. The intellectual certainly gets something from his culture and speaks from it. This fact relativizes what he will be able to say. What he will be able to say can only be a transcription of his objective situation. If intellectuals exist – and I would not necessarily claim this status for myself – they do so only to the extent that they say something more, or something other, something a little different. In doing so, they will have something in relation to their social interests and even with respect to the classes to which they belong. However, they will share this with anyone. Intellectuals must be able to both share this and negate it, otherwise there would be no point in talking about intellectuals. There would be no more intellectuals. I wouldn't be against envisaging a world without intellectuals as such. It's a possibility, and perhaps it's pessimistic. It would mean that the social order had eliminated every kind of discourse. On the other hand, it could mean a radiant and transparent world where there is no longer any need for thoughts, analyses, etc. We would envisage the end of the intellectual in an extremely optimistic or an extremely pessimistic version. Still, such as intellectuals are in this last century and a half of history, they cannot be denied the possibility of raving a little, of going beyond their objective situation and creating utopia. The world does not live in utopia, but intellectuals are carriers of a kind of utopia. This is the only positivity they can have. You see, it's a negative positivity because utopia does not exist. It may even be impossible. Intellectuals also carry what is impossible, as well as carrying the ambiguity of discourse. Discourse is necessarily ambiguous. When an intellectual sacrifices himself in order to become the mere spokesman of a group or a class, he is finished.

MS *But 'intellectual' does not equal 'ideologue'.*

No, of course not.

MS *Then how would we define 'intellectual' in sociological terms? Do intellectuals belong to socio-professional groups? And aren't you giving the term a particular French connotation?*

Yes, it's true, there is a French connotation to the word. Intellectuals in France have had a different history. The term has a history different from its history in other countries, in the United States, or in the Soviet Union, or in the rest of the world. Intellectuals are really those who are defined by their use of discourse, by the rhetorical use of discourse, by its reflexive, critical use, etc. For us, in France, intellectuals are bound to a definition of them as marginalized critics. People like technicians, who use their brain but do so through technical means, are not, for us, intellectuals. Even scholars and scientists are not, in France, intellectuals. We have more restricted and more élitist positions. And it is precisely this position which is being lost today. The élitist position has been hard hit, and we don't have any other to take its place. That's why there is confusion and unhappiness today. I am talking about the unhappiness of the élite.

NOTE

1 Baudrillard is referring to the dissolution of the Socialist government at the end of July 1984, when Pierre Mauroy was replaced by Laurent Fabius as Prime Minister, and the four Communist ministers, who had participated in government since the 1981 presidential elections, resigned from government.

© 1985 *Thesis Eleven*. Intellectuals, Commitment and Political Power. Interview with Maria Shevtsova, *Thesis Eleven*, 10/11, 1984–85. Translated by Maria Shevtsova.

9

GAME WITH VESTIGES
Interview with Salvatore Mele
and Mark Titmarsh

SM *In Australia what seems most striking about your work is your 'anti-sociology', if one could call it that. Could you explain this 'anti-sociology'?*

It's not so much an anti-sociology. I'm neither a sociologist nor an anti-sociologist. Sociology was where I landed in the university, certainly. But from the point of view of a discipline, I left it during the sixties, going into semiology, psychoanalysis, Marxism (into sociology too) and then . . . in '68, for example, I undertook a radical critique of American sociology. So, there *was* an anti-sociology movement. For myself, let's say it is also a critique of the notion of the 'social', not only a critique of the discipline of sociology. It is postulated within sociology that there *is* a society, that there *is* a 'social' which is evident, and that you need do no more than conduct quantitative studies, statistical research, etc. Well, effectively, that is not the case. In that sense, yes, I want to go past working in sociology. I don't want to stay there. But it is not a declared hostility. It's just that it is one of those disciplines which may be precious, but it's necessary to pass through all disciplines.

SM *On that point about working through various disciplines – sociology, psychoanalysis, Marxism – you seem always to be utilizing a system in order to destabilize it. For example, in* For a Critique of the Political Economy of the Sign *you utilize several linguistic systems in order to destabilize them;* Oublier Foucault *utilized Foucauldian systems of power in order to ironize that system;* The Mirror of Production *used Marxist systems. To me this seems a modernist strategy, not postmodernist. It seems a problematic based on a distinction between the internal and the external, based on the opposition between systems and anti-systems. Is it possible that the projects you've undertaken are no more than simulacra, or more specifically anti-simulacra, of the very systems that you are criticizing?*

The question is well posed. Yes, there's a kind of strategy there. I don't know how intentional. Rather, it comes as the *result* of the possibility to comprehend and take hold of the systems and to reverse them. It's not so much a discursive critique using negativity. Rather, it is an irony. It is a process of pushing

81

a system or a concept or an argument to the extreme points where one pushes them over, where they tumble over their own logic. Yes, it's all a type of artifice using irony and humour. In the notion of pushing systems to an extremity there is a kind of fatality. That is to say, it is a fatal strategy. When you push the systems to the extreme you see that there is nothing more to say. So there is a destabilization. Maybe there is a certain provocation. But among all those disciplines that one traverses or ironizes or whatever, no one of them is privileged. That goes for myself too. I don't have any doctrines to defend. I have one strategy, that's all.

SM *Well you are interested in the interior and exterior of systems. You infiltrate systems. You use their armoury, vocabulary, etc.*

That's a strategy of the oriental martial arts! It's not postmodern. I don't know exactly what one means by that. But I'm no longer part of modernity, not in the sense where modernity implies a kind of critical distance of judgement and argumentation. There is a sense of positive and negative, a kind of dialectic in modernity. My way of reflecting on things is not dialectic. Rather it's provocative, reversible, it's a way of raising things to their 'N'th power, rather than a way of dialectizing them. It's a way of following through the extremes to see what happens. It's a bit like a theory-fiction. There's a little theoretical science fiction in it – and that interests me. I don't know if science fiction is postmodern. Perhaps there is an affinity. In some senses there are quite a few things which interest me in the postmodern. But I don't know a definition of it. I don't know exactly what a postmodern culture would be. Maybe it is a 'mosaic' culture, as McLuhan would say, in the sense that there is a possibility of a universal patchwork culture . . . . The idea that I've been discussing – the notion of fatality not in a religious sense but in the sense of surpassing the extremities, etc. – that doesn't seem postmodern to me. My irony is not the same. There is an aspect of all that in it, but it's not exactly the same.

SM *You talk about the myth of narcissism, about a surface that one cannot pass through. Is this a question of reversibility or fatality?*

Ah, narcissism. Modern narcissism, our own, would be a kind of frightening banality, not really a fatality. One could find a fatality in mythic narcissism, in the legend of Narcissus, where fatality took on its own image, for example, and went too far into its own image eventually. That's a type of destiny, perhaps. Whereas our narcissism, that which Christopher Lasch and others speak of – that is rather a kind of distracted auto-reference. One can see it developing in all the modern means of communication – video, etc. In this sense they are really narcissistic media. That is to say that nothing emanates from the screen or the computer any more. People work on the computer as if to look at the functioning of their own minds. That is an operational narcissism. It is a kind of auto-referentiality which seems very narcissistic, not so much from a mythic or phantasmatic point of view, or in a libinal or imaginary sense. It is a narcissism of auto-reference. Everyone must find their own niche. But that is not a fatality; it is not a destiny. It is simply a necessity in the development of modern circuits: to each person their own circuit, their own computer. But there is no longer the strong imaginary feature here of the mirror, of the mirror phase, of traditional mythic narcissism or even of psychoanalysis. But that is all truly different. There we are, perhaps: the realm of the postmodern. It's a type of narcissism almost on a level of parody. Almost on the second or third level of the narcissistic imaginary . . . .

SM *To make a fairly banal enquiry, what do you think of modern, post-Lacanian psychoanalysis, that practised by Kristeva for example?*

I don't think it's such a big thing any more. For me it's no longer very interesting. I suppose psychoanalysis is continuing, but I have the impression that, in France at least, where I have observed its evolution, it really has lost its strongest referents, its concepts. I believe that Lacan – the death of Lacan also – has brought an end to psychoanalysis. Lacan, like some great simulator or seducer, at once practised, intensified and ironized psychoanalysis, pushed it to the point where the postmodern, that is to say, where *all* interpretations are possible. There has been a technical sophistication of the concept of the unconscious, so that one has moved past the boundaries, into a kind of ecstasy of psychoanalysis, but which no longer has any function or vocation which is simultaneously radical, critical, interpretive, etc. It's not enough to say it's in crisis. I think it has really passed into an empty form. It can carry on, in a sense. It can even enrich itself with a culture associated with Kristeva and others. But I don't rate it highly any more. Over two or three years there's been an extraordinary winding-down. The psychoanalytic world, which used to have a lot of authority and prestige, has completely fallen flat. Even so, the schools keep going. People continue to write. They even write increasingly subtle pieces. But it's a useless subtlety. It doesn't interest us any more. That's for sure.

SM *Could you elaborate your formula 'more X than X'? I see this as parallel to the concept of a 'hyper'-state. Is this 'hyper'-form the universal form of 'être en abŷme' (of being in a state of suspension)? That is, the idea of 'more X than X' entails a notion of largesse and expansion, but the 'être en abŷme' is something minuscule. Is there an oscillation of perspectives here?*

It's rather difficult to compare. It is a kind of potentiality, an outbidding, etc. The connection with the notion of '*mise en abŷme*', that would have to do with the problem of representation. The '*mise en abŷme*' is, rather, a kind of complication or frenzy in the systems of representation. There is a doubling, a multiplication of the system. But in my opinion it is a kind of impasse or extremity of a system of representation, which becomes more sophisticated, certainly, but which loses the thread of representation. It becomes a kind of 'baroque' representation. This 'more X than X', this kind of superlative or exacerbation in things, is something completely different in my opinion. It's not a matter of being more expanded or extensive – it's more *intensive* in gradation. It's a kind of power, an upgrading of power – a movement to extremes, an increase in power of effects once things have lost their referents – that is, lost whatever served as cause, origin, referentials, finality, etc. – there, something is left, which breaks down, not into an aleatory infinity but into a form which multiplies itself effectively until it becomes fatal to itself ... it finds a type of fatality in its own effects. But here I don't think there is a rapport with '*mise en abŷme*'. To me it seems an image of the problematics of representation. What I would like to try to find is a kind of superlative, a 'more than', something other than a representative system, other than a dialectic, something which cannot really be verified, which functions differently from any representative or dialectic or aleatory mode .... One can also imagine that things function in an aleatory manner.

MT   *I'd like to ask you something about your notion of fascination. In* In the Shadow of the Silent Majorities *you wrote 'fascination is not dependent on meaning. It is proportional to the disaffection of meaning. It is obtained by neutralising the message in favour of the medium.' Do you think that this dynamic could in some way be responsible for the acceleration and over-production of the media, exemplified by, say, television's devouring and proliferation of genres and formal qualities?*

On the point of fascination ... yes, I think there is a connection which is absolutely immediate with the development of the media. The development of the media is precisely this fascinating format which no longer seeks out any meaning, which finally suspends meaning in limbo (*en abŷme*) and in a type of proliferation. Yes, it's something which, right away, neutralizes meaning through an excess of diffusion. It is not just a negation or a denial of meaning. It is more complicated. For example, the media multiply events, 'pushing' the meaning – events no longer have their own space-time; they are immediately captured in universal diffusion, and there they lose their meanings, they lose their references and their time-space so that they are neutralized. And from this point on, all that is left is a kind of 'neutered' passion, a stupefaction in front of the sequences, the events, the messages, etc., which can no longer have any meaning because there is no time. It all goes too quickly and too far, so that they don't have time to return and reflect on themselves, hence to acquire a meaning. There is no mirror stage here, neither for events nor history. The media are a kind of liquefaction of the sequences of meaning. One remains, therefore, at the 'screen stage'. One is in front of the screen; one is no longer in front of the mirror; it no longer reflects. *We* are in the screen stage. That is to say we are at a point where we have no gaze on the screen. We have a fascination. It is a way of blending in with the screen, to be immanent with the screen. There is no more fascination in the gaze. There is no longer any transcendence of judgement. There is a kind of participation, coagulation, proliferation of messages and signs, etc. You are no longer in a state to judge, and no potential to reflect. You are taken into the screen, you are a gaze-simulacrum. *This* is fascination. It is a form of ecstasy. Each event is immediately ecstatic and is pushed by the media to a degree of superlative existence. It invades everything. It is really 'distended'. It is an ecstatic state which is no longer reflexive. It is the same stupefied, fascinated state that one can also experience in front of music that is rendered very, very well with technical perfection. With hi-fi, for example. For me that is the 'ecstasy' of music. It is a technological perfection and sophistication of music to the degree where music has disappeared. It is the same problem with history, when it disappears, when the event disappears in the ecstasy of information, the ecstasy of messages. We have disappeared in a sort of ecstasy of the media, of information circulating with acceleration across everything. And one is no longer able to put a stop to this process. This is what I call fascination. And perhaps this fascination can be a pleasure ... even a passion! We know the passion that exists today for computers; the manipulation of computers is fascinating. But, I must say, this isn't seductive. There is a profound difference between fascination and seduction.

Fascination, in my opinion, is that which attaches itself to what is disappearing. It is the disappearance of things that fascinates us. And for me the media are a place of disappearance. It is just as interesting as a place of production or a place of apparition. It is a place of disappearance; it is a place where meaning disappears, where significance, the message, the referent disappear. It is a way of making things circulate so quickly that they are made to disappear. And it fascinates us like a black hole. It is a place of disappearance. One is fascinated by the disappearance of things. And I think it's much the same with politics, with the social, etc. Today I think it's a society where we are haunted and fascinated by the disappearance of the social, by the disappearance of the political. But it's a game, a big game. It can make a lot of things happen, but it's no longer the *production* of things which interests us; production interests, but disappearance *fascinates*. I think that it is there that one could try to look for the difference. Or at least that is a way of seeing it.

Seduction is always a *dual* relation. There is always a game, a possibility of a game, and a very intense dual relation through defiance, etc. In fascination there's no defiance; on the contrary there is a kind of respective neutralization of things. With seduction there is a respective challenge, a provocation which leads to a very strong dual relation. Whereas, in our rapport with the media, with the world of 'fascination', it's the total opposite. It would be an inverse of seduction, where one seeks less and less for a response or a reversibility of things. Seduction is very reversible: signs are received and immediately sent back. Whereas in fascination there is no longer any need for signs to pass. Signs are recorded, but no more. Hence it is not seductive. There's no adventure or challenge. It's really the inverse. There's no doubt.

SM *With reference to seduction .... In a footnote in* Oublier Foucault *you depicted the history of the feminine as the seduction of man. Can you be more precise about this notion of femininity as the historical function of seduction?*

Ahah ... the privileged relation between femininity and seduction .... Yes, for me it's not so much a case of an opposition or difference between the sexes in the biological or physiological sense (that exists, of course, but ...). Rather it's a question of the mythic or symbolic distribution between the masculine and the feminine. For me they are not two poles set against each other, term to term. Rather there would be the *masculine*, the site of an opposition, a distinctive opposition which would therefore be the site of manipulation, of a certain power. It would proceed, not by a dual relation, but by a distinctive relation, so that it would oppose good and evil, oppose left and right, etc. Whereas the feminine is the power which would fuse these poles, the power which through seduction establishes a continual dual circuit between the poles so that one would not arrive at a distinctive opposition. For example, this seems to be the place where the question of power is not posed, where the very question of power is resolved in the problem of seduction. In itself the masculine doesn't seem to be seductive. Perhaps it is powerful, strong. Perhaps it holds in some ways the controls – those distinctive oppositions in the order of the world. For the feminine it is a matter of dissolving this order, of bringing everything down to zero. In the end it ensures that everything plays ironically, seductively, and so on. For the masculine, nothing plays, things must function; it is different. But I must make this point: the 'feminine' is not strongly connected with 'woman', nor is the 'masculine' linked so strongly to 'man'. Obviously it's necessary to question all problems of feminine liberation, sexuality, and to pose those questions in a rather more subtle fashion than they've been posed until now. As for the character I've given to the feminine, I've already given to death (not in the morbid sense of the term) or to symbolic exchange. The two play the same role: reversibility, fusion, excess of distinctive oppositions. So in all this there is a kind of genealogy. Terms such as 'consumption', 'symbolic exchange', 'death', 'the feminine', 'seduction' are almost homologous, operating in the same fashion. As an opposition there is another grand position: 'power', 'the masculine'. I'm simplifying a little. But it is a question of these two.

SM *Isn't that a dialectic after all?*

No, precisely not. (Laughter.) For the dialectic proceeded *from* the *masculine* side in distinctive oppositions with a dialectic interplay between them. But that is rational. I mean, it's a rational process. The feminine is what puts into question the very definition of things. The dialectic operates on a *determination* of things. Things have to be determined in order that they can be synthesized, etc. As for the feminine, it operates on the indetermination of things. So it's not in a dialectic regime. It is something else.

MT *You once wrote in 'Requiem for the Media' in* Critique: *'There is no need to imagine it [television] as a state periscope spying on everyone's private life. The situation as it stands is more efficient than that. It is the certainty that the people are no longer speaking to each other, that they are definitively isolated in the face of a speech without response.' Don't you think TV has even stronger effects of inducing communal gossip, talking about events, serial characters, cross-referencing actors and styles, treating characters as real people, writing to them as if they existed, or even, as Marshall McLuhan has suggested, that television induces a taste for exotic foods, do-it-yourself technologies and a desire for multi-functionality in all things?*

In general I agree with McLuhan's analysis. I think it is still the best analysis, still novel moreover, because it has not always been well understood. But, in effect, his analysis remains optimistic in the sense that he thinks that television, electronics, etc., put people in touch with each other more and more and that one has a kind of tribal village in surplus of communication, and finally liberty increases through the intensification of the media. Evidently I have maintained the inverse thesis (even if it operates on the same functional analysis) in as much as the media, and especially television, accord no right of reply, allow no code between those who send the message and whoever hears it. One can attempt to interpret it in other ways, but no, precisely because of the fascination that I mentioned there's no reversibility, no reply. So the media leave us in a kind of irresponsibility. I maintained that thesis quite a while ago; it was a radical critique of the media, of the political economy and the media; i.e. that it compelled people into silence, into an extremity of alienation and irresponsibility. But afterwards I changed that hypothesis a little. I still think that the media are unilateral, a one-way system coming from 'over there', outside. But as for the silence of the masses in relation to the media – that is, that it is the media which produce the masses in their silence – I gave this silence a pejorative and negative sense. Later on I turned this hypothesis around. It seemed to me that things were more complicated than that. It seemed that the hypothesis of manipulation, mystification, alienation was too conventional. It was necessary to seek out another hypothesis. Therefore, in 'The Silent Majorities' I proposed that this silence was a power, that it was reply, that the silence was a massive reply through withdrawal, that the silence was a strategy. It is not just a passivity. It is precisely a means of putting an end to meaning, of putting an end to the grand systems of manipulation, political and informational. And at the moment, the masses, perhaps, instead of being manipulated by the media, actually utilize the media in order to disappear. It is a strategy of disappearance through the media. For the masses it is a way of neutralizing the fields that one would like to impose on them. One wants to impose a political field, one wants to impose a social field, a cultural field: all of that comes from above; it comes through the media, and the masses reply to it all with silence; they block the process. And in that, it seems to me, they have a kind of negative sovereignty. But it is not like an alienation. At the moment it is not at all certain that the media are a strategy of power for controlling and manipulating the masses in order to force them into silence. Rather it is perhaps a case of the strategy inverted, that it is the masses who hide themselves behind the media. That is they *nullify* meaning. And this is truly a power. On one side there is the political class, the cultural class, etc., who *produce* meaning – their métier, their function is to produce meaning, messages, etc. And on the other side there are the masses of people who refuse this meaning which comes from above, or who block it all because there is too much meaning, too much information. So, 'let's put a stop to this process!' In this it is the masses who enact with their silence a reversal, an anti-media strategy through the media. It seems a 'mass strategy' if you like, in terms of theory. It is a case of utilizing a structure. The masses do not look for a determined, negative reply, a subversive reply; they do not seek to make up the anti-media – it's the intellectuals who do that. No, the masses are only silence; but they are absolutely in their own service. Basically they absorb all systems and they refract them in emptiness. That is their strategy. So, one defends the same analysts to begin with – McLuhan, for example – but one inverts the hypothesis. That seems more interesting.

MT *Does the silence of the masses then incite the media into a kind of hysteria in order to* cause *some sort of response?*

Yes, there is a kind of circularity between silence and the excess of information. It is a kind of hysteria of information, effectively. There is a rapture, an escalation, that's for sure. The more silent the masses, the more one talks to them, bombards them with messages, etc. But the more one produces information, the more one increases the masses. It's a little like in physics: with a moving body, it has a certain speed and a certain mass, and the more the speed augments, the more the mass augments. At the moment, in order to make this body move, it is necessary to produce a body with still more energy, to make it stronger and stronger; and the more this energy augments, the more the mass augments as well. There is a kind of escalation in emptiness, which terminates at a point of inertia where the speed is so great – by speed I mean the rotation of messages, circuits, etc. – the speed is so great that one can no longer produce enough energy to mobilize the system. It is a kind of implosion. It is a kind of inertial point of the systems themselves. I believe that this is the situation with politics, culture, etc. One is in a situation, apparently, of extensive mobilization, participation, circulation; and in reality it is a case of inertia, of abatement, an inertia of meaning. And the mass is moving less and less; it is increasingly in a state of silence. This all derives perhaps from the fact that there is too much power. That is to say, now the states, the institutions, the technical and technological systems, etc., are so perfected and control everything in such a way that there is no longer any means of reversing these systems, no longer any subversive or revolutionary strategies which can bring about the overthrow of these systems. Thus, there is only one solution . . . this is a strategy of inertia, of blocking. And in my opinion one cannot call it negative. It is negative from the point of view of action, from the point of view of a system of active value, but since this very system is obstructed, in saturation, the masses reply to it, in effect, with neutralization.

SM *Isn't this the same thesis as Foucault's with regard to power? That is, the more power there is, the more the masses resist it?*

Yes, but he doesn't talk in terms of the mass in the sense that we have used it. He thinks that power changes, that it becomes interstitial, a power which infiltrates everywhere, and that one can still reflect this power at that level. That is, one can still fight by other means, one can still have a molecular, interstitial strategy – he always thinks in terms of *active* strategies. He doesn't think of inertia as a strategy. He doesn't consider that polarity. This is not a criticism. His analysis is perfect at that level. Quite simply, I think it's still traditional. It is still an analysis of power; it's more fluid, but it's still determined. It is still *power*. Basically, there's no more power in that sense – it is neutralized, that is, as it is perfected, it's more and more neutralized. And finally one can no longer know where it is because it's no longer anybody's strategy – not of the media on one side, nor of silence on the other. It is no one's strategy. In truth there is no one who can profit from it nowadays. Of course, one sees the political class hurling itself at television in an attempt to monopolize, but they can't do it. Its function is always to turn around against them. That would be almost a fatal strategy – a strategy of a power which *believes* that the media ensure power, which produces more and more. That is fatal for power itself because it ends up being absorbed by the media, completely 'mediatized'. So in reality it is no longer its own strategy. And that goes on at all levels today. But they are not aware of it, nor are the socialists here. They have never understood. They always think of the media as a means . . . but not as . . . . With reference to the major analyses of McLuhan, they never understood.

SM *You didn't finish the sentence then. 'The socialists think of the media as a means, but not as . . . '?*

Well . . . as something else . . . as something which is no longer determined, which has entered that dimension of over-reaching, proliferation, saturation. One can no longer identify the means and the end. One is no longer in that former 'clear', 'rational' system. As if to say, '*That's* the aim, the objective, the referential. *There*, there's the means.' And so on. One cannot do that any more. Techniques are not the world. They structure the world directly. McLuhan knew that. He was right. And all the media techniques and electronics are techniques of *in*determination. They are not techniques which can be used as means for determination. They indetermine everything. Even power is defeated there – it loses its own will to power, volition over power.

MT   *When you talk about Marshall McLuhan and refer to him as being an optimist, do you think that somehow the things he wrote are inappropriate today? What would be your criticisms of Marshall McLuhan's position?*

His analyses are truly valuable. I remember when I was in Canada, where I saw people working as his heirs: they had criticisms which amounted to saying that McLuhan was right about the mass media and that his analyses were good. But they also said, 'Nowadays we are no longer in the mass media – today we are in "multi-media", or "micro-media". The mass media are finished. We're not in a mass any more. We are in the multiplications of the media. Therefore the analyses of McLuhan no longer function.'

But that is not true at all. It is a little like Foucault's analysis with reference to power. That is, they conduct a similar analysis: 'There is now a plurality of media. Everyone will find their own autonomy again, so that small groups and individuals will be able to become "emitters" of media, able to fabricate information. They will be on cable TV, household telematics, etc. So that changes everything. And at the moment the analyses of McLuhan are not valuable. They were concerned with a previous epoque, when there was a mass, when television was the great medium of the masses. Now one has other things. One has video, cable TV, etc.'

Well, I don't think so. But I don't think that the problem of general information remains in the way McLuhan mapped it out: that is, general information, be it 'global' or 'micro', creates the mass. The mass is definitely not something to do with the 'millions of individuals' and so on. The mass is a *form*, a kind of inertia, a power of inertia, which is created by the circulation of information as it circulates at the level of national television, the level of local video, etc. In this sense all information creates some mass. Therefore, analyses of the media in terms of the mass are always good. Quite simply there is no need to set up a definition of the masses as millions of assembled individuals. The mass is something else. It's a mode of circulation and inertia. In this sense it is *the* event of the modern world. That is, we have to deal with, at the same time, a kind of acceleration of information, etc., and at the same time, in parallel, with a kind of indifference which grows and grows – a power of indifference. *That* is the mass. And it can be in any circuit, any medium. So the fundamental problem of the mass – McLuhan didn't analyse it exactly like this, but it amounts to the same thing – the mass is 'always' increasingly present. One must not believe that it is all resolved by smashing up the major media, by making the small media. No, that has not changed the problematic as a whole. Is information really information? Or on the contrary (no, it's not 'the contrary'), will it produce a world of inertia? Will it produce, by its very proliferation, the inverse of what it wants to? Doesn't it lead to a world, a universe in reverse, of resistance, inertia, circulation, silence and such like? It is for this reason that it is fatal: it is by *information* that one is supposed to bring consciousness to the world, to inform and to awaken the world, but it is this very information through its very media which produces the reverse effect. It is a type of counter-finality, of fatality. This applies as well for sexuality. A little more sexuality liberates you, they say, but with sexuality *everywhere*, basically there's *none at all*. There is a destruction of the sexual effect through the universal discourse of sexuality. Something like that. It's the paradox of saturation, inversion. There is a kind of reversible fatality for systems, because the more they go towards universality, towards their total limits, there is a kind of reversal which they themselves produce, and which destroys their own objective. It is what I call 'hypertelia', a way of surpassing a function, past its own objective. One goes past finality. Things go too far. Cancer, for example, is a hypertelic process: the cells are too lively; they reproduce too quickly. For the organism itself, it is a *catastrophic* process. With systems of economy, knowledge, production, if they go too far in the one direction they get carried away and over-reach their own limits, and at this moment they lose themselves in reversal. For this reason the dialectical process is no longer operative. In my opinion, the dialectical process plays on certain divisions: production, sexuality, etc. There has been a phase when there really was a production and a dialectic of meaning. And then it contained too much. It is finished. Dialectics are finished. Another regime has taken over. And what interests me is the analysis of this other regime.

SM *The regime of hypertelia?*

Yes. Hypertelia, excrescence, proliferation.

SM *Another rather banal question. You've spoken of McLuhan's heirs. What do you think of your own heirs? Paul Virilio, for example?*

My heirs? Oh, Virilio is no heir. He's developed things in a very original manner. I find Virilio excellent, but he's perhaps more localized. At one and the same time he has simplified and radicalized the analysis of speed. I find all of that very, very strong. And in some sense it's more extreme, more extremist than my own analyses of the problem of speed and so on. But he is perhaps a little bit abstract. He is an analyst of a kind of catastrophe of time, of speed. But he remains an optimist of . . . mmmn . . . . Well, he is a christian. He is a christian! (Laughter.) This is not an argument, no . . . . But he is not an heir, as such, nor an associate in that sense. When I look around the French intellectual field there aren't many with whom I function with much affinity. There's Virilio, and then a few others who aren't known elsewhere. There is a great disparity among the theories. You know that well enough. Maybe that's also postmodern. (Laughter.) Outbursts of theory, each in its own nebula.

SM *One could say that the postmodern is not only this patchwork, but also the relativization of all systems.*

Yes. That is certain. And, perhaps from this situation an ironic process develops which is no longer subjective irony. Subjective irony was still a faculty of judgement. It was still determined also. In this case one might be able to make a kind of objective irony out of all these processes, these runaway processes, these processes of exaggeration, proliferation and relativization of everything by everything, by television, etc. There is a kind of objective irony. In America I saw television where you hear laughter all the time. It's very vulgar, very coarse, but it brings about the situation where it's the events themselves which laugh, on the screen. (Laughter.) That is quite strange. But all in all I think that everything is in a situation now where increasingly it is all in multiplicity, proliferation, neutralization – these are all processes of objective irony. It is no longer the irony of this or that – it is the irony of the event itself. It's a kind of game. Yes, perhaps therein lies one possible definition of the elements of postmodernity.

MT *In 'Gesture and Signature', you characterized modern art as midway between critical ideological terrorism and de facto structural integration, [you say] that it parodied, illustrated and simulated the contemporary world, but that it never disturbed the order which was also its own. Would you consider contemporary art that proclaims itself postmodern, or is interpreted as such, is outside the above characterization?*

In 'Gesture and Signature', which is fairly old now, I was regarding art somewhat as a form of collusion between art and the global system. There was a game of complicity in the system itself – not really a strategy of the system but something ambiguous, a kind of critical paradox. Maybe that is still true, I'm not sure. In art, at present, I would have difficulty saying where things are. In any case, I would rather not see things now in terms of ideology. For that was still an ideological analysis. It was asking 'Is art an ideology?' That was the question asked often in the sixties and seventies. No, I would see art rather as a site of a type of disappearance. Certainly, this is modern art since Hegel, let's say. That is, art enacts its own disappearance. From the nineteenth century, let's say, it is no longer the harmonious or reflective image of the world. It is a process of auto-destruction, with plenty of prestige, I must say. It destroys itself. Thus it also enacts a kind of symbolic auto-destruction of systems. But it *plays* with forms. This is caught up in the appearances of systems as well. But it plays with forms in order to destroy them. In reality modern art isn't constructive at all. With reference to modernity Baudelaire put it very well. Its magic and its prestige lie in destruction and auto-destruction. This gives rise to prodigious effects. Inasmuch as there is a system to support it, insofar as there is a strong system or order, then art is in some way a destructive metaphor of the system itself. But I would see postmodern or contemporary art in a different way. From now on, within these very systems, it is less and less stabilized; it exists less and less; it has lost its order. It doesn't have its legitimacy any more. This auto-destructive negativity of art no longer has any *raison d'être*. Truly, art can no longer operate as radical critique or destructive metaphor. So art at the moment is adrift in a kind of weightlessness. It has brought about a sphere where all forms can co-exist. One can play in all possible ways, but no longer against anyone. There is no longer an enemy, no longer any system . . . . Of course, there is still one, but it no longer has the specific power of, for example, capital or the political in their heyday. Accordingly there is a disappearance of the horizon of a political order, a cultural order. It amounts to this: art is losing its specificity. It is brought back to itself again in a kind of self-reference, and it continues to operate in all its tableaux. That is to say, it is becoming 'mosaic', as McLuhan put it. It cannot do anything more than operate out of a combinatory mode. So it transmits itself into a combinatory system. For me it is not as interesting as the history of modern art up until . . . well, one can't put a date on it: just after the war, after surrealism, after World War Two. In contemporary art, one feels, there is no more danger, no dramatic danger; there is no negative dramaturgy of art. There is no longer anything to destroy. That is the problem. That is to say, for the last twenty years one has joyfully destroyed everything, put everything into question: the economy, man, humanism, power. One has analysed everything. One has conducted radical critiques of everything. And it went very well, because there was a system in front of one. Now there aren't any more enemies to receive the radical critiques. Marxism? No, it's been done. Psychoanalysis has almost disappeared here. Political power? Well, it exists in a kind of simulation, but one can no longer talk of a class enemy and so on. And that's the real problem, right there. Effectively it is a problem of relativity. Negativity is no longer possible precisely because there is no longer any positivity. So one has departed from the dialectic already. I find it a weightless universe where one is forced to operate without really having an adversary. And that's very difficult. So there is no substance to sense and there is no substance for nonsense. (Laughter.) So one loses on both sides. This is a fairly dramatic situation. There is a specific anguish in it. For when one has an enemy one can apply a radical critique and critical judgement. But all that is finished. One can carry on with it, but it no longer has any interest. One doesn't know very well just what distance one can assume. If there are no longer any systems, if there is no longer any critical distance, does one go to some pure distance where one is truly 'elsewhere'? I do find myself in that position to some extent. Or one is entirely within systems, and one plays off and through the commutations of the systems themselves. Many people think that way today. Many people who were involved in the ideological critique have moved into an operationality which is more or less playful without too many illusions. But they play with the system. Or, if you really don't want to play in that manner, then you are in a distance which doesn't derive from dialectics but which is fatal in the sense that it doesn't operate except on itself. That is the problem today with reference to institutions, the remnants of the state, and other theories: there is a need to find other modes of distancing. But they haven't been found. Out of this there arises an intellectual crisis. One can no longer take refuge in the traditional role, which was rather comfortable. What one notices, in France anyway, is that people in the intelligentsia are trying to rediscover their referents. One tries to find a serious mode of working, in history, philosophy, epistemology. One is trying to find once again a moral, an intellectual virtue in order to make it to the year 2000 because one cannot put up with this kind of emptiness. It's an *original* situation, but it is empty. And it engenders anguish. I have the impression that there is a process of restoration. And that is also part of the postmodern: restoration of a past culture, to bring back all past cultures, to bring back everything that one has destroyed, all that one has destroyed in joy and which one is reconstructing in sadness in order to try to live, to survive. Really, that is the tendency. But I hope it won't finish there. I hope there is a solution that is more original than that. For the moment one really doesn't see it. (Laughter.) But this isn't pessimistic.

MT *Postmodernism seems to be spoken about simultaneously in many different disciplines without much communication between those disciplines. For example, in architecture postmodernism is described in terms of complexity and wilful contradiction, a return to symbolism and picturesque aesthetics, an expansive inclusiveness that treats the entire history of architecture as a vital source of forms and images and an unashamed usage of the vernacular. In painting, the transavantgarde rejects the univalent rigour of modernism and demands a pluralist inclusiveness that does not abide by historical or stylistic restrictions. Do you think these varying definitions can be drawn together in any way, and if so, what value does it serve to do so?*

There's no clear or appropriate answer to that. Basically, if postmodernism exists, it must be the characteristic of a universe where there are no more definitions possible. It is a game of definitions which matters. It is also the possibility of resuscitating images at the second level, ironically of course. It all revolves around an impossible definition. One is no longer *in* a history of art or a history of forms. They have been deconstructed, destroyed. In reality there is no more reference to forms. It has all been done. The extreme limit of these possibilities has been reached. It has destroyed itself. It has deconstructed its entire universe. So, all that are left are pieces. All that remains to be done is to play with the pieces. Playing with the pieces – that is postmodern. So, it's not the quest for a definition. It is a kind of ungraspable universe where things would be aleatory, certainly, and where they have exited from history. Certainly art doesn't have a linear history. It is not that clear. Even so, one could say that impressionism leads to cubism, abstraction and so on. Impressionism has gone further and further into the distance. But there has been a return of impressionism with hyper-realism. The hyper-real is the first movement in which there is a game played with representation nowadays. One plays parodically with photographic resemblance, with things that one doesn't believe in any more. One knows quite well that there are no longer any exact images of the world, no more mirrors – there are only tricks with mirrors. And all the forms float. It is true for theory as well. I think that theories are floating too. They don't address one another. There is no longer any intellectual discussion nowadays. There are no theories which are opposed, in a determinate fashion, which one discusses. It's impossible. They all float around one another. There is a kind of ambiguity and complicity, but at the same time it is a little like fashion. It has become a universe of fashion in a profound sense. Fashion is a grand game, a beautiful game. But there is really no history of fashion, it is a recurrent circulation of forms. Increasingly, art has become fashion in the profound sense of the term. That does not preclude great things in a creative sense, or in architecture and so on. Postmodernity is neither optimistic nor pessimistic. It is a game with the vestiges of what has been destroyed. This is why we are 'post-': history has stopped, one is in a kind of post-history which is without meaning. One would not be able to find any meaning in it. So, we must move in it, as though it were a kind of circular gravity. We can no longer be said to progress. So it is a 'moving' situation. But it is not at all unfortunate. I have the impression with postmodernism that there is an attempt to rediscover a certain pleasure in the irony of things, in the game of things. Right now one can tumble into total hopelessness – all the definitions, everything, it's all been done. What can one do? What can one become? And postmodernity is the attempt – perhaps it's desperate, I don't know – to reach a point where one can live with what is left. It is more a survival among the remnants than anything else. (Laughter.)

Paris, 18 January 1984

Part III

I STOPPED LIVING . . .

10

FORGET BAUDRILLARD
Interview with Sylvere Lotringer

SL *Let's begin at the end or, rather at the ends: the end of production, the end of history, the end of the political. Your reflections begin with a series of liquidations. Has the time come to put Western civilization in the wax museum? Is everything now for sale?*

I don't know if it's a question of an 'end'. The word is probably meaningless in any case, because we're no longer so sure that there is such a thing as linearity. I would prefer to begin, even if it sounds a little like science fiction, with a quotation from *Die Provinz des Menschen* (The Human Province), a recent book by Elias Canetti.[1] It is possible, he says – and he finds the idea rather painful – that starting from a precise moment in time the human race has dropped out of history. Without even being conscious of the change, we suddenly left reality behind. What we have to do now, continues Canetti, would be to find that critical point, that blind spot in time. Otherwise, we just continue on with our self-destructive ways. This hypothesis appeals to me because Canetti doesn't envisage an end, but rather what I would call an 'ecstasy', in the primal sense of that word – a passage at the same time into the dissolution and the transcendence of a form.

SL *History survives its disappearance, but somewhere its spirit got snatched away ...*

History isn't over, it is in a state of simulation, like a body that's kept in a state of hibernation. In this irreversible coma everything continues to function all the same, and eventually can even seem to amount to history. And then, surreptitiously (as Canetti has it), it's possible that everything is no longer real or true. In any case we would no longer be in a position to decide on that.

SL *The 'end' you're talking about would be the end of all finalities – together with an exacerbated, empty parody of their resurgence.*

There is no end in the sense that God is dead, or history is dead. I would prefer not to play the role of the lugubrious, thoroughly useless prophet. It is not a tragic event, something highly charged with emotion, something that you could mourn – for there would still be something to be done about it. Suddenly, there is a curve in the road, a turning point. Somewhere, the real scene has been lost, the scene where you had rules for the game and some solid stakes that everybody could rely on.

SL *How did that happen? Has this really happened?*

That's fiction. History has stopped meaning, referring to anything – whether you call it social space or the real. We have passed into a kind of hyper-real where things are being replayed *ad infinitum*.

SL *Traditional societies had no history but they had a mythology; we're discovering now that history may have been our own mythology. If we can cease believing in history, then maybe history had more to do with faith than fact.*

But then, what does it mean 'to believe'? That would mean maintaining some kind of subjectivity as a criterion of the validity of things. Now if credibility alone is what gives things meaning, then we're bound to remain trapped in the imaginary. What interests me instead (but can you still call this history?) is the possibility of a pure event, an event that can no longer be manipulated, interpreted, or deciphered by any historical subjectivity.

SL *Can individual subjectivity be totally short-circuited by the event?*

The problematic of the subject implies that reality can still be represented, that things give off signs guaranteeing their existence and significance – in short, that there is a reality principle. All of that is now collapsing with the dissolution of the subject. This is the well-known 'crisis of representation'. But just because this system of values is coming apart – the system which also supported the political and theatrical scenes – that doesn't mean we are being left in a complete void. On the contrary, we are confronted with a more radical situation.

SL *The* tabula rasa *brings out tendencies latent in the culture. It clears the ground. But there is a high price to pay in terms of emptiness and disenchantment. There you have all the seduction, and the sadness, of nihilism.*

It is true that logic only leads to disenchantment. We can't avoid going a long way with negativity, with nihilism and all. But then don't you think a more exciting world opens up? Not a more reassuring world, but certainly more thrilling, a world where the name of the game remains secret. A world ruled by reversibility and indetermination ...

SL *That's certainly radical; it leaves no roots.*

Radicality is not a more sublime virtue of theory. It means isolating in things whatever allows for interpretation, whatever overburdens them with meaning. I don't derive any malicious pleasure from this analysis; still, it gives me a curious sense of giddiness ...

SL *But who's there to feel giddy? To exult in one's own disappearance is still another, more paradoxical, paroxystic form of subjectivity. What's left once you've liquidated that overload of meaning?*

What remains is a good deal less than one would like to admit. Every system of value – in terms of energy, for example – seems to be crumbling down.

SL *You settled your score with Marx in* The Mirror of Production.[2] *Why haven't you written a* Mirror of Desire *to have done with the judgement of Freud?*

I can't bring myself to write something on psychoanalysis. It would be useless to attack frontally its ideology or proclaim its demise. You have to allow desire to catch itself in its own trap.

SL *Desire was caught from the start. That's the reactive side of any theory. You can only reveal a phenomenon if it is already disappearing. Where is hysteria now? Nowhere and everywhere. Often the pyramid of concepts is piled up sky high on top of an empty tomb.*

It is always the same sign that controls appearance and disappearance. It presides over both. In the meantime, you're left to your own devices. There may be events, there may be a history ...

SL *The history of sexuality, for example.*

Sexuality has gone weightless. It is now reaching the state of 'obscenity'. But everyone conspires to mask its disappearance by setting up *trompe-l'oeil* stage décor.[3]

SL *Psychoanalysis pretends to cure sexual neurosis, while it keeps on injecting it with a semblance of reality. Although far removed from the Freudian point of view, Foucault still participates in that nostalgic effect of theory. After all, paying so much attention to the genealogy of sexuality accredits the idea that it is still a space to be occupied. But it is more like Grand Central Station ...*

I don't see the point of retracing the genealogy of sexuality. It's so true, so undeniable that there is nothing to say about it.

SL *American sexuality is more Foucauldian than Foucault. In sex clinics here, masturbation has become a categorical imperative if you want to reach a synthetic genitality. Your position with respect to Foucault is of the same order. Foucault wrote the archeology of things; you take them to the point of their cryogenicization. In L'Ordre des Simulacres (The Order of Simulation), though your approach was pretty close to his . . .*[4]

You're talking about the three orders? I could have made a book out of it, others rushed in to find examples. As for myself, without denying it, I don't believe it holds up. For a time I believed in Foucauldian genealogy, but the order of simulation is antinomical to genealogy.

SL *An anti-genealogy then?*

No. If you take this logic to the extreme, what you get is the reabsorption of all genealogy. That's why I believe Foucault was unable to make the leap. What interests me is the mysterious point where he stops and finds nothing more to say.

SL *You keep criss-crossing Gilles Deleuze and Felix Guattari's path, breaking away from representation, rejecting dialectics, dismissing meaning and metaphor. You part company with them on the terrain of subjectivity: they put the subject in flux, you abolish it. They make desire the basis of becoming; you see becoming as annihilating desire.*

I couldn't care less about desire. I neither want to abolish it nor to take it into consideration. I wouldn't know where to put it any more.

SL *That's no surprise. You derive your own energy from the collapse of values. To make desire itself the basis of the system becomes redundant.*

What bothers me about desire is the idea of an energy at the source of all these fluxes. Is desire really involved? In my opinion, it has nothing to do with it.

SL *Well, then, what does?*

Earlier on you mentioned disenchantment. The other, enchanting aspect, for me, is no longer desire, that is clear. It is seduction. Things make events all by themselves, without any mediation, by a sort of instant commutation. There is no longer any metaphor, rather metamorphosis. Metamorphosis abolishes metaphor, which is the mode of language, the possibility of communicating meaning. Metamorphosis is at the radical point of the system, the point where there is no longer any law or symbolic order. It is a process without any subject, without death, beyond any desire, in which only the rules of the game of forms are involved. Among other things, what psychoanalysis has to say about mythology is an abuse of metaphorical language.

SL *And what would correspond to that mythology in the order of metamorphosis?*

The possibility of transmutation: becoming-animal, becoming-woman. What Gilles Deleuze says about it semed to me to fit perfectly.[5]

Love is no longer considered as a dependence of desire upon a lack, but in the unconscious form of the transformation into the other. In that metamorphic unconscious nothing is repressed. The metaphor is bypassed. Conversely, in metastasis – the proliferation of bodies, obesity, cancer – there again, unfortunately, the subject no longer exists. There is no more language. Metaphor is no longer possible.

SL *And what do you see taking shape with the disappearance of subjectivity?*

Something rather paradoxical. There are three modes of disappearance. Either the subject disappears in the cloning system, eliminating death. That has no charm. It is too much like an extermination which is the proliferating metastatic form of the disappearance of the other. Or, you could have disappearance as death, which is the metaphorical form of the subject. Or else, disappearance as a game, the art of disappearance.

SL *Alongside these modes of disappearance, the mechanical (cloning), organic (death), and ritual (game) forms, why not conceive of a more lively way of disappearing? The possibility of assuming roles without identifying with them. One agrees to disappear, but like nomads, in order to reappear somewhere else, where one is not expected.*

I conceive of that disappearance abstractly, with Deleuze, as a flux, but also as an absolute transparency. It is the loss of the real, the absolute distance of the real. One can no longer touch things.

SL *The only form of the real that remains, as I see it, is a shifting between things. Otherwise you are paralysed – or vaporized. Paralysis is the panicky plea for identity. It's neurosis: wearing yourself out trying to pour into concrete what is slipping away in all directions. Evaporation is chloroform, or ether. Disappearing without a trace. It chills you to the bone; it puts you to sleep, too.*

It's possible that in places like New York people can remain in a kind of positive, happy fluidity, a state of trans-pearing. But most people experience it as a kind of liquid terror.

SL *Is it worth abdicating all subjectivity in order to protect ourselves from terror?*

We're no longer in systems of real accomplishment; today they are necessarily potential, with the added bonus of risk, panic. The de-subjectification of things.

SL *What's there to risk if all subjectivity is being extinguished?*

We're condemned to effects of giddiness – in all the electronic games as well. There's no more pleasure, no more interest, but a kind of dizziness induced by the connections, the switching operations in which the subject gets lost. You manipulate all you want, without any objective, with the effect of aleatory giddiness of the potential systems where anything can happen.

SL *You prefer panic to terror.*

Panic doesn't have to be unhappy. I see it as ecstasy. It's just a mode of propagation by contiguity, like contagion, only faster – the ancient principle of metamorphosis, going from one form to another without passing through a system of meaning. This process of effects in the absence of causes is a form of extraordinary expansion. The 'speed' that Virilio talks about is an effect of panic with respect to movement.[6]

A giddiness effect. Panic can also be the inflation of the event by the news media. All the communication theories have to be revised, including my own, which is still too meaningful. People no longer seek to appropriate things, or even destroy them. Bataille's 'devil's share' was still part of the ultimate romanticism of political economy. Now it's something else.[7]

SL *What do you make of death? Of the three modes of disappearance, it's clearly the one you are least interested in. It doesn't disappear for all that ...*

Death has passed into either the history of metamorphoses or into metastatic history. I found an article by Franz Bader, a German writer from the early nineteenth century, entitled 'On Ecstasy as Metastasis'. For him ecstasy is the anticipation of death, a passage into the metastatic state of the living subject. Death is replaced by the passage of this point of inertia.

SL *Every time I meet William Burroughs, I feel I'm in the presence of a happy dead man. As a living person he seems rather bored. I asked him if he would go to the moon. 'Of course,' he replied. 'I'd go anywhere; I'd leave the solar system if they came to get me in a flying saucer.' 'Even if there is no coming back?' I asked. He looked at me. 'Why come back?'*

I experienced the same feeling of no return during a trip to the United States a few years ago. It was a real shock. I had the revelation that I was entering the period of the rest of my life from another point of view, in a state of complete irony with respect to what had gone before. When there is no fundamental passion, when life or love disappears, there is no longer any possibility of a multiplicity of modalities, with respect to love or existence. It's an extra helping, a little bit ecstatic, a little bit residual, but also profoundly melancholic. Death is an event that has always already taken place.

SL *I've often wondered how one could live theories like yours.*

I got into it fairly late. For a long time, I was very 'cool' about producing theories. Of course, there had to be an obsession behind it, but I didn't think it had very much to do with anything. It was a kind of game. I could write about death without it having any influence whatsoever on my life. When someone aked me, 'What can we do with this? What are you really analysing?' I took it very lightly, with great calm.

SL *You felt it had more to do with culture?*

I'd always kept my distance from culture – as well as from theory. I maintained a position of distrust and rejection. That's the only 'radicalness' I can claim. It might have something to do with my old pataphysical training: I don't want culture; I spit on it. If a theory really becomes part of it, for me it's unspeakable. Several years ago, all that changed. Somewhere along the line I stopped living, in Canetti's sense.

SL *Something came unstuck.*

The giddiness I'm talking about ended up taking hold of me.

SL *A logical giddiness.*

Yes. I stopped working on simulation. I felt I was going totally nuts. Finally, by various paths, all this came to have extremely direct consequences on my life. It seemed logical that something would happen, an event of this kind – but I began to wonder what theory had to do with all this. There is in theories something that does away with the feeling of being 'unstuck'. But what theory brings back on the other hand, to reaccentuate it, pervert it – in the full sense of the word – I'd rather not know about.

SL *You spoke a bit earlier about the art of disappearance.*

Disappearance is something completely different from death. Dying doesn't do any good. You still have to disappear. It is a mode assimilated to that of seduction. The death of meaning is not interesting in itself.

SL *Behaviourism puts an end to meaning. It does it more radically than we do.*

There meaning is truly erased, but it doesn't disappear. Pragmatism is the same as simulation pushed to the limit. Simulation puts an end to meaning absolutely, in its neutralizing, undifferentiated form. But it does it without prestige, without charm, without pleasure, without any of the effects of disappearance which are the best we can afford today.

SL *You rediscover desire in charm. Something of desire would have to remain, otherwise . . .*

I only resented desire in the cultural acceptance it gained. Actually, desire is a term that managed to get out of the test of reality – if you'll pardon the expression – while still retaining a certain poetic density. It wasn't killed, it remains – on condition that it stays out of the libidinal.

SL *It's desire as seduction.*

In seduction, all the energy that you gathered for yourself is turned over to the object. Objective necessity occurs – an absolute surprise which takes away the effectiveness of the subject.

SL *Exchange exerts a similar effect, but the subject's disappearance is of a statistical order. It melts into 'the masses', which are conceived as an infinite commutation of individual clones – the mass as circulation, not immobility or assembly, of course.[8]*
   Neutralization is a statistical fiction, a sociologist's point of view reporting the existence of a flat encephalogram on the level of culture.

Well, let's be frank here. If I ever dabbled in anything in my theoretical infancy, it was philosophy more than sociology. I don't think at all in those terms. My point of view is completely metaphysical. If anything, I'm a metaphysician, perhaps a moralist, but certainly not a sociologist. The only 'sociological' work I can claim is my effort to put an end to the social, to the concept of the social.[9]

SL *You proclaimed the end of the social, I guess, by contrast with another more archaic form, which Marcel Mauss defined as the 'total social fact'. What does that symbolic or agonistic, exchange of traditional societies mean to you now? Do you still believe it has a bearing on postindustrial societies?[10]*

Actually, in traditional societies, exchange is absent. Symbolic exchange is the opposite of exchange. The term is rather deceptive. There is an order of exchange and an order of fate. The only means of exorcizing fate is through exchange; in other words, through a contractual agreement. Where exchange is not possible, fate takes over. In the case of the hostage, whenever exchange becomes impossible, you move into the order of the fatal, of the catastrophe. There is a dual reversibility, an agonistic challenge.

SL *Negotiation is no longer possible. From there on, anything can happen.*

I call symbolic exchange fatal: I am led to it by chance. Fate is in the dividing line separating chance and necessity, to use Jacques Monod's terms.[11]

Neither one wipes out the order of events. One – necessity – is based on an order of causes, of finality, a system of values which is that of metaphysics. The other – chance – is based on an objective by undetermined and erratic order. What I wanted to define with the 'fatal' order is an objective order, but of the highest necessity. The question of finality no longer applies. An event – or a being, or a word – resolves all efforts at explanation; it imposes itself with a force which is no longer of the final or causal order. It is more final than final: it is fatal.

SL *The way speed is more mobile than movement – it's pure form, independent of any destination.*

Yes, speed is the ecstatic form of movement. In ecstasy, there is no longer any stage – no more scene, no more theatre. But there is no more passion either. It is intense, but dispassionate. It can carry a charge of seductiveness, for seduction is an ecstatic form. The fatal is ecstasy in the form of an event, in the same way that free-floating capital is an ecstatic form of the circulation of money. They no longer bear any relationship to production.

SL *It is the extreme form of the logic of capital.*

The ecstatic form of capital is totally generalized exchange. An orbital form. In merchandise, money is already in process of de-referentialization. It is the transpoliticized form of merchandise. Look at what happens in the movement of money – money no longer bears any relationship to value, even in the sense in which Bataille uses the term (in order for there to be something 'spent', one must still believe in value). That is what gives rise to intense miraculous effects of multiplication. The secret of gambling is that money does not exist as a value.

SL *But value returns after the fact: it's what you have to pay if you lose.*

Afterward, you commit suicide. But in the heat of the moment, the idea of winning or losing is relatively unimportant compared to the seductive sequence of events.

SL *Gambling is the ecstatic form of money.*

Gambling isn't exactly a passion: the pleasure one derives from it is too crystalline. It is a cold ecstasy which deals with money not as meaning, value, depth or substance, but in the pure form of appearance or disappearance.

SL *It's a form of imminence.*

Yes, but there's nothing behind it. It's the imminence of itself. Gambling is an organized catastrophic, apparitional form – a total metamorphosis.

SL *It's a game with a subject. This would explain the fascination it holds: to gamble is to forget yourself. The extreme form of neurosis – and its annulment.*

Gambling is a game, a challenge. There is no gambling subject: the transsubstantiation is complete. It's pure seduction. It comes from elsewhere. In theory gambling is without consequence. This is why it's so easy to condemn the 'immorality' of gambling. Gambling is immoral. It bears no relation to the reality of money.

SL *It feeds on itself.*

It's the passion of arriving at a given object – money, in this case – and managing to disconnect it completely, to discover its means of appearing. I didn't say its means of production; we know that only too well, and it's no fun. Wherever you can find the possibility of pure appearances, you are once again in the game. It's in this sense that I no longer situate myself in the irreversible order of annihilation. The possibility of returning to a level of metamorphosis or seduction cannot be lost. There's only fate.

SL *But first this has to pass through a rage to destroy, to exterminate everything.*

There has to be extermination. In the final account, it's extremely rare that something can get out of the chain of cause and effect to appear fully. It is the ephemeral moment in which things take the time to appear before taking on meaning or value. What is fascinating then – what makes that moment an event – is that a mode of sociality can be created which is not the mode of exchange but the occurrence of pure events. The statistical occurrence, on the contrary, is flat, numerical, without sequence. It is nothing but contiguity and measurement. We live in a world that is very loose, quite lax, in which things are more or less arbitrary, disconnected and therefore sporadic, erratic. The order of the fatal, on the other hand, is the site of symbolic exchange. There is no more liberty, everything is locked in a sequential chain.

SL *That was already the case with the primitive ceremonial.*

I don't exclude rituals and ceremonies. Whatever reaches the level of pure appearance – a person, an event, an act – enters the realm of the fatal. It cannot be deciphered or interpreted. The subject has nothing to say about it. Events emerge from any and every place, but from an absolute beyond, with that true strangeness which alone is fascinating. It belongs neither to the order of the normal nor to the accidental. It is a necessity greater than the law, something like objective chance without any effect of the unconscious, whose fate would be repressed.

SL *A successful event leaves nothing behind it.*

In the finalities that one can assign oneself, values are always tentative. They must be invested. They are necessary, but subjectively. For example, the fetishistic object topples the subject's need to place itself in the transcendental centre of the world. On the contrary, at any given moment the universe has the possibility of incarnating itself in a detail which is unjustifiable in its own right. The universal no longer exists, there is nothing left but a singularity which can take on the aspect of totality.

SL *Singularities, in the Hegelian sense, have a particularity and a universal aspect. They are moments.*

Yes, whereas now singularities very likely no longer have any universal becoming. The universal is a game preserve, it is the site of that indifferent strategy. It cannot be assigned an end, a reason, a meaning. It is total crystallization around an event.

SL *Deleuze dealt with this problematic in* Logique du Sens (Logic of Meaning).[12] *But for him, the logic of appearances, the play of surfaces, does not abolish subjectivity.*

For me events are no longer those of the subject; they reach a point where they function all by themselves. It is a pure connection of events in a logic of appearances, if you like, which meets seduction. The order of seductive connections stands in opposition to rational connections, whatever they may be, and also to delirious connections, and possibly to molecular ones. It is not an order of the accidental; an accident does not fascinate me in that sense. The catastrophe does not fascinate me as an accident, it fascinates me as a necessity. That appearances function all by themselves is based on a necessity much more implacable than the chain of causes, which is for its part relatively arbitrary, as is the connection of the signifier and the signified. The connection, the chain of appearances, are signs that do not, in fact, make sense. There is a rule to the game.

SL *Is the fatal the fulfilment of an empty rule?*

A rule can be perfectly arbitrary in its enunciation, but it is much more unbreakable than the 'law', which can be transgressed. You can do anything with the law. With the rule, on the other hand, either you play or you don't play. If you play, the rule is implacable. You can't get around it. It would be idiotic to transgress it. The rule of the game – the seductive sequence – is played in an extremely ceremonialized fashion. Situations can be replayed indefinitely, the 'rule' does not change. But it is secret, never known, never spoken. If it were known, things would become visible and reversible again. With causal or rational sequences, you have crisis.

With seductive sequences, on the contrary, you are – literally – in a catastrophic order.

SL *That's the logic of the avalanche.*

Forms that are beyond judgement have a much greater power of fascination, but they are for that same reason terribly dangerous for any order whatsoever. They can no longer be controlled. At any given moment a category or a form stops representing itself, it no longer enters the stage of representation, it no longer functions according to its end. It doubles back upon itself, taking a curve so rapid that it reaches a kind of potentialization. All the rest goes into a state of weightlessness. In the language of poetry we are familiar with those sequences in which things seem to take place without continuity, without consequence, without mediation. Language is always an order of seduction to the extent that it is a mutant order. If you suppose continuous, progressive, linear order then it is still based on a mutational 'superstructure'. The words in a poem are of that order. They do not go through the meaning. One word calls forth another in a catastrophe of charm. One leads to another in a thoughtless, unintelligible way. I am not seeking the irrational. On the contrary, we know that there is a necessity without its being transcendental or providential. The same thing can take place in the order of facts, of actions, of existential situations.

SL *It is ritual without the sacred, the tragic without the tragedy.*

It is not a sacred universe, even though there is indeed a tragic aspect in seduction. If you accept the rule of the game, you can never know in advance to what degree of concatenation of appearances a strategy may lead. Take, for example, the story of the woman to whom a man sends an ardent love letter. She asks him what part of her seduced him the most. What else can he answer? Her eyes, of course. And he receives in the mail, wrapped in brown paper, the woman's eye. The man is shattered, destroyed. The woman sets herself as the destiny of the other. Literalizing the metaphor, she abolishes the symbolic order. The sign becomes the thing. The subject is caught in the trap of his own desire. She loses an eye, he loses face.

SL *In* De la Séduction (On Seduction) *you took another metaphor literally, that of the woman-object.*[13] *It meant (in appearance at least) taking feminism against the grain with, I believe, unexpected potentializations.*

I consider woman the absence of desire. It is of little import whether or not that corresponds to real women. It is my conception of 'femininity'.

SL *Isn't it surprising that in the midst of metamorphoses, the feminine figure for you remains fixed. That's very nostalgic, that polarity of roles.*

110

But I don't believe in it. For me, femininity is non-polar. Contrary to masculinity, woman has no anxious focalization on sex, she can transform herself into herself.

SL *That means becoming-woman is something that can occur in women or in men.*

Of course. Femininity appears in certain individuals, men or women. But woman is the object which plays out all the liquidities of desire. The drama of love is entirely in men, that of charm completely in women.

SL *Speaking of love, you replace intersubjectivity with a reciprocal transformation. A passage into the other, but an other which is no longer there.*

That is the problem of otherness. As in the world, or on the terrain of sex, no one is the other of the other sex any longer. It is not narcissism, which is a concretion accomplished in solitude; not otherness either. Each one functions within his/her own nebula, accomplishing his/her own virtuality.

SL *If I understand, the process of becoming-woman common to both sexes is the accomplishment of each one as a separate object. Their reciprocal challenge is to become more woman than woman, in a word, to attain that femininity which each one can attain only in relationship to himself/herself.*

I think here of the strategic position of the process of becoming-object. What interests me now is no longer the subject but the object and its destiny. You become the destiny of the other. It is clearer when you think of childhood. The child always has a double strategy. He has the possibility of offering himself as object, protected, recognized, destined as a child to the pedagogical function; and at the same time he is fighting on equal terms. At some level the child knows that he is not a child, but the adult does not know that. That is the secret.

SL *That's what is fuelling the hysterical campaign against 'child abuse'. Adults panic in the face of the extermination of childhood, which they on the other hand are encouraging. Childhood constitutes the last anchor of our culture. If childhood is lost, what is morality to be based on? The social repression of 'child molesters' is all the more ferocious.*[14]

The problem is that everything has been unleashed on childhood. There has been quite a 'palingenesis' on childhood, no psychoanalytic joke intended; now there it has been taken seriously. The category of childhood is defined historically, and there psychology begins: child psychology, therapy, pedagogy, it all follows. If, going against every assumption, you maintain the little utopian fact that childhood does not exist and that the child is perhaps the only one to know it, then everything blows up in your face. That is what I was trying to say about women. Women, children, animals – we must not be afraid of assimilations – do not just have a subject-consciousness, they have a kind of objective ironic presentiment that the category into which they have been placed does not exist. Which allows them at any given moment to make use of a double strategy. It isn't psychology, it's strategy.

SL *When you speak of the strategy of the fatal, what interests me most is the strategy. What is to be done?*

No, it's completely antinomical. It's not really strategy. That's a play on words to dramatize the total passage from the subject to the object. Whether you call it the revenge of the object, or the Evil Genius of matter, it is not representable. But it is a power all the same. In fact, I would go along with calling it the principle of Evil, of irreconciliation, the way the Good is the principle of reconciliation. That exists, it is inextricable, it cannot be destroyed.

SL *Can you still invoke a strategy to account for situations in which the subject has no place?*

Only an 'objective' strategy that no one could recognize. What I foresee is a transposition of all forms and the impossibility of any politics. There is something like a threshold of inertia. Beyond that, forms snowball, terror is unleashed as an empty form.

SL *Panic.*

Right. It's the other form of the ecstatic, it's catastrophic form, in the almost neutral sense of the term, in its mathematical extension. It is a completely alien response of the object world to the subject world, of a completely external destiny which occurs with an absolute surprise and whose symbolic wave strikes the human world.

SL *You see several sides to ecstasy?*

I see two. Take a model. Its ecstatic side is to be truer than the truth; it creates a kind of giddiness, a kind of inflation of truth. A model is a rather pathetic thing. But take fashion for example. Fashion participates in this phenomenon absolutely. It doesn't depend on any sort of aesthetic judgement. It's not the beautiful opposed to the ugly, it's what's more beautiful than the beautiful. The obese – that famous fat American – is not opposed to the skinny one. He is fatter than fat, and that is fascinating. Fashion is the absolute formalization of the beautiful. It functions by means of the unconditional transmutation of forms. Ecstatic forms can be static and cold; sometimes they can be more

112

enchanting, warmer. There is a splendour of fashion and, behind it, an uncontrollable rule of the game. A rule which conveys the objective irony of fashion. Everything that can be invented deliberately falls flat on its face, and it's something else that catches on instead.

SL *Can fashion serve as a model for politics?*

Fashion has always been at odds with politics and scorned by politics. But you cannot politically oppose fashion to politics. Fashion is a splendid form of metamorphosis. It is both a ritual and a ceremony. It can't be programmed.

SL *Could happy, ecstatic political forms be conceived of?*

It's rather difficult to sort out happy and unhappy forms. Seduction, like fashion, is a happy form, beyond the beauty of desire: 'I am not beautiful, I am worse.' Seduction uses signs which are already simulators to make them into the falser than false. It displaces them, turns them into traps and produces a splendid effect snatched from the imperative of veracity of signs, and even of desire, which is no longer at stake.

SL *Must all political rituals necessarily be programmed?*

Politics functioned in terms of distinctive oppositions: the left or the right. As in other areas you have the true or the false, the beautiful or the ugly, etc. Now, at a given point the energy of a situation stopped depending on this kind of dissociation. It is no longer the dialectic of the two terms that organizes things, but the fact that the forms each go their separate ways, meaninglessly, senselessly. It is the truer than true, or the falser than false. A form shoots off in a kind of relentless logic, uncalculated, without any history, without any memory, the way cancer cells go off in an organic direction. That logic seems to me more interesting because it does after all correspond more to the way things are evolving nowadays.

SL *Where do you see that logic at work in the political field right now? In the media?*

The media are supposed to be a fabulous distortion. But behind that analysis still lurks a symbolic demand for truth. Where does that distortion come from? Placing the media in the system of will–choice–liberty is really hopeless. All you can do is invoke a total alienation of the political subject, accuse the power structure of manipulating, etc. The power structure doesn't manipulate TV, it functions exactly the way it does. It relies on representations, it also secretes them with the scant political relief of a TV image, without accuracy or energy, to the point of merging with the civil society in the indistinction of the political scene. Meaning manages to disappear in the horizon of communication. The media are simply the locus of this disappearance, which is always a challenge to the powers that be. It's becoming urgent to reformulate a theory of the media as '*agents provocateurs*' of information overload, turning political debate into a gigantic abyss. Let's get rid of the notion that the media mystify and alienate. We've had enough of that.

SL *The theory of alienation has become the echo necessary to the media for their existence. It amounts indirectly to giving them the benefit of an intention. They don't deserve that.*

You're right. In the transpolitical, there is no more who. Then if it isn't the power structure, which seems pretty clear, if there is no longer a subject, is there a strategy of the object, objective irony?

SL *The media industry never does anything but reproduce its own necessity. As William Burroughs said: all things considered, the public could get along very well without the news.*

There you have it. All that is done now is to display a range of choices which are all equally potential or fulfilled. Have you heard this story about Beau Brummell? He travelled a great deal, always in the company of his manservant. One day he was in Scotland, in a region where there are many lakes, each one more beautiful than the last. Brummell turned to his servant and asked him, 'Which lake do I prefer?' Having to choose is really a bore. That's what servants are for. In any case, that's not what counts. Power – Knowledge – Will – let the inventors of those ideas take responsibility for them. It makes perfect sense to me that the great masses, very snobbishly, delegate to the class of intellectuals, of politicans, this business of managing, of choosing, of knowing what one wants. They are joyously dumping all those burdensome categories that no one, deep down inside, really wants any part of. That people want to be told what they want is certainly not true; it is not clear either that they really want to know what they want, or that they desire to want at all. The whole edifice of socialism is based on that assumption. They start from the fact that this is what people ought to want, that they are social in the sense that they are supposed to know themselves, know what they want. I think we have pressed beyond that point, beyond truth, beyond reality.

SL *Objective irony, that would be the masses' offhand way of getting rid of their responsibilities, turning power back to its fantasies, knowledge to its obsessions, will to its illusions. The silent majority, as you see it then, is not the accomplice of law and order, but rather its silence is a dead silence. The masses are playing dead. And this stubborn silence, this insolent reserve, would sanction the disappearance of the social.*

Exactly. The large systems of information relieve the masses of the responsibility of having to know, to understand, to be informed, to be up on things. Advertising relieves people of the responsibility of having to choose, which is perfecty human and perfectly horrible. As for power, it has always seemed ironic to me to delegate it to someone. That's like catching him in a trap, and that trap closes on the political class itself. I see all of this as a profound reversal of strategy on the part of the masses. They are no longer involved in a process of subversion or revolution, but in some gigantic devolution from an unwanted liberty – with some evil genius lurking behind it all. I think we are beginning to realize how much terror lies at the heart of the paradise of communication. Beyond that, events are inconsequential, and that is even more true for theories.

SL *But there is power in the fact of being inconsequential.*

That was what interested me about May '68. Behind the political, revolutionary and historical scene, and also behind the failure, there was the power of an event which managed to absorb its own continuity. It makes it implode, succeeds in swallowing its own energy and disappearing.

SL *May '68 swept down on France like an avalanche, and no sooner had it appeared than it disappeared, mysteriously, practically without a trace.*

Then where has all that energy gone? Nowhere – certainly not into socialism, in any case. It must have been reabsorbed somewhere – without necessarily remaining underground so as to emerge later. For me May '68 was the first event that corresponded to this inertial point of the political scene. Continuity disappears. Only such things are fascinating.

SL *Comprehension is no longer involved there.*

No. But more comprehension is going to be re-secreted. It is intolerable for everybody that events should be inconsequential, or that their own desires should be inconsequential. And, in the last analysis, that theory should be inconsequential. No exceptions allowed.

SL *All of that is part of what Paul Virilio calls 'the aesthetic of disappearance'.*[15]

From time to time theory allows itself beautiful effects of disappearance. What more can one do? In terms of results there is no difference between what came to an end with May '68 and whatever Giscard d'Estaing or Mitterrand accomplished. Acceleration permits another kind of disappearance effect, another order that can't be reached in any other way. Therefore, I agree with Paul Virilio on the idea of theory going to extremes. You will ask me, why are people going to those extremes, if you don't suppose that at some point the world, and the universe, too, is in the grips of a movement to extremes. There you are, apparently, forced to make an almost objective, rational hypothesis. It is impossible to think that theory can be nothing more than fiction. Otherwise no one would bother producing theory any more. You have to believe that going somewhere is not just a metaphor. And then, if it is a challenge, in any case there is a partner. It is no longer a dialectic, but there is a rule of the game. Somewhere there must be a limit that constitutes the real in order for there to be theory. A point where things can stick, or from which they can take off.

SL *For Virilio there is definitely a trend towards extremes at work in the world today: the military class is swallowing up civilian society before disappearing itself in a suicidal race.*[16]

Virilio's calculation is to push the military to a kind of extreme absolute of power, which can only ultimately cause its own downfall, place it before the judgement of God and absorb it into the society it destroys. Virilio carries out this calculation with such an identification or obsession that I can only credit him at times with a powerful sense of irony: the system devours its own principle of reality, inflates its own empty forms until it reaches an absolute and its own ironic destiny of reversal. I myself am not so interested in military hardware, but in software. It's the form of his idea that strikes me as valid.

SL *The state of emergency, the risk of nuclear extermination – you can dismiss all that?*

Why, of course, I think about it, but for me there is no fatal term. The nuclear threat is part of a 'soft' mode of extermination, bit by bit, by deterrence, not at all an apocalyptic term. It is the scenario of deterrence that Paul Virilio shares with me, apparently, because he moves back and forth between the real term and the mythical term, which is mine. For me, it's in the realm of the intellectual wager. If there were an absolute term of the nuclear apocalypse in the realm of the real, then at that point I would stop, I wouldn't write any more! God knows, if the metaphor really collapses into reality, I won't have any more to do. That would not even be a question of resignation – it's no longer possible to think at that point.

SL *The implosive side of the nuclear threat paralyses everything. It's more than deterrence, it's political tetanus.*

Virilio is very interested in strategic vicissitudes; I don't have the patience. Does the nuclear threat have a political term? Or does it make it disappear when the bomb hits the ground? It's the same as for the media, I no longer attach any importance to it. Can there be a political management of a material that is 'transpolitical'? I don't see where it could come from.

SL *Let's go back to your analysis of terrorism, which led you to discard the concept of the social. For a number of years we witnessed a trend towards extremes in the confrontation between the Red Army Faction and the German government. Now what was the final outcome? A challenge, implosive forms of confrontation? Not at all. Once the extremes were eliminated (Stammheim), the possibility was established of bargaining, of striking a compromise. Politics regained the upper hand, and history with it.*

Terrorism can have a visible, a spectacular form. It is still part of the dramatic, practically, in the historical realm. So it can be succeeded by a kind of negotiable terror. The term 'hostage', as I have used it, would then qualify not only the visible dramas of the taking of hostages, but rather the hyper-reality of everyday life which is situated well beyond negotiable terror. It's the same as for deterrence. It's not the actual terror of the orbiting bombs' power of destruction; Virilio says that very clearly. War having also become an impossible exchange, the hostage would only qualify a situation in which all exchange has become impossible.

SL *War is perhaps impossible: it continues nonetheless everywhere you look.*

People get killed, people die in war, of course. But it would still involve a kind of conspiracy to set up a *trompe-l'oeil* décor, the way city planners make provisions for parks and greenery. The history of Europe is perhaps of that order – an effort to circumscribe Europe as a space of freedom, a political space, etc., to escape that panic of the insolubility, the impossibility of a declared war, of a war which can really signify itself. It is set up as a war space in an attempt to alter somehow, however minimally, the situation of generalized dissuasion, which is intolerable. The consequences are felt at some point with this blockage, this leukaemia of political life which is unbearable for everybody, for the ruling classes as well as for those who are ruled. But at this point war certainly no longer has the same meaning, nor does art, or politics, or the hostage. Everything takes on another existence, with different stakes.

SL *You once tried, along with Virilio, to theorize the concept of the 'transpolitical'. Is the transpolitical situated on the other side of the political logic of consequences? Can that be a way of saving the political?*

The efforts to save it, that is what we are witnessing all around us. Those efforts are occupying the scene. The present, or recent, form of socialism in France – I call it 'ecstatic' – in that sense it is transpolitical. It proceeds from a model. Socialism realizes, hyper-realizes, a model which no longer has any veracity or original passion.

SL *The transpolitical would be a negative notion then? It's the same scene but emptied out from within.*

In that sense, yes. That is part of the exterminating analysis. I'm not crazy about the term itself. It's almost too 'figurative'. It signifies that there could still be a beyond, and that we ought to go and take a look at what's going on there. I prefer the formulation in terms of that point Canetti describes. We don't know what happened after that. The traditional points of reference are no longer usable, but we don't know what we are in. To demand a degree of truth is always problematical. Fascism was already something like that. It was a kind of potentialization. That is why it remains relatively inexplicable in political terms, such as capitalism or class struggle.

SL *There is a secret to fascism.*

Yes. It derives its overwhelming necessity precisely from its being isolated and disconnected, as in the case of the catastrophe, but this necessity is far beyond any rational finality. The secret lies in that total autonomy of a narrative, of a form, a myth, that can no longer be described in a logical, coherent and acceptable manner, but runs amok. Past a certain threshold of inertia, forms start snowballing, stampeding, and terror is unleashed as an empty form. There comes about a swept-away effect, an effect that feeds on itself and can become the source of immense energies, as fascism did, unfortunately. When effects go faster than causes, they devour them. I could easily see the 'speed-up' analysed by Virilio from this angle, as an attempt to accelerate faster than linearity can. Movement goes somewhere, speed goes nowhere. May '68 was an illogical event, irreducible to simulation, one which had no status other than that of coming from some place else – a kind of pure object or event. Its strangeness derives from a logic of our own system, but not from its history. It is a prodigious effect, and it is situated on the other side of that crucial point Canetti describes and that I mentioned earlier.

SL *The cause of an event is always imagined after the fact. After that jolly May, we were treated to the curious spectacle of causes racing after effects.*

May '68 is an event which it has been impossible to rationalize or exploit, from which nothing has been concluded. It remains indecipherable. It was the forerunner of nothing.

SL *There are no children of May.*

Perhaps a kind of 'secret' is involved here too.

SL *Tell me about secrets.*

There are fundamentally two kinds of secrets. The obscene form of the secret involves a saturation of the event with explanations. The other kind involves something which is not hidden and therefore cannot be expressed directly in words. It is this second kind of secret which makes the event somehow innocent. Now what can you do with that? Ordinarily, when things happen, you pick them up as best you can as a subject. In the case of May '68, we have been forced to give all our subjective energy to the object.

SL *The event becomes a kind of slippery object that refers each subject back to his/her own fantasies without ever allowing itself to be touched. There are no children of May.*

That event disappeared without leaving a trace other than this secondary and parodic effect, this second or thirdhand product manufactured to occupy a political scene that has been utterly absorbed and destroyed: French socialism.

SL *The socialists' error is to have occupied the vacuum and to have allowed themselves to be sucked into the black hole of politics.*

There are two ways of seeing this. You can say there used to be a political sphere and there isn't any more, following a Foucauldian genealogy. That was how Foucault talked about man. There is no longer a scene of politics the way it was organized around the history of power relations, production, classes. Power is no longer an objective, locatable process. This is what I say is lost, if we can speak of an end of something. We are elsewhere. If, on the contrary, the political sphere consists in knowing how to play on an event or a thing on the basis of its objective or conscious end – but in order to ward it off – then power, in political terms, becomes a kind of challenge.

SL *A challenge from the powers that be not to exercise power?*

I wonder, in fact, if true power, the power that deepens the meaning of politics, is not the one that pulls back from itself, that plays out its own death, without even willing it consciously. The secret of power is that it can no longer be occupied, no longer be taken. When 'power' is confused with the 'power structure', you know it is no longer power. It becomes extremely vulnerable.

SL *Could we not conceive this phenomenon in a more active fashion? The political as the art of not occupying a position yourself, but creating a void for others to rush into it.*

The political sphere must keep secret the rule of the game that, in reality, power doesn't exist. Its strategy is, in fact, always creating a space of optical illusion, maintaining itself in total ambiguity, total duplicity, in order to throw the others into this space. This is Machiavelli's strategy.

SL *It is also the story of Sophie Calle.*[17]

Right. For no particular reason, as you know, she followed a stranger in the street; she became his shadow and thus, in a certain sense, erased his traces, acted as his destiny. Creating a void, she asked the other to fill it. She herself is nothing. She has no desire of her own in all this. She doesn't want to go anywhere, even though she follows him all the way to Venice. She doesn't want to find out what he is or to know his life. She is the proof that, although he thought he was going somewhere, in fact he is going nowhere. Where he supposedly is, there's no one. We could envision this story in terms of Balthazar Gracian. Is God's strategy really to lead man to his own ends, in other words to move man closer to the image of God according to a progressive-evolutionary process? God isn't so dumb, Gracian says. Nowhere does it say that man wants to arrive at his own end, which would be the idea of God in its canonical form. God's strategy is much more subtle, which no doubt corresponds to man's desire not to give a shit about his own end. God's strategy – that of all the Jesuit manuals that were incredibly widespread in the seventeenth century – is to keep man in an eternal suspense. And that is in the order of politics. Which reveals God as being fairly malicious, perverse, given man's faculty to erect almost anything as a finality. Any poss-ible illusion to avoid the last judgement, which is truly Hell. In fact, politics is always in a contrary, twisted, or simply 'seductive' relation to its own ends. God is much more interested in the game, in the possibility of playing with ends, even using means. Furthermore, this proposition – the end and the means – has always favoured the ends at the expense of the means. Since the means are immoral, the ends must be moral. But we could very well turn the proposition around, and this is precisely what the Jesuits do: play with the means, whatever, for the ends cannot be found any more. For the Jesuits – and this is their basic proposition – it is impossible to establish a proof of God's existence. So all right, God exists, the grace of God exists, but it has nothing to do with us because what we're dealing with is a strategic worldliness. And with this you can play. There are only means.

SL *In* Simulations, *what especially interested me, in fact, was the possibility of effecting this kind of diversion. I was struck by the fact that the Italians – in particular certain figures of the Autonomia movement[18] – when con-fronted with an emergency situation, found in certain of your propositions, even if they were disenchanted ones, instruments that they immediately tried to use politically. Instead of respecting your own ends (or their absence as ends . . .), they took certain of your concepts as floating theoretical tools capable of being reinvested in particular situations. In short, they diverted your own diversion. I admit that I like this practical perversion of your own theoretical perversion.*

That indeed seems to me to be the situation in Italy. Everyone seems to be party to prolonging a situation that isn't exactly political – in any case, no one can pull the strings any more. The situation is seductive because of that kind of indecisiveness with which everyone plays without necessarily being aware of it. I like that Italian ability to turn around, turn away an objective state that would otherwise be catastrophic: the State could have disappeared a long time ago, along with politics.

SL *In fact, the State has never existed there ...*

I think that every other country is in the same situation, despite appearances to the contrary. They are all in a situation of political simulation, but on the sly. Italy, on the other hand, seems to be exercising the simulacrum as such, seduction as such.

SL *The simulacrum supports politics, instead of wiping it out.*

The Italians have a long tradition of all this with the Jesuits and the Church – in the way Nietzsche meant. For them, the end is always imminent, but at the same time there is a possibility of almost joyful resurrection with each event, and that is phenomenal. We certainly couldn't say the same of Poland ... who are ideologically active and cannot help fantasizing about a world that would make more sense, or that would return to sense. And so you get to terrorism, which is an enormous fantasy of a political order of the State the better to murder it, to massacre it. But what game is terrorism playing? Terrorism makes no more sense than the State does. They are accomplices in a circular set-up.

SL *In Germany, as in Italy (neither country ever having been unified or centralized), terrorism helps the State appear.*

It's the role of a partner more than of an adversary. It's always like that: events are played out on a conscious level of adversity, of war, of irreconcilable, incompatible ideologies, but in reality what's happening underneath it all? Who would dream that the situation can become so totally terroristic that in fact it joins its other extreme? I don't see how all this can end. It is not objectively representable.

SL *You see in the terrorist act, as in nuclear confrontation between the Great Powers (which is, in fact, State terrorism), not an explosive phenomenon, but the point at which the social implodes. But what is 'the social'? You hypostatize a complex reality in an abstraction, only to immediately send the abstraction back to the domain of unreality and proclaim its end. Isn't that a bit too easy?*

But I take the social as already hypostatized. From hypostasis to ecstasy!

SL *If the social doesn't exist – if it has never existed outside of the theoretical imagination – then it can't implode.*

All right, that's entirely plausible. And yet you could also state the hypothesis that at a given moment the social did exist, but not at all as a representation of society, nor in a positive sense, but rather as a challenge to the reality of things, as a virulent myth. This is how Georges Bataille saw sociology: as a challenge to the very nature of the social and to society. History also existed in that sense. But then, that's not really existence, because when history begins to exist, very quickly there's nothing left but to treat it as an instance of jurisdiction and meaning. I have never resolved that ambiguity between being and existence; I believe it's insoluble.

SL *For Nietzsche, the philosopher must decipher action. He must actively evaluate the forces confronting each other in society. You conceive of the social as the depletion of an empty form. What role, then, do you attribute to theory? Must it be a virulent myth, as it is for Bataille? But if the social has become weightless, what does myth attack? And for what cause?*

I admit, that question of theory troubles me. Where is theory situated today? Is it completely satellized? Is it wandering in realms which no longer have anything to do with real facts? What is analysis? As long as you consider that there is a real world, then by the same token there is a possible position for theory. Let us say a dialectical position, for the sake of argument. Theory and reality can still be exchanged at some point – and that is ideality. There is after all a point of contact between the two. And then you can transform the world, and theory does transform the world. That is not at all my position any more. Moreover, it never was. But I have never succeeded in formulating it. In my opinion, theory is simply a challenge to the real. A challenge to the world to exist. Very often a challenge to God to exist. But there is more than theory. In the beginning, religion, in its former heretical phase, was always a negation – at times a violent one – of the real world, and this is what gave it strength. After that, religion became a process of reconciliation rather than a pleasure or reality principle. This can hold true for theory as well: a theory can attempt to reconcile the real with theory itself. And then there is a principle of antagonism – an absolutely irreconcilable, almost Manichaean antagonism. You maintain a position of challenge, which is different from unreality.

SL *Still, isn't that exactly what you do: make stakes unreal by pushing them to the limit?*

But I hold no position on reality. Reality remains an unshakeable postulate towards which you can maintain a relation either of adversity or of reconciliation. The real – all things considered, perhaps it exists – no, it doesn't exist – is the insurmountable limit of theory. The real is not an objective status of things, it is the point at which theory can do nothing. That does not necessarily make of theory a failure. The real is actually a challenge to the theoretical edifice. But in my opinion theory can have no status other than that of challenging the real. At that point, theory is no longer theory, it is the event itself. There is no 'reality' with respect to which theory could become dissident or heretical, pursuing its fate other than in the objectivity of things. Rather, it's the objectivity of things we must question. What is this objectivity? In the so-called 'real world', don't things always happen that way? By a divergence, a trajectory, a curve which is not at all the linear curve of evolution? We could perhaps develop a model of drifting plates, to speak in seismic terms, in the theory of catastrophes. The seismic is our form of the slipping and sliding of the referential. The end of the infrastructure. Nothing remains but shifting movements that provoke very powerful raw events. We no longer take events as revolutions or effects of the superstructure, but as underground effects of skidding, fractal zones in which things happen. Between the plates, continents do not quite fit together, they slip under and over each other. There is no more system of reference to tell us what happened to the geography of things. We can only take a geoseismic view. Perhaps this is also true in the construction of a society, a mentality, a value-system. Things no longer meet head-on; they slip past one another. Everyone claims to 'be in reality'. But the test of reality is not decisive. Nothing happens in the real.

SL *Is anything happening in the theory then?*

Theory dismantles the reality principle; it's not at all a means of objectivizing things in order to transform them. No, I don't believe that. At a certain point I felt – if we suppose that the real, and social practices, are indeed there – that I was launched on a trajectory that was increasingly diverging, becoming asymptotic. It would be an error to try constantly to catch hold of that zig-zagging line of reality. The only thing you can do is let it run all the way to the end. At that point they can raise any objection they like about the relation to reality: we are in a totally arbitrary situation, but there is an undeniable internal necessity. From that point on, theory maintains absolutely no relation with anything at all; it becomes an event in and of itself. We can no longer fix the way things are going.

SL *I wonder if there isn't a kind of 'skidding' endemic to theory. When theory manages to complete itself, following its internal logic, that's when it disappears. Its accomplishment is its abolition.*

Yes, I really believe that's true. Can theory (I'm speaking here about what I've done) produce, not a model, but a utopian, metaphorical representation of an event, even as its entire cyclical trajectory is being accomplished, completed? I think there is a destiny of theory. There is a curve we can't escape. You know that my way is to make ideas appear, but as soon as they appear I immediately try to make them disappear. That's what the game has always consisted of. Strictly speaking, nothing remains but a sense of dizziness, with which you can't do anything.

SL *Isn't that a little bit suicidal?*

It's suicidal, but in a good way. If this game didn't exist, there would be no pleasure in writing, or in theorizing.

SL *Theory, or the pleasure of disappearing ...*

There is an art of disappearing, a way of modulating it and making it into a state of grace. This is what I'm trying to master in theory.

SL *It's the end of theory, at least in Canetti's sense.*

Yes, in that sense.

SL *Theory implodes.*

It's possible that theory will implode, that it will absorb its own meaning, that it will end up at best mastering its disappearance. But it doesn't happen like that. We must manage to choke back the meanings we produce – which always tend to be produced. If a theory – or a poem, or any other kind of writing (it's not endemic to theory) – indeed manages to implode, to constitute a concentric vortex of implosion, then there are no other effects of meaning. Theory has an immediate effect – a very material one as well – of being a void. It's not so easy to create a void. And, besides, there's catastrophe all around it. I don't see how theory and reality can go together. Can we implode in the real with charm? Without going all the way to suicide, we continually play on the process of disappearance in our relations to others. Not by making ourselves scarce, but by challenging the other to make us reappear. That's what seduction is, in the good sense. Not a process of expansion and conquest, but the implosive process of the game.

SL *You theorize the way others go to a casino. It's your gambling side; you swoop down on a theoretical object – Foucault, for example – with a cold passion and you totally disconnect it from its own thrust ...*

There has to be some pleasure at stake, of course, which is neither the pleasure of prophecy nor, I think, of annihilation (destruction for destruction's sake). A perverse pleasure, in short. Theory must be played the way we said gambling was before.

SL *The secret of gambling is that money doesn't exist. Does theory have a secret too?*

The secret of theory is that truth doesn't exist. You can't confront it in any way. The only thing you can do is play with some kind of provocative logic. Truth constitutes a space that can no longer be occupied. The whole strategy is, indeed, not to occupy it, but to work around it so that others come to occupy it. It means creating a void so that others will fall into it.

SL *If theory can no longer occupy anything, can it at least constitute a challenge to the system to bring about its own annihilation?*

I have my doubts about its capacities in that respect. Those in power manage it much better than we could. The French socialists were wiped out because they couldn't see the malice of the social, which the Jesuits know so well. They should have had a more sporting idea of struggle: the slipperiness of forms. By trying to establish stability the socialists lost every time. They were always completely out of step with their system of cultural projection. The ground they fell on was quicksand. So what else could they do? What position can theory hold when it comes to thinking up events of that order? In concrete terms, I can't see any. Except perhaps in the twisting in which systems, in the simulated references they latch on to (the masses, the media), end up turning on themselves without intending to, and skidding. To me this seems pure genius, in the evil sense. It's a hypothesis, but a rather effective one.

SL *Theory can anticipate or hasten the catastrophic aspect of things.*

We could say that theory is ahead of the state of things, that it moves too fast and thus is in a position of destiny with respect to what could happen. In reality, things happen in such a way that they are always absolutely ahead of us, as Rilke said. We're always late, and therefore they are always unpredictable. No matter how, things are always much further along than theory simply by virtue of the fact that the use of discourse is in the domain of metaphor. We can't escape it. In language we are condemned to using ambiguous extrapolations. If we claim a truth, we push effects of meaning to the extreme within a model. All that theory can do is be rigorous enough to cut itself off from any system of reference, so that it will at least be current, on the scale of what it wishes to describe.

SL *You've cut yourself off from every system of reference, but not from referentiality. What I see you describing is not a challenge to the real, but a challenge internal to theory. You don't criticize the genealogical attitude or the libidinal position, you send them spinning away like tops. You wholly embrace the movement that animates them, you amplify their concepts to the maximum, pulling them into the vortex of your own dizziness. You draw them into an endless spiral which, like the treatment of myths by Lévi-Strauss, leads them bit by bit to their own exhaustion.*

That's right. Thus theory is exterminated. It no longer has any term, literally. You can't find an end for it any more. That's one mode of disappearance.

SL *By pushing theory to its limit the way you do, you are hyper-realizing it. You take away from theory its substance, to exhaust it, to extenuate it in its form, and then you 'forget it' as a body in suspension might be left behind. You don't even simulate the real, you play God's advocate, the evil genius of theory. More Foucauldian than Foucault, you evaporate his microphysics; more schizo than Deleuze and Guattari, you straddle their fluxes, denying them any resting point. You are not the metaphysician you would like people to take you for; you are a metatheoretician, a simulator of theory. No wonder theoreticians accuse you of being an* agent provocateur. *You aren't theoretical, you are 'worse'. You put theory into a state of grace into which you dare the world to follow you.*

Theory is simulation. At least that is the usage of it I have. Both simulation and challenge. It isn't deliberate. It started that way, that's all. I don't want to give it a general form.

SL *You catch concepts in their own trap – that is, in yours – abolishing every certainty by dint of fidelity. That is the position of humour, which can be sad, as well as tongue-in-cheek. You adopt the imperceptible insolence of the servant challenging his master (his intellectual masters) to take him seriously. Calling your bluff would mean getting entangled in your game. But to evade your challenge still amounts to lending you a hand. You 'forget' those whom you vampirize, but you never allow yourself to be forgotten. You are like the media, about which one can say nothing without oneself becoming implicated in it. What allows you to understand it so well, is that you are included in it. You are both playing the same game. You both use the same strategy. You don't speak about the media, the media speak through you. As soon as you turn on your theoretical screen, the great myths of history are turned into a soap opera, or into 'serials'. You make them share the fate of that TV programme, 'Holocaust', which you analysed so well.* [19]

I don't deny history. It's an immense toy.

SL *Yes, if you remain glued to the screen, or fascinated by the giddiness of commutations.*

Our anti-destiny is the media universe. And I don't see how to make this mental leap which would make it possible to reach the fractal or fatal zones where things would really be happening. Collectively, we are behind the radioactive screen of information. It is no more possible to go behind that curtain than it is to leap over your own shadow.

SL *You are one of the few thinkers to confront the gorgon of the media from within, to extract from it a vision – at the risk of being paralysed. Yet you, too, need an adversary to succumb to your own fascination. And that partner*

*can't be the media since you are yourself behind the screen; nor can it be
reality, which you have left far behind. That partner is theory. Cultivating
paradox in order to revluse theory, to upset its vision, to bring it to a crisis
by playing and displaying the card of its own seriousness. That, I believe,
is what your pleasure is, the only one maybe, or the only socializable one,
at any rate a pleasure that is as strong as fascination.*

I admit that I greatly enjoy provoking that revulsion. But right away, people
ask, 'What can you do with that?' It relies after all on an extraordinary
deception – in the literal sense of the term. There is nothing to be had from it.

Paris and Rome, 1984–5

NOTES

1 Elias Canetti, *The Human Province*, New York: Seabury, 1978.
2 Jean Baudrillard, *The Mirror of Production*, New York: Telos, 1975.
3 Jean Baudrillard, *Simulations*, New York: Semiotext(e) Foreign Agents Series,
  1983.
4 Gilles Deleuze and Felix Guattari, *Anti-Oedipus: Capitalism and Schizophrenia*,
  New York: Viking, 1977.
5 *In Mille Plateaux*, Paris: Editions de Minuit, 1980. See also *Nomadology: The
  War Machine*, New York: Semiotext(e) Foreign Agents Series, 1986.
6 Paul Virilio, *Speed and Politics*, New York: Semiotext(e) Foreign Agents Series,
  1986.
7 Georges Bataille, *La Part Maudite*, Paris: Minuit, 1967. The 'devil's share' is
  the portion of one's goods that cannot be spent usefully, but which must be offered
  sacrificially.
8 Jean Baudrillard, *In the Shadow of the Silent Majorities*, New York: Semiotext(e)
  Foreign Agents Series, 1983.
9 *ibid*. 'The End of the Social' comprises the second part.
10 *ibid*.
11 Jacques Monod, *Chance and Necessity*, New York: Vintage, 1972.
12 Gilles Deleuze, *Logique du Sens*, Paris: Minuit, 1969.
13 Jean Baudrillard, *De la Séduction*, Paris: Galilee, 1979.
14 *Loving Boys*, New York: Semiotext(e), 1980.
15 Paul Virilio, *L'Esthétique de la Disparition*, Paris: Balland, 1980.
16 Paul Virilio/Sylvere Lotringer, *Pure War*, New York: Semiotext(e) Foreign
  Agents Series, 1983.
17 Sophie Calle, *Suite Venitienne*, Paris: Editions de l'Etoile, 1983.
18 *Autonomia: Post-Political Politics*, New York: Semiotext(e), 9, 1980.
19 Jean Baudrillard, *Simulacres et Simulation*, Paris: Galilee, 1981.

Part IV

RADICALISM HAS
PASSED INTO EVENTS . . .

11

AMERICA AS FICTION
Interview with J. Henric and G. Scarpetta

JH/GS *Jean Baudrillard, you're a very difficult person to categorize within the present French intelligentsia. On the one hand, you appear very interested in innovations, in the day-to-day reality ignored by other thinkers; but on the other hand, you are one of the few thinkers who still fulfil the traditional role of the intellectual: the critical role, although at the same time your way of filling this role has nothing in common with the typical Sartrean commitment which consisted of endlessly differentiating between good and evil. In your opinion, what is the function of the philosopher today?*

I don't really think of myself as a philosopher. My particular critical impulse comes from a radical temperament which has more in common with poetry than philosophy. It is neither a question of some sort of dialectical critique of reality; rather, it would seem to be the search within my object for a sense of disappearance, the disappearance both of the object and of its subject. In a way, America is hell; I vomit it out, but I am also susceptible to its demonic seduction. In other words, I don't criticize, I'm throwing things up at the same time that I'm greedily devouring them. There does not seem to be much room here for the critical subject, does there? Dynamic integration? That's scarcely me! A return to philosophy, and the search for a new conceptual platform . . . ? That doesn't interest me either. Nor can I envisage any kind of compromise position. The only game that amuses me is that of following some new situation to its very limits. I hope that our own decomposition will eventually offer sufficient singularity to hold my attention. America, of course, is already quite well advanced in this respect.

JH/GS *At one point in your book,* America, *you posit both that Europe has disappeared in California, and that we should continuously ask ourselves how we can be European . . . . How do you come to terms with this?*

For me, California is a strange place where I find myself freed from all culture. Europe, or at least European culture, evaporates there. The primitive background for my book is the desert, but this desert is neither a place of refuge nor a drug; on the contrary, it's a kind of sidereal location. In such a place one lets oneself drift freely while still retaining – even at the most extreme limits – a sense of simulation. Out there, problems of nature and of culture cease to exist; one passes beyond reality, whereas here one is painfully aware of its presence. Everything there seems removed from the reality principle.

JH/GS *Isn't it the case, however, that there are certain sections of reality in America which still refer to something of Europe? Can't one detect obvious transplants in the American art world, for example?*

In New York, undoubtedly. But are these really transplants? Everything there seems so extravagant to me. I don't really feel that I'm within academia, the way I do here. There are museums, of course, but when Americans get to work on things they always treat them like some sort of fiction. There is culture too, obviously, but it is not innocent; on the contrary, it is trapped within a kind of cruelty. The last thing I want to suggest is that America is some sort of paradise. It is precisely its rawness which interests me and its primeval character, although one shouldn't confuse it with some sort of primitive society, even if my book claims as much the attempt to conceptualize it within a global cultural perspective. We should try to pass beyond the horizons of indifference, 'inculture', silence and the desert . . . .

JH/GS *Would art, in the traditional sense of the word, still have a function within the kind of universe to which you refer?*

Art, a function? For me, no. But has it ever had a function?

JH/GS *Well, it once had one, as art: whereas today . . .*

Yes, it once had one. Today, perhaps, it operates more or less exclusively in a state of flux, in various networks. Unfortunately, its function has become purely promotional. And yet this enigmatic process known as writing still goes on: I wrote this book. The word art bothers me a bit.

Let me specify that *America* should not be read as a realist text. Its subject matter being a fiction itself, I've exaggerated this quality, without actually entering into science fiction. It's no longer possible to write about Europe in this way. I've no wish to conceal the element of defiance and artificiality within my sort of fictionizing.

JH/GS *Certain key terms recur insistently in your books: 'catastrophe', 'the end of history', 'decadence'. Are you a nihilist?*

Yes, I'm aware of it. People tell me: you're a pessimist, with you, it's the end of everything. Let me repeat that I'm not interested in realism. I am not speaking of the real extermination of things, of the physical, biological disappearance of living beings. My books are scenarios. I *play out* the end of things, I offer a complete parody of it. Even the signs of catastrophe contain irony. Think of that recent incident with the space capsule. It was extraordinary: a sort of symbolic victory that only the Americans could afford! That fantastic burial in the sky! They've revived our appetite for space. Offering themselves the luxury of such disasters. What a way to go! Simple endings are without interest; they're flat and linear. The really exciting thing is to discover orbital space where these other forces play. We need to invent new rules. I'm always thinking of the next horizon to be crossed . . . .

To look ahead in this way requires a somewhat metaphysical and a somewhat transcendental curiosity. People have spoken so often about the end of things that I'd like to be able to see what goes on the other side of the end, in a sort of hyperspace and transfinity. And even if things are not really at their end, well! Let's act as if they were. It's a game, a provocation. Not in order to put a full stop to everything but, on the contrary, to make everything begin again. So you see, I'm far from being a pessimist.

JH/GS *There's also another word which, unlike the terms just mentioned, occurs very infrequently in your earlier essays but which appears a great deal in America: the word 'modernity'. Considered with regard to its application in this book, what exactly do you understand by this term?*

It's a fluctuating, ambiguous term. I don't attribute any particular meaning to it. Nor do I situate its meaning with reference to any so-called postmodernity. If there is such a thing as European modernity, then it may be defined more accurately in legal terms. It is a concept which comes down to us from the French Revolution, and which has a political, ideological meaning. The transplantation of the term to America seems to me to be mutational rather than dialectical. Here in Europe, we contrast modernity and tradition; we can envisage the dialectic between conservation and revolution. Over there, the term bursts out in the middle of nowhere; it represents a zero point from which a kind of mobile space is expanding. Having said that, it's also the case that the word modernity rings a little false. Is there an alternative? Be this as it may, in order to evoke this transpolitical, transhistorical reality, I ended up using this overworked term once again. Perhaps the word hyper-modernity, expressing an infinite potentiality, would have been more accurate. It would give a better idea of that state of escalation in which things exist over there.

JH/GS *In your book, you insist upon a point that seems particularly import-ant: the puritanical religious foundation of the American people. It's curious, because what we see there is a religion, Protestantism, which has always had difficulties with modes of display (one thinks of its responses to the*

Counter-Reformation, to the baroque, to religious ceremony), and yet you suggest that American society is the society that pushes the sense of simulation to its most extreme limits ...

This is not so much a case of ritual or of ceremony. American society is not a society of appearances; it has no counterpart to the games of seduction with which we're familiar over here. The simulacrum is another game: its signs don't refer to any sense, they flow continuously without reference to any sense. Aesthetic effects become rarified in this kind of universe. I must admit that I still find the puritan centre of such a world rather difficult to explain. What kind of metabolism can there be between the omnipresent puritan energy and the fantastic immorality of this society? It seems as if the puritan impulse swept away much of the symbolic ritual, the baroque apotheosis, of Catholicism. What one confronts, then, is the pure play of forces, where signs rearrange themselves according to a different logic which we find difficult to understand.

JH/GS *You also suggest that, in the United States, cinema becomes true ...*

That's a European perception, but Americans also consider it a fact of life. They experience reality like a tracking shot; that's why they succeed so well with certain media, particularly television. By contrast, we have never left the perspectival, scenical theatrical tradition. We find it difficult to de-subjectivize ourselves, to de-concentrate ourselves completely. They do this very well. Cinema exists as a screen, not a stage; it calls for a different kind of acting. You're surrounded by a perpetual montage of sound and vision.

JH/GS *What are your most vivid impressions of California?*

First of all, it is the sense of having rediscovered a realm of fantasy and of disruptive energy which I find it difficult to come to terms with here, where I find myself up to my neck in culture. The seemingly flat, extensive, immanent world of California delighted me, despite its lack of seduction, in the theatrical sense of the word. It's not a question of letting go and completely vanishing in this kind of universe; but simply to drift in a world without anchor and without destination. Here in Europe, we can constantly locate ourselves between our past and our destiny. California is more like the masses, which cannot speak, have no meaning, neither rhyme nor reason, but radiate an intense, inverse, fictional energy.

JH/GS *You remark that America does not suffer from any sort of identity crisis. But these days one has the impression that in the States a certain discourse continually emphasizes the American identity ...*

There is, in America, as everywhere, an explicit and another mode of discourse. You certainly find this frantic search for identity, but its 'reality', if I may

134

use the term within quotation marks, is rather promiscuity, re-mixing and all modes of interchange, that is to say, the great game of de-identification. Naturally there is a certain resistance to this, but I find that discourse of identity secondary and derivative, and a kind of neurotic reaction, when compared to the basic situation. Is there really a sense of American nationality? All the signs are there, but in my opinion they derive from the publicity effect.

America is a trade mark, and they insist upon its superlative quality. What one witnesses here is the pathos of national publicity: the stars and stripes, we are the best, etc. This sense of national identity is no longer a matter of heredity or territory .... Anyway, it seems better that the whole space should become a publicity board, or even a movie screen. American chauvinism and nationalism, yes indeed, but it lacks the territorial pathos of its European counterparts. Even racial questions, those unresolved questions which perhaps will never be resolved, have been transubstantiated into ethnic interface.

It's something living, it's not sclerotic like racism and anti-racism here. The chessboard is constantly animated, and everyone can play their game. This *savage* – rather than primary – level of reality interests me considerably. All of the themes that I first examined in my previous books suddenly appeared, in America, stretching before me in concrete form. In a way, then, I finally left theory behind me and at the same time rediscovered all the questions and the enigmas that I had first posited conceptually. Everything there seemed significant to me, but at the same time everything also testified to the disappearance of all meaning.

One might perhaps conclude that America as a whole is a matter of abjection, but such criticisms are inconsequential: at every instant this object is transfigured. It is the miracle of realized utopia.

© 1986 *Art Press* and J. Baudrillard. Interview with J. Henric and G. Scarpetta, in *Art Press*, May 1986. © 1988 Nicholas Zurbrugg this English translation in *Eyeline*, 5, June 1988.

12

THE EVIL DEMON OF IMAGES

Interview with Ted Colless, David Kelly and Alan Cholodenko

AC *In your Kuttna lecture, 'The Evil Demon of Images', you invoke the notion of the immorality of images, at one point declaring that 'the image has taken over and imposed its own immanent, ephemeral logic; an immoral logic without depth, beyond good and evil, beyond truth and falsity . . . '. My question is this: if this logic lies beyond good and evil, why is it not an amoral rather than an immoral logic?*

From the very moment that one goes beyond good and evil one can also play a sort of game with this 'amorality' itself – somewhat perversely perhaps. So there is a twofold development here: there is at the same time both a transmutation of values (a denial of good and evil, *à la* Nietzsche, for example) and the game with the resulting amorality, a game which as it proceeds becomes more and more romantic and more pathetic. With this game one enters the domain of 'hypermorality', if you like. You play the game *with* amorality: you do not discard morality – rather you retain it, but purely as one of the rules, as one of the conventions which are completely perverse but nevertheless necessary if the game is to proceed at all. In fact, in this sort of game the whole question of what one does with morality remains completely open.

I can perhaps try to explain this more clearly in the following way: once you go beyond the question of morality, of good and evil, you have indeed entered the realm of amorality but you have not for all that exhausted the question. The game can continue, to involve amorality itself. And this is why I prefer the word 'immorality'. There is a play on words in the text – morality, amorality, immorality – which I think is absolutely essential here. The point is that amorality as a concept is not very interesting or challenging. The concept of immorality, on the contrary, is far more dramatic.

Take Nietzsche's treatment of God, for instance. What Nietzsche says is that God is *dead*. This is a far more interesting situation than if Nietzsche were simply to say 'there is no God' or 'God has never existed', etc. – that would be mere atheism – whereas to say that God is dead as Nietzsche does is to say something far more dramatic, and really something else altogether: it is an attempt to go *beyond* God. Similarly, the word 'immorality' as used in the text is an attempt to go beyond not just morality but also amorality. It is certainly an attempt to state the disappearance of morality, but also to situate the ensuing game at a level different from mere amorality itself.

AC *So Nietzsche is not a mere atheist.*

Yes, Nietzsche is not in the least an ordinary 'atheist'. He is not committed to the denial of the existence of God as an ordinary atheist would be. He is actually denying not that God exists but that God is alive. He is saying that God is *dead*, and that is a fundamental concept.

The concept is similar to my concept of 'challenge' in *De la Séduction*. This is the idea that the disappearance of something is never objective, never final – it always involves a sort of challenge, a questioning, and consequently an act of seduction. In almost everything that I have written, there is this challenge to morality, to reality, etc. So Nietzsche, for example, challenges the existence of God by issuing a challenge *to* God. It is just as uninteresting to say 'God does not exist' as to say 'God exists'. The problematic for Nietzsche is completely different. He is challenging the 'liveliness', the being, of God. In other words, he is *seducing* God. Similarly, in my work, what I try to do is to issue a challenge to meaning and to reality, to seduce them and to play with them ...

TC/DK *To play the devil's advocate, there does seem to be, in this text, both an ethical vocabulary, implying a position to be adopted, and a more or less urgent directive to come to grips with the indistinguishability between the real and the order of simulation. To an audience this might imply one of two modes of address.*

On the one hand a soliloquy, maybe dispassionate, that nonetheless plays a part in the dramaturgy of the final act – the eclipse of history, the vanishing of the real. In this case, can we understand this text to be the words of a provocateur *– intervening to precipitate, or arrest, this devolution; or rather those of an analyst – commenting upon and clarifying this action? In other words, does this text have a role to play?*

On the other hand, could this be an ironic aside, neither participating in the action nor critically detached from it, a knowing remark that clues us in but is, for all that, inconsequential?

Well, congratulations on an excellent question. It deals with an important problem: the position of a text (and especially of a text such as this one), as well as the position being adopted in the text in relation to its object – or at least the object as described by the text itself. In the sense that the text attempts to move towards the end of something – towards a sort of catastrophe, a *something lost* – there is indeed an element of provocation, since the text must be situated within its own logic, within its own processes. There is provocation in that one wishes to accelerate this logic. One goes therefore in the same direction as the text – but one accelerates, one goes much faster towards the end of the text. And one plays on the logic itself to be able (at least) to reach a point beyond it, so as to make the system reveal itself more clearly. It is more or less a strategic position that one adopts: one of precipitation, of acceleration, as demanded by the text itself.

Nevertheless, I do not for all that abandon in any way the position of the analyst. There is here perhaps an ambiguity, an ambivalence, which is quite fundamental. On the one hand we have a position which is strategically necessary, and on the other hand we retain the position of the analyst. This ambiguity probably remains throughout the text at every point. One is compelled to *produce* meaning in the text, and one produces this meaning *as if* it arises from the system (even if in fact the system lacks meaning) in order precisely to play that meaning against the system itself as one reaches the end. So there is a position here – a third position – which I would describe as that of *objective irony*.

Objective irony is not objective irony: it is not an irony based on solipsism or on any separation of discourse from the subject. Objective irony is precisely the irony whereby one is able to turn the system, to make it work against itself, to play against itself. This creates an ironic effect within the text, since its position is bound to be ambiguous. In other words, one always in a sense remains the subject of a discourse, any discourse, so one always in a sense assumes the position of an analyst. But then, one must also exert the same strategy to the *object* of discourse: in the same way that one works with the subject, one must also work towards the position of pure object, towards the 'vanishing point' of discourse itself.

Consequently, I do not think that one has to choose one way or another. What the text involves, simultaneously, is both provocation and analysis. There is a simultaneous requirement to give meaning to the text (analysis) and also to give an end to that meaning (provocation). And what really differentiates this procedure from other processes of negation – for example, the negative dialectic of Adorno – is precisely what I call objective irony. That is, there is a movement within the text, from subjective irony as used by Adorno and others (based on the irony of the subject) to objective irony – the irony of the object itself. What I try to do, if you like, is to try to get out of the subjectivity/objectivity dialectic, in order to reach a point where I can make of the system an object, a pure object, one with no meaning whatsoever. I try, in other words, to constitute the subject of discourse in turn as an object; I try to create a sort of distance (which is not a 'critical' but an 'ironic' distance) between the subject and the text – and when this occurs, then of course the position of the analyst disappears.

And yet, while one remains within a theoretical type of discourse, within a discourse such as this one, one cannot exclude oneself from any of these positions. I do not have to choose – and I would hesitate to choose – between

any of them. All three positions have their place in the game as it proceeds
– and this is in itself, of course, the supreme irony of the text.

TC/DK *You have titled this paper 'The Evil Demon of Images'. In the*
Méditations *Descartes refers to an evil demon that can conjure an inexistent
world that includes the inexistent figure of Descartes himself. Descartes was
able to exile that demon through corrosive doubt, confirming the world and
its objects; here you have conjured that evil demon's return, exiling instead
both doubt and the real. How would you describe the relation between this
text and the Cartesian project it seems to invoke?*

In the Cartesian project there is at least the inauguration of a rational principle.
It is from this rational principle that the whole question of doubt arises. This
doubt comes from the subject – as subject of knowledge, as subject of discourse.
Whether Descartes in fact succeeds in making the subject constitute itself,
in its reality, in relation to a diabolical world which is full of superstitions
and hallucinations and so on is a controversial matter. But the fact remains
that Cartesian doubt is based on the promise of a world which can be confirmed
only in terms of its own reality: there is doubt on the one hand and there
is reality on the other hand; and there is the conflict between the two, which
Descartes tries to resolve.

For me the question is totally different. When I evoke the principle of evil,
of an evil demon, etc., my aim is more closely related to a certain kind of
Manichaeism. It is therefore anterior to Descartes, and fundamentally it is
*ir*rational. There are in fact two principles at stake: on the one hand there
is the (Descartes') rational principle or principle of rationality – the fundamental
attempt, through doubt or anything else, to rationalize the world – and on
the other hand there is the inverse principle, which was, for example, adopted
by the 'heretics' all the way throughout the history of Christianity. This is
the principle of evil itself. What the heretics posited was that the very creation
of the world, hence the reality of the world, was the result of the existence
of the evil demon. The function of God, then, was really to try to repudiate
this evil phantom – that was the real reason why God had to exist at all. So
in this situation it is no longer a question of doubt or non-doubt, of whether
one should exercise this doubt or whether this doubt could lead us to confirm
or deny the existence of the world. Rather, it is once again the principle of
seduction that needs to be invoked in this situation: according to Manichaeism,
the reality of the world is a total illusion; it is something which has been tainted
from the very beginning; it is something which has been seduced by a sort
of *ir*real principle since time immemorial. In this case what one has to invoke
is precisely this absolute power of illusion – and this is indeed exactly what
the heretics did. They based their theologies on the very *negation* of the real.
Their principal and primary convention was that of the non-reality, hence
of the non-rationality, of the world. They believed that the world, its

reality, is made up only of *signs* – and that it was governed solely through the power of the *mind*.

This idea of the world as being constituted only by signs is, if you like, some sort of magic thinking – and indeed it was condemned as such. For it does entail that the 'real' – and any sort of 'reality' – that one sees in the world is quite simply an absolute utopia. The rationality that one has to invoke in order to make the world 'real' is really just a product of the power of *thought* itself, which is itself totally anti-rational and anti-materialist. This is completely opposed to Descartes (whose rationalism leads eventually but directly to materialism). For me to invoke the question of doubt or of non-doubt and either to assert or to question the reality of the world would be completely futile. The principle fundamentally and from the very beginning is that there is *no* objectivity to the world.

But nevertheless one has to recognize the reality of the illusion; and one must play upon this illusion itself and the power that it exerts. This is where the Manichaean element in my work comes in. It is a question which, really, is purely strategic.

We can compare this position easily with that of Freud if you like – with his juxtaposition of the principles of Eros and Thanatos. These two principles are at first absolutely opposed to each other. But there is also the crucial moment in Freud's work when, having desperately attempted to unify and integrate the two, he finally abandons the project and invokes instead the principle of their total irreconcilability. This is something that works very much to the advantage of the principle of Thanatos itself, since of course Thanatos is itself the principle of irreconcilability.

This is the key to the whole position: the idea is that of a most fundamental and radical antagonism, of no possibility existing at all of reconciling the 'illusion' of the world with the 'reality' of the world. And I have to say this once again: here the 'illusion' is not simply irreality or non-reality; rather, it is in the literal sense of the word (*il-ludere* in Latin) a *play* upon 'reality' or *mise en jeu* of the real. It is, to say it one more time, the issuing of a challenge to the 'real' – the attempt to put the real, quite simply, on the spot.

There is here a fundamental distinction – which it seems to me exists in the whole history of thought in general. There is the principle of the possibility of reconciliation on the one hand, and there is the recognition of total irreconcilability on the other hand. For me the reality of the world has been *seduced*, and this is really what is so fundamentally Manichaean in my work. Like the Manichaeans I do not believe in the possibility of 'real-izing' the world through any rational or materialist principle – hence the great difference between my work and the process of invoking radical doubt as in Descartes.

AC *Did semiology arrive to save meaning precisely at a point when it was already lost? Is semiology a nostalgic, a romantic project?*

I do not really know about the nostalgia of semiology: one must believe in the first place that meaning did once exist, and so you could then attempt to try to find it again, at least as a lost object . . . . Obviously I do not believe this, so the nostalgia might have been there in semiology but it would have been in my view totally unfounded. One thing is certain: semiology did attempt – and does still – to save meaning and to *produce* meaning as a sort of repudiation or conjuration of non-sense, and in that light semiology as a discipline does appear to be *evangelical*. And this is so in spite of the fact that today in semiology there is to a certain extent an awareness of production, of its own production of signs.

The problem arises in the way that semiology operates: in so far as it immediately establishes a distinctive opposition between signifier and signified and between sign and referent, etc., from the very first point of departure what semiology tries to do is to *domesticate* the sign. By comparison, in the world which I evoke, the one where illusion or magic thought plays a key role, the signs evolve, they concatenate and *produce themselves*, always one upon the other – so that there is absolutely no basic reference which can sustain them. Thus they do not refer to any sort of 'reality' or 'referent' or 'signified' whatsoever. So in this situation what we have is the sign alone; and it is the power which is proper to the sign itself, it is the pure strategy of the sign itself that governs the appearance of things. This position is vastly different from semiology, as for instance in Lacan and in the *Tel Quel* school, where a primary role is given to the 'signifier'. In other words, for me the sign is, if you like, without recourse. There is no basic reserve, no 'gold standard' to the sign – no basic reserve of reference from which the sign can be recovered or accommodated. On the contrary, *reality is the effect of the sign*. The system of reference is only the result of the power of the sign itself.

This is what Artaud meant when he talked about the 'savage power' of the sign, when he alluded to this 'cruel' capacity that the sign has to 'erupt', and so on. The framework here for an understanding of the effect of the sign is hardly a representational one. Rather, the framework is the fundamental antagonism between the sign and reality: here the sign is precisely that which operates against reality, not for it. From this point of view, there is really no semiology at all, properly speaking. No real *logos* (as is implied in the couple 'signified/signifier', etc.) is available. Instead, we have a sort of single brutal sign which exists in its purest state and which goes through the universe, simply reproducing itself, constantly and forever. In the representational system, one cannot do this. One cannot go from one sign to another directly; one must mediate from one sign to another through meaning, through the duality 'signified/signifier', and so on. This is why I invoke the concept of destiny, the concept of the *destiny* of the sign – whereas what semiology invokes is a concept of the *history* of the sign, the history of the sign as a domesticated product of meaning. This domestication process, of course, is also to be found in other disciplines – in psychology, for example – and to me it seems to be only a desperate attempt to seek salvation . . .

Having said all this, it is true that semiology has become much more sophisticated in the last few years. So today we have a semiology of poetry, for example, or of the speech act, of *langue* and *parole*. A lot of attempts are being made to go beyond the representational mode, which was obviously deficient. But in my opinion semiology will never be able – to adopt the coinage of Nietzsche – to go beyond its shadow. It will never be actually able to find the sign in its purest state – in the way in which I, for example, try to do in *De la Séduction* and in the world of illusion.

TC/DK *In an earlier essay ('Design and Environment or How Political Economy Escalates into Cyberblitz') you specified a historical moment when the object resigned its use value status by entering into a pure order of the sign function. In this essay your reference point is rather the media image. Has the media image supplanted the order of events and of objects in the same manner as the Bauhaus project of total design supplanted the realm of nature? And does the delirious proliferation of the media image have a similarly specific historical moment?*

A propos this, can you explain the qualitative difference between the media image and those other forms (theatre, architecture, painting, language) that were incapable of overwhelming the real to such effect?

Yes, in a sense there is a historical shift. There is a historical evolution, which begins and also culminates with the phase where signs, as I said, lead from one another according to the logic of illusion. So this was indeed a first stage – not necessarily a chronological 'first' stage but certainly a logical one. And then the phase of rationality followed, with the production of the reality-effect by the sign. It seems to me that towards the end of this stage the sign found itself being separated and being sent back towards its own transcendence and immanence. What followed therefore was the game of the dialectic of the sign, the game whereby reality would be posited against the immanence or transcendence of the sign. Consequently, there is indeed a sort of historical movement.

The movement reaches its apotheosis in the arrival of the media. Now, once again, the sign is all alone. But this is not to say that we are back at the first stage once more. The situation now is different. Now the sign seems to me to posit what I have called the 'principle of hyper-reality'. That is, what we have now is the disappearance of the referent – and it is in relation to this disappearance of the referent that there is a sort of omnipresence to the sign. The problematic of the disappearance of the referent was not an issue according to the first logic of illusion; rather, there was simply no referent. So in a sense we are going back towards an anterior state – but nevertheless with a difference.

Is this evolution a historical one? I do not think it is. It is, rather, a metaphysical one: the universe of the media which we are currently immersed in is not the magical universe or the cruel universe which we had at an anterior stage, where the sign was operational purely on the basis of its own functioning as sign. With the advent of the media, it seems to me that we have lost that prior state of total illusion, of the sign as magic. We are, in other words, in that state of 'hyper-reality' as I have called it. Now we are dealing with a sign that posits the principle of non-reality, the principle of the absoute absence of reality. We went beyond the reality principle a long time ago, and now the game which is being played is no longer being played in the world of pure illusion. It is as if we are now in a shameful and sinful state, a post-illusion state.

We can try to put this another way, if you like: as we all know, philosophy is based on the negation of the real. There is at the heart of philosophy a primordial act regarding the negation of reality; and without that negation there is no philosophy. Now, it seems to me that throughout a certain period this negation was the privilege of philosophers. But today this is no longer the case. Today the negation of the real has penetrated inside things themselves, so much so that it is no longer the privilege of just philosophers but an axiom that belongs to all. What has happened is that the negation of reality has now been incorporated into 'reality' itself. In short, what we have now is a principle of non-reality based on 'reality' – a principle of 'hyper-reality' as I call it. The mutation is interesting, since it implies nothing other than the end of philosophy. The philosophical principle of the negation of reality has now pervaded everyday 'reality' itself.

This is why I say that today we have a form of irony which is objective. Irony can no longer today be simply the subjective irony of the philosopher. It can no longer be exercised as if from outside of things. Instead, it is the objective irony which arises from within things themselves – it is an irony which belongs to the system, and it arises from the system itself because the system is constantly functioning against itself.

Now to the second part of the question – the Bauhaus question. The Bauhaus project of total design is certainly one of the important episodes in the evolution of simulation, which marks the passage of the sign from the dialectic of the real to the order of the sign itself. Nevertheless, the Bauhaus project does not go to the stage of seduction of the real, and there are radical differences between simulation and seduction. The Bauhaus remains at the stage of simulation. To say it once more: seduction seems to me to invoke an enchanted universe, whereas simulation invokes a universe which is totally disenchanted and, as I said, almost shameful.

And, finally, the last part of the question: in my view there is no substantial qualitative difference between electronic media such as TV on the one hand and other forms such as language, painting or architecture on the other hand. In my opinion there is no real difference between them; they all operate at the same level, that of simulation. Of course, one would have to discuss this at some length, and in any case I am not an expert in any of these areas.

However, it does seem to me, for example, that simulation has invaded theatre just as much as it has invaded painting, and that as a result neither of them has the power to exert total illusion any longer. Both the theatre and painting have entered the order of simulation and in fact they now typify simulation.

So all the forms can in fact be substituted one for another. They have all been contaminated by simulation, and so now they function in terms of 'communication' and 'information', which are nothing other than the by-products of simulation. Neither architecture nor painting, for instance, has today any effects which are proper to themselves; instead, today they function merely as indications of the transformation of the world.

We must remember this: the aim of art was once precisely to posit the power of illusion against reality. There was a time when art was trying to make reality play a game which was different to the game that art itself was playing. In other words, there was a time indeed when art was always trying to force reality to play the game along different rules, when it was always trying to *seduce* the reality of things. But today this is no longer the great game that art is playing. All the art forms are now playing the game at the level of the simulation of reality – and whether the particular art form be painting or architecture makes no difference whatsoever.

That is, there is no longer any great 'challenge' being posited by these art forms – a challenge to go beyond the reality principle. For example, the very project of the Bauhaus (which incorporated, of course, all of the various art forms) was precisely and by definition the attempt to design the world – and this attempt does not make any sense unless the world is being considered in terms of the reality of its things. This is very different from the attempt to confront the world with the non-reality of its things, and really it is simply a sort of exercise of simulation. But all this is open to discussion and I would like one day to be able to analyse the issues in greater detail . . . .

The interviewers are grateful to Philippe Tanguy for his immediate rendering of their questions into French and of Professor Baudrillard's answers into English.

13

THE WORK OF ART IN THE ELECTRONIC AGE

Interview with *La Sept*

We are in the age of electronic communications; do you think that this communi-cation has fundamentally changed the way in which we see and understand the world or is it merely an accelerated form of technical reproduction?

I think we have a kind of transformation, yes, perhaps not a revolution in the subversive sense of the term, but a transformation of the relations of ex-change. It is often said that we are within communication and we are perhaps no longer exactly within exchange. At this time, what has changed is that the means of communication, the medium, is becoming a determinant element in exchange and quite often dominates its function, even technologically – as McLuhan has it – dominates the content, the message, the subject communicated, the very substance of communication. So there is an inversion of terms of some sort, where what was a means of communication gains a kind of finality, and possibly also a counter-finality, and then the strategies which revolve around the medium, the communication media, become more essential than the strategies which concern the contents.

The reality of images counts for more ...

Yes, it seems that from this point a sort of proliferation occurs, a saturation of the field of the medium. That is, as long as one has things to say and there is something to be exchanged between speakers, there is meaning, so it gets said and the process is limited. The medium gets the upper hand, basically, when images – or discourses – begin to proliferate, apart even from the meaning which they bear. There is a sort of – I don't want to say cancer; that would be borrowing a bit too much from modern pathology – but something similar. There is a kind of autonomy now of the systems of images and systems of discourse which has got the upper hand over meaning.

So then, where is reality still situated?

That's the entire problem. Is there still reality? I would rather say that we are in hyper-reality. Effectively, everything can be an object of communication.

Communication is completely generalized; it is no longer only discourse, but everything, which is an object of communication: architecture, art, have as their first end, it seems, to communicate, before even that of bearing a meaning. So where is the reality of what must be said, of what one wants to say? One almost has the impression that communication is a collective enterprise: the medium must function. There is a kind of obligation, a collective categorical imperative to make the media function at all costs. It's of little consequence whether the contents are completely real or unreal, or hyper-real; the important thing is that the medium continues to roll. So communication is drawn into this cycle of panic. It seems to become immediately an unlimited, proliferating system. There is a kind of imperialism of communication.

When you say hyper-reality, you might specify, in relation to reality, the reality of my daily life . . .

Yes, we can say for example that for events, politics, history, from the moment where they only exist as broadcasts by the media and proliferate, nearly globally, their own reality disappears. In the extreme case the event could just as well not have taken place – there are examples. It has taken place on the level of the screen. They are screen events and no longer authentic events – I am not sure if one can speak of authenticity, but nevertheless an ordinary reality which has a historical actuality that disappears behind the mediating hyper-reality of things. And here then, one can question indefinitely the degree, the rate of reality which continues to be shown. It's something else which is taking place: circuits are functioning. They can nourish themselves with anything, they can devour anything and, as Benjamin said of the work of art, you can never really go back to the source, you can never interrogate an event, a character, a discourse about its degree of original reality. That's what I call hyper-reality. Fundamentally, it's a domain where you can no longer interrogate the reality or unreality, the truth or falsity of something. We walk around in a sphere, a megasphere where things no longer have a reality principle. Rather a communication principle, a mediatizing principle.

Therefore we are all becoming images?

Yes, in one way or another . . . not only are there screens and terminals in technical terms, but we ourselves, the listeners, the TV spectators, become the terminals of all this communications network. We ourselves are screens. Lastly, the interlocutors are no longer exactly human beings. That sounds pejorative, but it's like that. The play has settled to one from screen to screen. It is almost dialogues between terminals or between different media.In a way it is the medium conversing with itself, this intense circulation, this type of auto-referentiality of media which includes us in its network. But it's somewhat of an integrated man–machine circuit. And at the present the difference between man and machine is very difficult to determine.

And that goes for artists, works of art?

Absolutely. I believe a work of art no longer has any privilege as a singular object of breaking through this type of circuit, of interrupting the circuit in some sense – because that is what it would amount to, a singular, unique appearance of an object unlike any other. However, for the communication system and that of the media there is no privileged object. All are substitutable and the work of art has finished up in there, it has been plugged into the same circuit. That does not mean that it may not have an authentic origin, but this will become less and less retrievable through the consumption of media, perhaps on screens but equally the large exhibitions where thousands attend and the crowd itself constitutes a kind of medium; the perception which one has of greatness is even constituted today by a crowd of spectators who are no longer amateurs, lovers of culture, in the traditional sense of the term. We are obliged to take this massive consumption into account. It is not merely the irruption of television or reproducability, reprography, or things of that ilk. Rather, the irruption of the mass even into aesthetic consumption changes, in my opinion, the status of the art work. Can we still talk of a 'work'? It's becoming something else. It is not exactly a commodity but it passes into the condition of a sign which must be able to circulate like any other. Therefore its own time and place, its uniqueness, is effectively removed.

Thus change of medium – the work becomes image – change of consumption ...

Yes, the change would perhaps be that while the work of art creates its own space, it invents itself, it takes its inspiration from itself, it has a quite unique reality, it becomes itself an object on the screen, it is transmitted by the screen. The change is perhaps this. One passes from what was a stage, the stage of the work, the stage of the theatre, the stage of representation, even the stage of politics – one can generalize this phenomenon – to the screen. But the screen has quite another dimension: it is superficial, it only communicates images, not a particular time and place. In the end it makes everything circulate in one space, without depth, where all the objects must be able to follow one after the other without slowing down or stopping the circuit. But the work of art is made for stopping, in the end it is made to interrupt something, to arrest the gaze, to arrest contemplation. If there is an aesthetic pleasure or aesthetic relationship there it must arise from this species of sublime moment which is a moment of immobility, of contemplation, which corresponds also to the moment of creation in the artist. But then for the media none of this works. It is not that which counts. You have to move on in any case. It is a bit like what was being said about the Mona Lisa in Japan, with five seconds to look at it.

But if the work of art has fallen, has been banalized like the other products of communication, how is it that we consume so many of them? The state, individuals, businesses ...

You have answered yourself. Because it's been banalized, so many are consumed, I would say. Because it is reproduced in an indefinite number of examples, it becomes a bit like holograms in the end; it has also cloned itself, in a way. And that is really the principle of consumption; it is as if everything becomes sign and image – in fact, it is more and more necessary for this to happen. There is no limit to consumption. There is a kind of limit to creation, but not to consumption. You enter into an indefinite series, the seriality of things, and then it is imperative for it not to stop. It is rather like the principle of television: the screen must always be filled, the void is not permitted, and as we are somewhat screens ourselves now, transformed into reflecting screens, there must always be images there, so they are filled in by something or other. And then, perhaps, there is the fact that banalization quite simply involves commercialization, entrance into the market, and that strategies of competition, of course, also enter into it, but there is more to it than simple market strategies, a profusion of images is needed. The screen, the image, the sign, the modern message, the media require profusion, proliferation; there must be plenty for everyone. This is not the case for the work of art, of course, which creates a personal, privileged relationship ....

There you seem to be returning to a kind of nostalgia for the aura ...

Not exactly. What I have said sounds like that and it is difficult to say it in another way because the discourse brings in an element of nostalgia. But you could conceive of ... well, many things; of course something has been lost, but Benjamin said this well. In my opinion, Baudelaire before him had a more modern vision of things – the idea of the absolute commodity. If we enter into the era of the commodity, or that of the media, one could say this of us. For him, the modern artist should not try to revalorize, resacralize traditional art or aesthetics, but go further into the commodity. You had to go some way towards the absolute object, the absolute commodity, and he had a lovely formula: the modern artist owes it to himself to give the commodity a heroic status while the bourgeoisie only gives it, in advertising and all that, sentimental status. So when I say that, yes, of course nostalgia is there, the discourse is necessarily ambivalent. There is a background of nostalgia, and it is not possible to say it in another way since we are in discourse and thus still in something not yet entirely mediated, and then I think that it is possible nevertheless to have a vision there, not a more cynical vision, no there is perhaps a new aesthetic as a result of mediation, of disappearance, really. To go further in this direction and to really play the commodity, but at the power of two or the power of ten. To play the media, but in a sense with an almost ironic strategy.

It makes me think of Andy Warhol ...

Yes, Andy Warhol, for instance. It's not a solution but it is the other road and the spirit, that's not nostalgic, but rather an ultra-radical practice of mediation. It has its grandiose, but also its sublime, which is nevertheless of the cool sort; it's a cool strategy, while one may suppose that the strategy of the traditional art work was more warm, of another order, really.

And so, in your opinion, what remains of the order of traditional aesthetic or nostalgic creation? There cannot be an avant-garde – more disenchantment is still needed.

There are perhaps two paths. There is perhaps a path which continues the history of art, if I can call it that, where artists like Bacon and all those continue to work as creative individuals. We can't abandon this path, it still exists, but in my view it is true to say that it's no longer exactly contemporary. It is anachronistic in some ways, but wonderful all the same. In my opinion our modern – or postmodern, I don't know – condition is really that of mediation and it is there that strategies are worked out or, indeed, another destiny, where one can talk of the disappearance of art. Art is perhaps in the process of playing out its own disappearance – in my opinion this is what it has been doing for the last century. The problem posed today is perhaps that we have reached the end of this process and that we are entering a period where art no longer does anything else than stimulate its own disappearance because it has already disappeared in reality, because the media have already carried it off, because the system has. So in my opinion it's difficult to say the game is up. Not exactly, but it is also difficult to think that there still might be a real history for art.

Therefore, instead of resistance do we accept the deed of mediation, banalization and go as far as possible?

Yes, that would seem a less banal strategy, let's say, than that of nostalgia.

So what about you in all this, your own identity?

Well, yes, obviously to say that is still to speak as the subject of a discourse. But I don't think that need be a contradiction, but it is a paradox, surely. Because if the media have done away with it and if the work of art itself is really threatened, so is critical discourse, analytical discourse, just as much. That is to say that my position, to the extent that I make an analysis like this, is also paradoxical, because it no longer normally has any reference itself. It is there on the screen, that's obvious: I am on the screen, you are too, so we are already in another stratosphere and we are really talking, perhaps, there of something which has been lost. But I don't see the possibility of passing to the other side. You have to accept the deed, in my opinion, and then there are ambivalent strategies. There are double strategies.

You mean more experts than mediators?

Yes, but there is perhaps a way of playing with the media, to accept the deed of this system, of this entire integrated circuit and set it in play and perhaps not disrupt it, yet make it reversible – it's possible – and perhaps still to obtain some critical results, or sublime ones. But you have to take into account that these are fragile strategies.

Difficult therefore to .... How are you ... are you an image?

We are in a false situation now, it's true; you have to work within the paradox, the paradox of communication, which is in effect that everywhere there is communication and no one any longer has anything to say to anyone, or almost, whilst the paradox of language or of the work of art would be that there is something to say but the medium is no longer there. The message is there but the medium no longer responds. Or else in the opposite sense the medium is there, but there is no longer any message. Finally, we will now be in this paradoxical situation perpetually.

Do you think that one can still think?

Because I think it, it must be true. But nothing will be able to prove it any more than one can elaborate a truth outside a system like this. One will have to work with the hyper-reality of this system and enter the sphere of the floating signifier, of floating meaning or non-meaning, with risky strategies, etc. This is what I believe must be done. One must abandon the objective radical position of the subject and of the message.

But economic power relations are determining, all the same?

I myself am in no position to speak about it. I don't think so but it's a bit stupid to say that. As for myself, they are not determining. They are themselves mediated, they themselves pass into another sphere. I no longer believe that there are objective power relations nor objective strategies of this kind. In a way, they themselves have lost their own reality principle. Before, we could have made an infrastructure of it, a determining causality and everything, but today, no, they are entering too into a hyper-real zone where it is all connected with the media, all connected with advertising, etc., and even power relationships, even objective strategies are obliged to do their own advertising, to make their own image before being decrypted or decoded, before taking action. So they no longer have the material force they might have had before, if they ever had any. But perhaps sides have already been taken. Myself, I privilege in analysis things other than the economic, but perhaps that is debatable.

© 1988 Illuminations (TV) Ltd. Interview: The Work of Art in the Electronic Age, *Block*, 14, Autumn 1988. Translated by Lucy Forsyth.

14

THE POLITICS OF SEDUCTION
Interview with Suzanne Moore and
Stephen Johnstone

SM/SJ *Your latest book is on America and you have commented that: 'All of the themes explored in my previous books suddenly appeared stretching before me in concrete form.' Questions about the loss of reality, the primacy of the image and the passivity of 'the masses' all recur and you say that there is no hope in American society. But what gives you hope?*

I've said in the past that hope is a rather unimportant value. We are in a period when hope is not a very lucid idea. I realize that utopias are very active in the US – the green movement, the feminist movement and so on. These are the so-called hope-bringing movements that aspire to be revolutionary, but in actual fact in the American hyper-reality they are part of the same publicity game. They may not be part of the official power but nevertheless they play a role in the mega-publicity operation that is America.

They are not innocent of this or uncontaminated by it and in this way they have an enormous superficiality about them. They keep changing. Movements disappear or emerge not because the ideas are good or bad but simply as a sign of vitality – the physical vitality of American reality which is in constant flux. I can't see that this sort of thing can really be described in terms of politics.

I don't believe in the ecological movement but I *do* it. One doesn't have to believe in it to do it and I would like to say that I do it! In America it's the doing that is important and it doesn't matter whether the ideas are good or bad. As an example of energy transformation and transmutation America is still extremely alive. Much more than Europe.

SM/SJ *In* America *you describe American culture as 'vulgar but easy', as a culture which its own intellectuals are unable to analyse. Doesn't this imply a nostalgia for European culture, particularly academic culture?*

Yes. The European position is very ambiguous. The European model sees American culture as a superficiality and it analyses it in a superficial way. But American culture or rather non-culture is in itself completely original. It's not just a lack of culture and doesn't need to be interpreted negatively. The word superficial should really be in inverted commas because I've

152

taken the banal, the normal way of looking at America and turned it around. This non-culture is in itself positive and shouldn't be viewed through the eyes of European nostalgia.

SM/SJ *If American intellectuals can't understand their own culture, do you agree with Umberto Eco who says that American professors should be pensioned off? Is it possible that high school kids have an intuitive understanding of their own society that the intellectual can never have?*

Yes. There is a possibility of understanding by intuition. But the American intellectual cannot understand his own culture because he is locked into an intellectual ghetto. His defensive style is to mimic European culture which is why there is such a great divide between the American intellectual and American culture. Of course, young people have a much livelier intuition and are not put in this false position.

When I wanted to investigate American hyper-reality for myself, my colleagues refused to participate, so I wouldn't say along with Eco that they should be pensioned off. I would actually send them into the desert.

SM/SJ *Ah yes, the desert! You say that: 'Deserts are sublime forms distanced from all society, all sentimentality, all sexuality.' And you also suggest: 'One should always bring something to sacrifice in the desert and offer it as a victim. A woman. If something has to disappear there, something equal in beauty to the desert, why not a woman?' What is the point of such a gratuitously provocative statement? Is the corollary to sacrifice a postmodern philosopher in the centre of the city?*

It would be a very good idea to publicly sacrifice a postmodern philosopher.

Naturally, there is a certain amount of provocation in the image of sacrificing a woman, but I don't necessarily regard the term 'sacrifice' negatively. I see it as a positive thing. There is a certain amount of reciprocal sacrifice in seduction, for instance. Something has to die but I don't see it as having to remove someone – perhaps desire or love must die. Sacrificing a woman in the desert is a logical operation because in the desert one loses one's identity. It's a sublime act and part of the drama of the desert. Making a woman the object of the sacrifice is perhaps the greatest compliment I could pay her.

SM/SJ *In New York recently there was a show called* Resistance (Anti-Baudrillard) *to which a number of prominent artists contributed. How did you feel being confronted with your own work as something to be struggled against, as something to be contested as melancholic, full of inertia, as offering no way forward?*

As I said before, there is always an element of provocation in what I write. It is a sort of challenge to the intellectual and the reader that starts a kind of game. Naturally, if you provoke then you must expect some counter-provocation and some negative reaction. The fact that it is so virulent is really quite interesting. It shows that in a way my negativity has passed on to them, subliminally perhaps, which is what I expected. I would say that there has been a *hyper-reaction* to my work and from that point of view I have succeeded.

SM/SJ *So what about the position of women in your work. Are they experts in seduction?*

I am not in agreement with hardline feminist ideology which says that woman as seducer is a degrading role. In my view the strategy of seduction is a happy, liberating power for women. It feeds into the simulation. Unfortunately, in feminism everything that happens to be female is defended – *l'écriture féminine*, poetry, any kind of artistic creation, and this makes it a kind of mirror of masculine simulation. This is a negative simulation, an unfortunate simulation. It seems to me that the feminine strategy of seduction is not an alienation of woman, as the feminists believe. One must rise above the battle of the sexes and get away from sexist alienation. Men and women shouldn't oppose each other. I believe one can regain feminine seductiveness as a positive virtue and that this is one way to rise above it. But of course I risk being misunderstood.

SM/SJ *Isn't that just a romantic view of woman as transcendent? A lot of feminists have already criticized the essentialism that you criticize.*

It's important to make a critique of woman as woman. Seduction is not just a sexual strategy and it's not one-sided. More a complicity. There are rules to the game. It's a very physical game and one of equality. Both sides are deeply involved and the stakes are high. It's almost an ideology played out to the detriment of democracy. Right now men are striving themselves to find an ideology which defines them and I think that femininity should go beyond its narrow confines, beyond the way that it sees itself at the moment.

SM/SJ *Is there such a thing, then, as love?*

There is an acting-out, but I don't really know. I don't have a great deal to say about love.

SM/SJ *Do you have children? Do they make you feel optimistic?*

I had two. Today they are grown-up. Perhaps I was a bad father because I didn't project my own personal hopes on to them, so they were carried along by their own impetus. They do their own thing.

SM/SJ *Do you gamble?*

Yes, I do in Las Vegas. Sometimes I am not a gambler.

SM/SJ *Is your work a gamble? If so, what are the stakes?*

I don't know whether you could call them cultural stakes. You must not confuse the stakes with the results. The problem is not to destroy the work – perhaps the work doesn't have a stake – it spins around itself until it's exhausted. The stake, I think, would be its potential for energy. It's almost like a game of poker. The stake is, in a way, a game beyond the bidding in order to see other people's hands. And the stake is for other people to show their hand.

SM/SJ *In* The Ecstasy of Socialism *you denounce 'the unbelievable naivety of ... socialist thinking'. Does this position simply reflect a total disenchantment with post-'68 politics? Haven't you just exchanged any engagement with the political for a fascination with the mindlessness of consumer culture?*

There is a certain problem because the generation of '68 brought everything into play. There was a spectacular negation of culture, a sacrifice of political values. Of course, after a sacrifice there is always a vacuum, a cultural vacuum. In America this vacuum has been replaced not by a culture but by *events* which have a reciprocity with the '68 political scene – a cultural fireworks.

The radicalism of '68 has passed into major events like the stock exchange crash, the advent of Aids – that is American radicalism. That is a radicalism in which the intellectual has no place, the intellectual in the traditional sense. Intellectual radicalism has passed into events so the intellectual has been neutralized.

The intellectual has no future.

© 1989 *Marxism Today*. Interview: The Politics of Seduction, *Marxism Today*, January 1989.

15

THE END OF THE END
Interview with John Johnston

JJ As you know, many New York artists regard you as the theoretician of their practice; that is, they cite your texts in order to justify what they do. It is even said that the art of Peter Halley, Jeff Koons, Sherrie Levine and others – the so-called 'neo-geo' artists – is an art of simulation. How do you respond to that?

I have no response. My texts can serve as a justification for anyone. To take them as a reference is already in itself a simulation, and not among the best. For if there is one characteristic of the universe of simulation, it is surely the loss of the referent and of reference, which establishes a linkage of meaning. Thus it is a total misunderstanding to take anything as a reference. There are two possibilities: either I function as a serious reference (which is always a pleasure) and there is a misunderstanding of simulation, or I myself function as an object of simulation (one treats Baudrillard as one treats Mondrian or Renoir, because there is nothing else to do; one gives *all the signs* of Baudrillard), and then I can only assume a certain distance, without moreover trying to preserve any purity or to claim that I am right and they are wrong. To move quickly, let's say that there is no art of simulation, no more than there is an art of seduction – it is simulation itself that *is* an art; it is seduction itself that *is* an art.

JJ Critics of contemporary art also frequently cite your work. For example, Suzi Gablik, in an article titled 'Dancing with Baudrillard' (Art in America, June 1988), refers to your work when discussing the paintings of Allan McCollum. His paintings, she says, are simulacra, and they illustrate the 'art of disappearance'. (Presumably because of their black and empty surfaces, and the fact that though there are many of them – a senseless proliferation, in fact, in various sizes and scales – they are always the 'same painting'.) But the problem is that they actually end up looking very beautiful and modern. They are bought and the system functions very well despite their critical effect. Gablik states: 'How do you convince an art dealer that McCollum's pictures are not "real", but simulations? You won't succeed, because collectors will buy them, dealers will show them and critics will write about them; even simulations cannot escape the system's ability to integrate everything. And so it is that art survives its own disappearance: somewhere the real scene has been lost, but everything continues just the same.'

How do you see this recuperation and loss of a 'real scene'? Is the 'art of disappearance' in the object or in the system where the scene functions?

Of course, simulation is *real*, has material consequences, and is valorized as such. Suzi Gablik's reflections are naive. What else at the limit can assume value but the artificial? Value itself is an artifice. We are simply witnessing the systematization and the exacerbation of this principle of the artifice of value. Thus a 'simulated' work of art is even more artificial; it has even more value on the market – not as work of art, but as simulacrum. And this is fascinating. One understands very well why art lovers and collectors are fascinated and will pay dearly for this fascination. But one must not take that for a criterion of *aesthetic* originality.

JJ *You have written about Andy Warhol as a great contemporary artist. In a few words, how do you insert him in the frame of your thought? Where does his importance for you reside?*

I've spoken about this at a conference at the Whitney Museum, and it's difficult to repeat it here. Let's say that Warhol is for me the most evident and modern illustration of Duchamp's slogan, which is very much the epitaph of all contemporary art: 'The Bride Stripped Bare by her Bachelors Even'. Warhol is art stripped bare by anti-art even. It's an aesthetic orgy, but a destructive orgy, drawing its irony from the object itself, from the banal extravaganza of the commodity. He will have made of art a serial and banal dimension, but he succeeded in extorting from this seriality and banality a genial element of shock, surprise and prodigality. He has made a paradoxical leap. The others, his successors, have only succeeded in making of banality a new sentimental aesthetic (like the bourgeoisie has made of advertising, according to Baudelaire). It is useless to be inspired by Warhol. After him, the objects speak for themselves, like Duchamp's bride, once she is stripped.

JJ *One often speaks of our time as a new, 'postmodern' era: there is postmodern art, postmodern theory, postmodern society and the postmodern condition. In the United States, Jean Baudrillard is often cited as a theoretician of the postmodern, even if you don't use the word. Is your theory of simulacra and simulation, of seduction and the ecstasy of communication, a perfect illustration of our postmodernity?*

I can do nothing against this 'postmodern' interpretation. It is only a collage *a posteriori*. In the notions of simulacrum, seduction and fatal strategy, there is something 'metaphysical' at stake (without wanting to be too serious), that

157

the 'postmodern' reduces to an effect of intellectual fashion, or to a syndrome of the failure of modernity. In this sense, the postmodern is itself post-modern: it is itself only a model of superficial simulation, and designates nothing else but itself. These days, that assures it a long posterity.

JJ *To be precise (and to simplify), one could say that the disappearance of the subject (as foundation of meaning) and the disappearance of the referent (as a principle of reality) are the major distinguishing marks of the postmodern. In these terms one might situate the theory of seduction and the challenges of the object, as you describe them in* Les Stratégies Fatales, *within the frame of the postmodern. But maybe the relationship is the inverse: is seduction itself, with its rules of play and raising of the stakes, a response and even a theoretical challenge to the so-called postmodern condition?*

I notice the importance in your recent work of an 'objective irony', in contrast to a subjective irony, which would seem inadequate to our thought. Could you give an example of this objective irony?

An example of objective irony: the electronic virus, the computer virus that has resulted in the recent panic in the whole field of data-processing. The measures of protection and control (soft bombs) inspiring a chain reaction of contamination and destabilization of information. I believe that the recent stock market crash has also had largely humorous effects in relation to 'real' economics and the law of value. It wasn't a question of a real catastrophe, but of an *ironic* catastrophe. The voting of the masses in the last French election, Aids itself perhaps (in regard to the naive ideology of sexual liberation) . . . the examples are countless. Our era, which is very impoverished in the number of instances of subjective irony (which tends everywhere to disappear), is on the other hand and, no doubt, for the same reason increasingly rich in phenomena of objective irony.

As for the incidence of seduction and fatal strategies in the postmodern, it is clear that they run counter to the postmodern lines of flight, the latter being characterized by the jamming interference of all finalities and the progressive polymerization of the subject, by fractalization and 'soft' indetermination, soft strategies, the administration of the absence of destiny and even of history. I oppose to it the complete contrary: the fatal as maximum outcome, as predestination of the object in its own universe, as raising the stakes and potentialization, as logic of extreme processes, as acceleration of the process of disappearance, all of which the postmodern is content to manage 'aesthetically' the residue.

JJ *In your latest books one notices a certain stylistic tendency, a manner of presentation, that is formulaic and repetitive in its syntactic form, which produces the effect of a very seductive transparency. Is the style a challenge to the reader, especially the French reader? Another tendency in these books is that you rarely cite other writers, except for Elias Canetti. Is he someone who has influenced you greatly?*

The progressive absence of references to authors or to the history of ideas is logical: the 'fatal' does not encumber itself with citations. Canetti is not really an exception, for it is not the ensemble of his work but fragments of it that have excited me. The style of the fragment, particularly since Nietzsche, has always stimulated me. It's writing that is non-dialectic, disruptive, indifferent to its origin and to its end, a literal transcription of objective irony that I believe I can read directly in the state of things itself. The fragment is like the nucleus of an ephemeral destiny of language, a fatal particle that shines an instant and then disappears. At the same time, it allows an instantaneous conversion of points of view, of humours and passions. Of course it's a challenge to the language, to the reader, to ideas themselves; it's also a challenge perhaps because at bottom it's a solution by facility, a 'subtle laziness' of writing (but the most difficult to attain).

JJ   *Currently in the US there's a kind of impatience regarding theory, a desire to return to history and historical research; yet at the same time a sense that everything has changed: a simple return to history is no longer possible, since history no longer exists in the classical sense (as defined in the nineteenth century). One vacillates therefore between theory and history. You have written that theory must be a challenge to the real. But the real can be a challenge to theory. Where are we now, in your view? And how can we get out from or escape this revolving door?*

It's true that everywhere today (and not just in the US) there is a resurgence of history, or rather of the demand for historicity, linked no doubt to the weak registration rate of factual history (there are more and more events, and less and less history). We are caught in a sort of gigantic, historical backwards accounting, an endless retrospective bookkeeping. This historicity is speculative and maniacal, and linked to the indefinite stocking of information. We are setting up artificial memories which can take the place of natural intelligence.

JJ   *In the Paris bookstores it's striking to see so many books on Heidegger and the whole Nazi question, the death camps and attempted extermination of the Jews. One would think that intellectuals are obsessed with the entire phenomenon. Is it an example of this return to history, but in a 'necro' mode?*

The quarrel around Heidegger has no philosophical meaning of its own; it's only symptomatic of the weakness of contemporary thought which, for lack of any new energy, returns obsessionally to its origins and the purity of its references, and painfully relives, at the end of the century, the primitive scene of the century's beginning. More generally, the Heidegger case is symptomatic of the collective revival which has taken hold of this society at the hour of its secular self-accounting: revival of fascism, Nazism, the extermination. Thus there is both the temptation to relive the primitive historical scene of the century, to whitewash the cadavers and to wipe out all debts, and at the same time the perverse fascination of a return to the sources of violence, the collective hallucination of the historical truth of evil. Our contemporary imagination must be weak indeed, our indifference to our own situation and to our own thought really great for us to have need of such a repressive thaumaturgy.

What does it matter whether one accuses Heidegger or tries to exonerate him for being a Nazi: everyone, on both sides, falls into the same trap, expending the little energy available in trials, griefs, justifications and historical verification. Self-defence of a philosophy squinting at the ambiguity of its masters (just as earlier one discovered that Marx was really a bourgeois and slept with his maid, or that Freud was really a paternal sexist); self-defence of a whole society which, for lack of being able to generate another history, has vowed to dwell endlessly on its previous history in order to prove its own existence, indeed its own crimes. But what does this proof really mean: only that *we disappeared*, politically and historically (and that's our problem), between 1940 and 1945. Just like the Armenians who exhaust themselves proving that they were massacred in 1917.

It is because philosophy, today, has disappeared (its problem is how to live out this state of disappearance) that it must prove that it was definitely compromised with Heidegger, or was rendered aphasic by Auschwitz. Just as there is no longer enough philosophy to found some relation between theory and practice, there is no longer enough history to inform a historical proof of what really happened. We tend to forget that our reality, including the tragic events of the past, has been swallowed up by the media. That means that it is too late to verify events and to understand them historically, for what characterizes our era and our *fin de siècle* is precisely the disappearance of the instruments of this intelligibility. It was necessary to understand history when there was still history. It was necessary to denounce (or defend) Heidegger when there was still time. A trial can only be instructive when the process is consecutive. Now it's too late, we're in another world. It's evident in the television production of 'Holocaust' or even in 'Shoah'. Those things will no longer be understood because notions as fundamental as responsibility, objective cause, the meaning (or non-sense) of history have disappeared or are in the process of disappearing. Effects of moral conscience or collective conscience are now entirely the effects of the media. We are now witnessing the therapeutic of obstinacy with which some try to resuscitate this conscience, and the little breath it still has left.

Auschwitz, the extermination camps, can't be expiated. There is no possible equivalent in punishment, and the unreality of punishment points up the unreality of the facts. We are living out something else entirely. What is happening collectively and confusedly through all the polemic about

Heidegger and the Nazis is the passage from the historic to the mythic, mass-media stage of all these events. And in this sense this mythic conversion is the only operation which has the power not to exonerate us morally but to absolve us phantasmatically of this original crime. But for that, for a crime to become mythic, its historic reality has to be put to an end. If not, all these things, fascism, the camps, extermination, having been and remaining historically insoluble for us, will have to be repeated eternally as a primitive scene. What is dangerous is not the fascist nostalgia but the pathological reactualization of a past in which everyone – defenders and accusers – is complicit in a collective hallucination that refers the whole era's absent imagination, in its play of violence and reality, to this period in a sort of compulsion to relive it and to feel a profound guilt for not having been there.

JJ   Here in France I've heard people speak of a return of French and European culture after a period of fascination with America. For example, many people love Wim Wenders' last film, 'Wings of Desire', precisely because, they say, it's a return to European concerns after a series of 'American' films. They applaud Wenders' interest in angels as a particularly European figure. Can there be an authentic return of European culture that would act against the 'mondialization' (or what used to be called the Americanization) of everything, or indeed has culture itself (as least in its more traditional meaning) become a form of 'mode retro'?

Personally I did not like 'Wings of Desire' (except for certain purely filmic sequences over Berlin). For me it's a beautiful example of a sentimental and metaphysical regression on the part of someone who has put his finger on the American 'desert' (by which I mean pure cinema) at the end of 'State of Things', the beginning of 'Paris, Texas', and in other sequences in his 'European' films. For exactly this 'American-ness', this extreme from of immanent and radiant lack of culture, this form that has become a worldwide effect, can be found everywhere, even if there is a particular poetic of the American tracking shot. For me the Wenders of 'Wings of Desire' is Felliniesque, with all this imagination dripping with European culture, the circus, the clowns, the angels, the ideal woman, the mirror. The best Wenders, by contrast, is like Antonioni, who himself was a European precursor, the only one no doubt, of the hyper-reality of passions and of landscapes. As the director of 'The Red Desert' and 'The Passenger' he advanced into the desert of significations and not into third-rate sexual and cultural theatricalizing like Fellini.

   Yes, there is something 'retro' in the whole evocation or resurrection of a 'European' culture, to the extent that it only serves today as the search for a lost identity (in the work of Europeans) or the search for the undiscoverable (in the work of Americans). Soon we will no longer have any sense of European culture except through the phantasms of people outside it. I remember that the first conference on European cultural identity was held at Venice, along the dead waters of a lagoon, and Borges came to give what turned out to be the only coherent discourse: he said he was the only European of the assembly.

JJ *In* Les Stratégies Fatales *you write that the US is a beautiful example of 'this immoral energy of transformation [directed] toward and against all systems of value. Despite [Americans'] morality, their puritanism, their obsession with virtue, their pragmatic idealism, everything there changes irresistibly according to an impulse which is not at all that of progress, linear by definition – no, the real motor is the abjection of free circulation. Asocial and still untamed today, resistant to every coherent project of society: everything is tested there, everything is paid for there, everything is made to have value there, everything fails there. Western music, various therapies, sexual "perversions", buildings in the east, the leaders, the gadgets, the artistic movements, all pass by in succession without stopping. And our cultural unconscious, profoundly nourished by culture and meaning, can howl before this spectacle. Nevertheless, it is there, in the immoral promiscuity of all the forms, of all the races, in the violent* spectacle *of change, that resides the success of a society and the sign of its vitality.'*

However, in America, *it's not the spectacle that interests you but the desert, the highways of the Southwest, the empty spaces. Do these two kinds of things go together: on one side the promiscuity of signs, on the other the primordial spaces not strongly marked by culture?*

Not only is there a profound and necessary relation between the immorality of the circulation of signs and the primitive scene of the deserts, but it's the same thing, and it's this correlation of two extremes, one of the immobile intemporality of the desert and the other of the ultra-mobility and ultra-modernity of the American scene, that establishes the absolute singularity of America. This is what has marked me profoundly, for the two seemed to me to come together in the same dazzling denial of culture (America as a 'primitive society'). The deserts, let's not forget, are the place of an extermination (including that of the Indians), the place of a disappearance of meaning (including that of nature). The metropoles, the megalopolises, along with the whole 'American way of life', they too are the place of a subtle extermination of man and the ends of man; their prodigious outgrowth, the exact inverse of the desert, is however just as much a subtle extermination of meaning. I love countries where there are these extreme poles (the contrary of Europe) and where these extremes meet.

JJ *President Reagan and his whole administration, his wife included, seem like an immense simulation. Even personally, Reagan is a simulacrum: before he was a Hollywood B-grade actor, now he looks like a living cadaver.*

The astonishing thing is that no one really cares when he lies to the press or makes incredible gaffes. Even more, he's been involved in many suspicious or illegal activities, like the Iran-Contra scandal. But basically no one in the US seems really upset; in fact, it's as if the exposé itself, as a genre of critical or investigative reporting, had suddenly become dépassé in the eighties. Everyone knows or suspects the worst but finally remains indifferent. One might even say that the very 'visibility' of Reagan and his suspect activities makes him invulnerable to criticism. Do you see here any confirmation of your own theories?

Indeed. Reagan is a sort of fantastic specimen of the obscene transparence of power and politics, and of its insignificance at the same time. It's as if everyone has become aware of the indifference of power to its own decisions, which is nothing but the indifference of the people themselves to their own representation, and thus to the whole representative system. This is accompanied by a demand all the greater for the spectacle of politics, with its scandals, morality trials, mass-media and show-biz effects. There is no longer anything but the energy of spectacle and of the simulacrum, but this is still not a negligible energy (every event is accompanied by the energy of its spectacle, for the actors themselves), and in this sense I would say that Reagan, in the obscenity of his smile, his gaffes, his false cancer (even if he really has it!), his good faith, his absolute lack of political imagination – because he is the exact and perfect reflection of a certain state of things – has become a historical A-grade actor. History itself and politics have fallen definitively to the B-grade level, a B-grade actor is the best placed for filling the role ...

JJ *Finally, there is much talk of the end of art, the end of philosophy, the end of the social. The end of the century is approaching, which will also be the end of the millennium. You have written that our destiny is the end of the end. How are we to think this end of the end?*

Where did I say that 'our destiny is the end of the end'? Well, it doesn't matter, since I believe it to be true. One of the forms of destiny is when the end is already there at the beginning. Predestination, if you like, or anticipation. Yet, when the end is already there at the beginning, it's the end of the end, if one can say such. We are living in this state of having anticipated in some way our own ends, of having anticipated the ends of man, of having already realized them, or even having already passed beyond them, through a sort of hypertelic (*hypertélique*) process in which we will have gone faster than our shadow (through a logic of the outgrowth of progress, of the political, of the social, indeed of the sexual), in which we will have passed as living beings into a sort of transpolitical, transsexual, transaesthetic state (which is not at all the eclectic and derisory state of postmodern indetermination, but a tragic state of a passing beyond our own finalities), and where in consequence it would no longer even be possible to live or confront our own end.

163

The end will longer even have the time to produce itself. It will escape us, and of course with it the feeling of our origin. There will be such an exponential acceleration of all effects, such an instantaneous realization of all effects (this is already the case in information and communication) that the future will no longer even have to take place. This is what I wanted to say in a somewhat paradoxical fashion in the essay 'The Year Two Thousand Will Not Take Place'. What we must fear is not the term date of the year 2000 (which is in itself a symbolic end); it is that this term date even has been rendered impossible or useless, like all the other symbolic term dates (death being the most beautiful of all). That would really be the end of the end . . . .

© 1989 John Johnston. Interview with Baudrillard, *Art Papers*, Jan.–Feb. 1989. Translated by John Johnston.

16

FRACTAL THEORY
Interview with Nicholas Zurbrugg

NZ *Perhaps I could begin by asking you about the widespread influence of your writing upon artists and art critics. Are you surprised by this reaction?*

Well yes, because in many respects aesthetics and art have never really entered into my area of research. My interest in the object has always been for the non-aesthetic object, the banal object, or the metaphysical object. I've never really been concerned with the aesthetic object. So yes, I was astonished by the enthusiasm with which artists took me up as a point of reference, along with all the terminology like simulacra, simulation, and so on. I was surprised because, first and foremost, simulation refers to a world without reference, from which all reference has disappeared. But on second thoughts, one might think of art criticism as something which tries to give a sense to works, while at the same time showing that they are beyond all interpretation. And in that respect I'm a kind of art critic who is not so much concerned with art, but who – in a certain way – transforms the real, or the hyper-real, into a sort of artwork. My relationship with the banal or the hyper-real is the same relationship that one might have with a work of art. I offer it the kind of visual, sensual, analytical attention that one could also bring to the work of art. So perhaps the thing that artists find interesting in my writings is not so much their aesthetic quality or their aesthetic analysis, as the process by which their analysis of simulation and the hyper-real gives a meaning to something which ought not to have any meaning. And in reality, this is what art does. Art gives a meaning or a sense of identity to something which is meaningless, which has no identity.

NZ *The problem here seems to be that many of those artists influenced by your writing appear to have quite contrary aims. My impression is that they're trying to create artworks without depth, without meaning, in a more or less cynical or negative spirit, so as to demonstrate that art no longer exists and can no longer hope to attain any profundity or aura.*

Yes, of course. But all the same, I think that some sort of misunderstanding has arisen here. What interests me in the theory of simulation – and remember, it's already quite old, ten or fifteen years old – is a sort of mutation, a sort of revolution, in the order of signs, in the order of appearance, and so on. So that the end of representation, the end of aesthetics, or of something like that, interests me as an intellectual event or drama – as something cerebral, metaphysical, and so forth. Whereas for the 'simulationist' artists in New York, it is taken for granted as something which they're happy to reproduce. For me, it was an event. For me, simulation was a sort of eruption.

It's for this reason that I have great admiration for Andy Warhol, but none at all for the current New York artists who simply reiterate and reproduce familiar modes of simulation. To assert that 'We're in a state of simulation' becomes meaningless, because at that point one enters a death-like state. The moment you believe that you're in a state of simulation you're no longer there. The misunderstanding here is the conversion of a theory like mine into a reference. Whereas there should never be any references.

NZ *Do you see your writings more like a catalyst, or as points of entry into something new?*

Well, yes – the idea of simulation should at very least signify something of a rupture or drama in the principle of reality, representation, and so on. It's wonderful when that happens, it's marvellous when there's some sort of eruption – there was a wonderful era of simulation. By contrast, once one dedicates oneself to legislating the order of simulation it's no longer interesting. My kind of theory is in many respects indefinable. It's not really an aesthetic, it's not a philosophy, it's not a sociology, it's a little volatile. Perhaps this corresponds to a certain kind of floating instability with more in common with the contemporary imagination than with any real philosophy. Possibly that explains why it is not someone like Derrida – who has had great academic success throughout American universities – why it is not so much his references of deconstruction and so forth that have been taken up by artists, as notions of simulation. Well, I don't know.

NZ *Could it be because your writings are more poetic? One of your early publications is the collection of poems,* L'Ange de Stuc. *Would it be fair to say that your writings are often quite poetic in spirit?*

Yes, it's true there's this other link with literature – with a less disciplinary language. It's true that my first writings were much closer in spirit to those of Artaud, Bataille, Rimbaud, and so on. I only began writing theory quite late, in my mid-thirties. And in reality, behind all my theoretical and analytical formulations, there are always traces of the aphorism, the anecdote and the fragment. One could call that poetry. I'm not quite sure if it corresponds to what you understand by poetry, but, certainly, the form of my language has broken open. There's another verbal element: a certain sense of dispersal, both in language and the discipline. This was never part of any particular programme, you understand, but perhaps there's an affinity there with some sort of aesthetic or artistic order.

NZ *Are there any particular writers or artists for whom you feel a special sympathy? I was thinking, for example, of certain similarities between your ideas and those of William Burroughs. Have you read his work?*

Yes, I've read his work, but I don't think there's any particular affinity. I'm not really an enthusiast for Burroughs and his circle.

NZ *What about Cage?*

No, no. I got to know his work quite late. I think they've had a much greater influence on people like Lyotard, who has really studied their work. For me the most important Americans were Pollock, Andy Warhol – whom I've always considered something of a master – and a number of others that I like a lot, but for whom I have no special affinity. I have rather a primitive knowledge of the fine arts, and I've deliberately maintained this slightly primitive attitude. I'm instinctively suspicious of everything which is aesthetic or part of culture as a whole. I'm something of a peasant or a barbarian at heart, and I do my best to stay that way. For example, when I'm asked to do something for television, I'm always more interested in the passive magic of its image, rather than the active magic of its production.

NZ *What do you mean by the image's 'passive magic'?*

I refer to that state in which one willingly remains beyond all questions of quality, as a pure perceiver of images for images' sake. When I watch television I'm not really concerned with its quality. I'm interested in a sort of travelling of pure images – a sort of fascination. I remain, as it were, at the level of fascination, rather than that of production, consciousness, quality and so on. So at this point there's a step that I haven't taken. I stay behind. I prefer to remain in this state of absorption.

NZ *To what extent do you think that this attitude has influenced your analysis of television and video? For example, in an interview that you gave for the French television programme* 'L'objet d'art à l'âge électronique' [*translated as Chapter 13 above*] *you propose that 'the screen ... makes everything circulate in one space, without depth, where all the objects must be able to follow one after the other without slowing down or stopping the circuit' [above, p. 147]. Do you really think that this is the case?*

Well, those who work with television and video may have another point of view. My point of view is that the screen, and everything that belongs to the order of the screen, be it video, television or whatever, no longer really belongs to the order of observation (*l'ordre du regard*). One's response to the image on the screen is not the aesthetic response of an observation characterized by distance, judgement and pleasure. It's something else. It's something extensive, something superficial. It's another game, another very fascinating game. When I'm in the realm of images, when I'm in the realm of the screen, when I'm in that kind of hyper-reality, I'm totally absorbed in that domain. If I'm in the domain of the profound, then I'm in literature – that's my job, after all. But when I'm watching the screen, I'm more or less a pure spectator.

NZ *So there's a difference between your position as a pure spectator, in front of the screen, and your position as an 'impure spectator', in front of the page?*

Yes – but there isn't simply a dialectic between an experiential response and an analytical response. On the one hand there's a kind of material that I know and can manipulate quite well – writing, literary forms, and so on. That's something with which I'm familiar, which I can judge. It's my domain. The other is something else. It's a foreign domain, and I want it to retain this foreign quality. I want to remain a foreigner there. For example, I take photographs, but not in terms of the photographic subject, or any vision of the world, etc. For me, a photograph is an expression of the pure object – it is the object which appears. I've no wish to impose myself as a subject in the world of images. I want the object to appear – not in a particularly aesthetic way but, on the contrary, perhaps even in a non-aesthetic way, as a purely objective object, an image seen more or less anthropologically.

So you see, I'm a very bad aesthetic analyst! And it's perhaps for that reason that I often have a more brutal reaction!

NZ *The ferocious theorist!*

That's right! Almost the terrorist!

NZ *Do you enjoy being a theoretical terrorist?*

Yes, I think it's a valid position – for the moment, I can't envisage any other. It's something of an inheritance from the Situationists, from Bataille, and so on. Even though things have changed and the problems are no longer exactly the same, I feel I've inherited something from that position – the savage tone and the subversive mentality. I'm too old to change, so I continue!

NZ *In your interview in* Marxism Today, *January 1989, you proposed that: 'It would be a very good idea to publicly sacrifice a postmodern philosopher.' [See above, p. 153.]*

Ah yes! I remember!

NZ *Would you be happy to offer yourself as the first of these sacrifices?*

Why not! Yes! If that could cause some sort of impact – although I don't really have any literal confidence in this kind of sacrificial ritual. But if it were capable of regenerating just a little subversive inspiration than that might help to change the general atmosphere here. The atmosphere here is so consensual, so conciliatory, so uniformly dialectical, that things are really difficult! For example, in an article that I recently wrote for *Libération* on the Rushdie–Khomeini affair, I defended its subversive potential. When all is said and done, I'd very much like to be the Rushdie of the left, and become unacceptable – by writing unacceptable things. But it didn't work! I sent this article to *Libération*, thinking that it would probably be rejected. But they accepted it all the same!

NZ *So your fate is to be published unconditionally!*

Yes – there's nothing one can do about it! And that is our real malediction – the fact that it is no longer possible to suffer from a sense of malediction. The whole Ayatollah business interested me in the sense that it upset this kind of consensus in rather a dramatic way. Although one probably shouldn't place too much hope in it.

NZ *Perhaps one could also claim that in a certain sense you have become the Ayatollah of postmodernism in its cynical or negative mode, insofar as it has become something of a commonplace to argue that this or that is dead, 'as Baudrillard has demonstrated'?*

Yes. Well, if the Ayatollah was basically defenceless in the global context, he had one symbolic weapon, the principle of evil, which was a very strong force, and which he used with great skill. Perhaps this concept is a little extreme, a little too moral and too close to negative theology. But all the same, I'm on the side of the principle of evil!

Admittedly, if I say that, it's very pretentious, because today it's virtually impossible to occupy this sort of position. All the same, I feel we are forced to work in that direction, because it is no longer possible to assume a purely critical position. We need to go beyond negative consciousness and negativity, in order to develop a worst-possible-scenario strategy (*une stratégie du pire*), given that a negative, dialectical strategy is no longer possible today. So one becomes a terrorist.

NZ *But if one adopts this strategy, doesn't one run the risk of becoming a retrospective terrorist – in the sense that it's well known that Tzara, Breton and the French Dadaists have already explored this path? And while this strategy obviously reacts against the present climate, perhaps its very emphasis upon the worst scenario possible prevents it from paying sufficient attention to new positive possibilities? Doesn't one run the risk of caricaturing things and judging them prematurely?*

There's the risk of virtually parodying things, certainly. But so far as positive solutions are concerned, there are already people working in that direction. So there's a division of labour. Almost everybody is working in that area – on positive solutions.

NZ *Well, I'm not so sure. My impression is that there are quite a number of artists who feel neglected, and who feel that the majority of critics are banal and without imagination. Like you then, these artists seem opposed to intellectual stagnation. Perhaps your work overlaps with theirs, in the sense that it provokes alternative initiatives?*

Yes, maybe, in the sense that there's a sacrificial strategy involving the principle of evil, the politics of the worst scenario possible, or the strategy of intellectual terrorism. Ultimately I don't believe in it. It is not the consequence of any particular faith, but simply an act of defiance, a game. But it seems to me to be the only enthralling game. At the same time, it's often an act of provocation. Perhaps the only thing one can do is to destabilize and provoke the world around us.

We shouldn't presume to *produce* positive solutions. In my opinion this isn't the intellectual's or the thinker's task. It's not our responsibility. It might occur, but it will only come about by reaction. I've the impression that if energy still exists, it is reactive, reactionary, repulsive. It needs to be provoked into action. One should not attempt to inaugurate positive solutions, because they will immediately be condemned – so they're virtually a waste of energy. In other words, one needs to make a kind of detour through the strategy of the worst scenario, through the paths of subversion. It's a slightly perverse calculation, perhaps. But in my opinion it's the only effective option – it's the only way that a philosopher or thinker can, as it were, become a terrorist. Of course, today, the real terrorists are not so much us, as the events around us. Situationist modes of radicalism have passed into things and into situations. Indeed, there's no need now for Situationism, Debord, and so on. In a sense, all that is out of date. The hyper-critical, radical, individual sensibility no longer exists. Events are the most radical things today. Everything which happens today is radical. There's a great wealth of radical events, and all one needs to do is to enter into its interplay. Nowadays, reality is radical. Reality is Situationist, not us!

NZ *But you'd still agree, wouldn't you, that the force of events can coexist with individual identity? You wouldn't wish to deny your own individuality?*

Of course not, because I'm still speaking!

NZ *So I'm not simply listening to the voice of events?*

No, it's not simply the voice of events! Yes, I agree – I may be halfway between a slightly false, slightly ambiguous position, and a more meaningful discourse which interprets things, and takes up a more definite position. But I don't consider this to be the best part of my discourse. One has to respect it, insofar as language itself demands some sort of collective intellectual consciousness and meaningful discourse. But in my opinion, the part which speaks most clearly is the form of one's language. That's why, without really intending to do so, I've elaborated my kind of aphoristic and fragmentary form. The form of my language is almost more important than what I have to say within it. Language has to be synchronous with the fragmentary nature of reality. With its viral, fractal quality. That's the essence of the thing! It's not a question of ideas – there are already too many ideas!

NZ *I'd be tempted to argue instead that this kind of fragmented form can be found everywhere, and that any of your disciples could parody this form rather boringly.*

Yes, but it has to fragment something. In that respect you need to have some sort of hard object in mind, awaiting fragmentation. If one creates fragmentation for fragmentation's sake, then that's mere simulationism. It's not Situationism, but simulationism. At that point there's an obvious danger. But that danger has always existed. One needs both to master meaning and then destroy it. But you must also destroy it. That's the main difference between my thought and the majority of so-called 'constructive' contemporary systems. They continue to be constructive. But rather than being constructive, or being purely destructive, one needs to follow the whole cycle through. One needs to accomplish the symbolic murder of all cultural meaning.

©1990 Nicholas Zurbrugg. Interview with Baudrillard, *Eyeline*, 11, August 1990. Translated by Nicholas Zurbrugg.

17

WRITING HAS ALWAYS GIVEN ME PLEASURE

Interview with *Le Journal des Psychologues*

You are known for your analysis of the object in the society called 'mass society'. Since 1968, in your book The System of Objects *you stress its role as a mask.*

It would be too much to talk about the mask of the object. From the beginning, objects obsessed me somewhat. This obsession was to do with finding the object: what is it? where is it? and to go across the interpretations of it that are given by the subject, whether at the psychological or the economic or the functional level. To go through the mirror and to see how it was with the object as a sign. That seemed to me to be the important thing, and it certainly took on a more dramatic appearance in terms of the revenge and the *'parti pris'* of the object. There is a reversal of the process. There is a semiology, Marxism, psychoanalysis, all of which I work with as everybody does, if I may say so, although in a somewhat contrary way. I reconstruct the object by using different techniques of interpretation, and at the same time these interpretations are put on trial, it is to take the logics which have been set in motion around the object, and to push them to the limit of their functioning and resolving them.

You were already proposing a critique of the technological society and its obsession with the continual advancement of 'progress' . . .

At the beginning the critique was a social, political, Marxist critique, a very extensive one. But the simulation in all these elements is a more advanced form than alienation. At least in my first books. It is true that that was to do with taking up a question, a critical position, perhaps a moralizing one. It was to do with the analysis of signs, as one of the advanced forms of alienation, in terms of a radical critique, and of the subversion of signs by signs. This was, to my mind, an essential period. So much that is stupid, naive and obvious was being written about consumption. To talk about it in terms of a differential and structural logic, of signs, was rather like effecting the same revolution as Marx did when, instead of talking about natural philosophy, about wealth and exchange, he talked in terms of production (but that

172

involved a theoretical revolution). Today the problem would rather be to do it in the area of communication because on that problem we are still at the same archaic stage as 1960 was for consumption and 1850 for production. You even talked of the 'cancer' of the object, a substitute for human relations, a shoring up of the series that strips the subjects of their differences, of their lived experience of time.

That is no longer valid. I don't repudiate it at all, but perhaps there are different levels at which questions might be approached and tackled. For me now it is not the problematic of alienation under any form whatever that interests me. I think that now the system has gone well beyond that.

Did your work prefigure your critique of the search for the same, for transparence?

The subject becomes an integrated circuit, a sort of convolutional system. It becomes self-referential, that is in effect its success. There has been this project of accomplishing the subject in a 'becoming subject of the world' in the process of being realized by means of computer techniques, by means of a total concentration in a sort of self-referential bubble called the subject. But it is not the subject of psychoanalysis, because that is no longer divided within itself, it has doubled back on itself. And here, one makes an unhappy departure from alienation. Thus, the problem also has changed considerably.

The idea of writing something is, of course, a sort of nefarious fatality. This isn't political denunciation, but there is a sort of inscription of fatality internal to this logic. All we who have made that radical critique of object-ivation, of alienation, we have all to an extent worked towards this frenzied self-subjectivation, which is all we have now, of all technology. It's the problematics of the clone.

So are we now in a logic of amalgam, of confusion?

And of expulsion. The transparence of evil, that's it: the expulsion, the exorcism of the other who no longer fits within the field. Does that mean that the deep logic is the reduction of the other, the definitive exoneration of the other?

A world where the subjects are normal?

Yes, where there are different irruptions of alterity. But I draw a distinction between difference and alterity. Difference is not the opposite of identifica-tion, on the contrary. It is diversification, it is the spectre of modality, you can see it everywhere, in fashion too. But it is in this spectre of differentia-tion that you find the iteration of the same, but not alterity. It is therefore an absolute distinction.

Can you clarify that, since you insist on the man/machine difference?

The idea of alterity is almost cultural and therefore indestructible. It is true we have lost it a little, but I don't want to treat it with nostalgia or melancholy. Therefore, from the very start, one is dealing with events which will bring about alterity, but which come from somewhere, which will no longer be pseudo-controlled events like those we have to deal with in our systems. It is the same for the subject, or subjectivity; it is achieved in difference, possibly in discrimination. The extreme logic of difference is in a certain way one of despair. Difference is to my mind without hope, which can only bolt into a sort of tetany, a sot of hysteria of difference. You can see this polarization explode, you can see it writhe. Meaning cannot break through precisely because, in this logic, meaning is difference. These differences are emptied of their content by today's systems, which put them in the shade because they are simplified, purely binary, digital.

You say that we have entered the world of indifference, and you give the example – since you were speaking just now about the digital aspect – of the minitel. Why speak to each other, when we manage to communicate so easily?

It is only vessels that communicate. It's machines that communicate, it's the medium that communicates. It is so easy to let the machines work, they are gigantic substitution systems. In integrated circuits there is no more need for the intervention of a subject. On the contrary, everything works best when the subject is shut out, excluded. Fundamentally, communication consists of networks, and in a network there is no longer any identifiable position of the subject.

You draw a distinction between two sorts of looking – when two people look at each other and when somebody looks at a screen.

Yes, for me the screen is the surface of communication *par excellence*, by definition; it is even the only surface of communication. The screen doesn't reflect, you don't *look* at a screen. Watching a screen is in a way all-absorbing. In principle, the screen plays the role of interface in communication, but the interface isn't a double surface. There is no other on the other side. Osmosis takes place at the level of this thin layer; there is no depth of sound, and thus no depth of meaning either, or contradiction. You can't see beyond the screen as opposed to the mirror. There is therefore not a beyond-the-screen. On the other side of a mirror you have your double. Beyond the screen it's the same; there is a redoubling of surfaces, which means that you no longer have that depth, the depth of the scene (if one understands by the word 'scene' everything that is distance, everything that allows judgement, pleasure, desire). With the screen, it seems that that culture, that symbolic, metaphorical space, is largely reabsorbed. There is no reflection, but refraction and, what's more, a mutual refraction of screens.

Is there an idea of fracture, the notion of a subject which breaks itself up on the message?

Yes, but it is not a rupture, a fracture, in the sense of transgression, in the dramatic sense of division, which would send us back to classical subjectivity. It is a division (demultiplication) of the subject, an aleatory proliferation, just as, more or less, the fractal line. It is the end of linearity, the end of finality, of the final perspective. And it is also the end of the origin, of the possibility of going back, in a linear fashion, to the origin. So it is the disappearance at the same time of the origin and of finality, a sort of random field, where the images of modern science operate fully. I think there is no discrepancy between the state that a certain scientific, micro-scientific conception has reached and the world as it functions.

Is there no defence against this promiscuity and perhaps this proliferation?

This is the whole problem of reversibility, that is to say, knowing whether all these processes which are in the logic of the system can have a reversible effect. Virulence, for example, could well come to have a destructive effect on the system: the system becomes vulnerable to its own logic. That is what fascinates me: it is no longer we, the subjects, who are leading a revolution against the system, by facing up to it, but a catastrophic principle, not in the apocalyptic but in the logical sense of the term, catastrophe as form. This reversible form means that systems bring about their own self-destruction. They are self-referential and self-destructive. You could see Aids as a sort of acceleration, as a way of thwarting this latent, global logic of the systems by a more rapid catastrophe, which causes, in a certain fashion, the appearance of antibodies. More precisely, Aids itself is the loss of antibodies, the loss of defences, but there is no denying that Aids acts as an antibody to the body social. It's a paradox which is unacceptable in moral terms, and which can, like all paradoxes, give rise to serious misunderstandings. All forms of virulence interest me in that sense – Aids but also electronic viruses. Not without a certain irony. It seems to me that in the reversibility of things there is an ironic form which is not the poetic, romantic irony of the nineteenth century. It is not a hope, it is not an alternative, but it does mean that a strange game is being played; we don't know the rules of this game. So indifference, in this case, isn't neutral ground, where nothing happens; it's strategic terrain now, where everything is upside down. And this reversal is passionate.

You have made a radical critique of this functional and antiseptic world where, eventually, man loses his defences because his universe offers no risks. So one should speak evil and think negatively in order to avoid catastrophe?

Yes, that seems to be the only recourse, at least in terms of immunity. You could give it a functional meaning, but I personally prefer to give it a metaphysical meaning. We must ourselves reinject some evil, or at least some decay, some virulence, and forge another type of discourse, perhaps to reawaken all that a bit. Otherwise, we risk total immersion. In certain sectors it has already happened. The political world, for instance, has become de-dramatized, undifferentiated, consensual and of lower intensity. It has become disaffected so that evil will creep back in of its own accord. Don't think I am making a political value judgement but Le Pen is a completely objective alarm signal, to be taken extremely seriously but not at all in the ideological mode. And everybody sets their face against doing that just when they find themselves smothered and choking in traditional politics.

And people play on that just as the terrorists do, as you demonstrate. They revive the past as a way of using symbols to leave a symbolic mark on society.

They play in an armchair, because society puts at their disposal everything they need. There is no need for them to do anything. There are groups of terrorists who do no more than claim responsibility for air-plane accidents, it's even no use doing that.

You say that 'the attack on the principle of reality is more important than aggression itself'. That is certainly going to give the psychologists something to think about.

Yes, something is wreaking its revenge. I don't know if it's the symbolic or even perhaps an illusion for a culture that has made the principle of reality the heart of its control over the world. Evil is another way of saying illusion, for the power of illusion, for the world as a total illusion. Almost all cultures, in my opinion, except ours, functioned on this principle of illusion. From that point of view I am almost Manichaean. We, of course, reject all this. On the contrary we try to realize the world, to escape from this total illusion which we find quite unbearable, by trying to materialize everthing. We have all sorts of systems to enable us to escape from this illusion of the world. And for a while this attempt worked very well, and there is no question of renouncing it, but now it's getting choked up. Have we gone too far in that direction, have we failed to keep the right balance? Art was a sort of balance between an illusion of the world and a different illusion. It was a way of working on illusion in order to control or counter the real illusion. That effort had fallen into indifference.

Have you moved from a Nietzschean mode of thought, through beyond Good and Evil, into a philosophy of the necessary inseparability of good and evil?

I have said that this inseparability of good and evil is, is what evil is. Good shows itself as the principle of the separability of good and evil. If you can't draw a distinction between these poles, then there are no more values, no more value judgements. Evil (which is also a *deliaison*, Freud's principle of Thanatos) is the same as the inseparability of good and evil, that is to say, the impossibility of distinguishing between them. That is vertiginous.

I read a lot of Nietzsche thirty years ago, but I haven't read him since. A lot of things have changed since Nietzsche's time, particularly the functioning of the totality of the system – which has passed beyond good and evil. This is no longer a question of a metaphysical utopia or a transmutation of values à la Nietzsche. The situation we have to deal with now is no longer a tragic one, but it is more despairing because we already have to deal with these transmuted values, as we touch the end of the logic of value.

Freud said: 'The object is born in hate.' That was also the theory of psychic development, adopted by the Kleinians. The mother is recognized as exterior because she is absent, she is hated from the moment she is recognized as exterior ...

I wouldn't put it like that, because I don't use these psychological terms now. I have tried to leave this terminology behind, because it seemed to me too sectarian, more and more shut in on itself the more it became sophisticated. But to go back to what you were saying, we could search for a principle of the production of the world. The world has been seduced in advance; seduction was there at the beginning. There is a precession of illusion, of seduction: you'll find this idea in numerous philosophies. Starting from that principle, it is clear, all the rest is an immense effort of correction, of setting things right in order to find a dialectic of continuity, of reference, of reason. But this effort arises in a field which is quite irreversible. One is always caught unawares by something which is formed in total 'irreason', which we might also call hate. There are two possible positions. Against the values of the good, of *liaison*, or love, one might take the other side, saying: no, what exists before anything else is evil. It is an almost Manichaean position, and it's rather simple. My position is based on reversibility, which seems to me to be the true symbolic form. It is more an indetermination or a total instabilty of principles, and it is evil because it contradicts all possibility of rebuilding the world.

At the level of the subject, to recognize a certain degree of negativity in oneself ...

Psychoanalysis is one field where that has a certain significance, in transference, in the mourning process . . . . But there comes a point at a certain moment, when one is led once again to a psychic constructivism, and there, once again, it doesn't work.

Group analysts often enlarge on the idea that the illusion of the good group is one that has got rid of evil. Evil is always somewhere else.

177

This old idea about the return of the repressed object is verified continually when one wants to see it. It is the principle of repression and of the return of the repressed object that characterizes our culture, which lives reversibility, this reversion, as something shameful (shameful in the unhappy sense, in denial) including in the edifice of psychoanalysis. The edifice is actively involved in this denegation, this repression. It envisages it, it theorizes it, but, in theorizing it, it gives it a validity, a coherence. We must be able to envisage that things do not work in terms of repression, of the hidden (without putting into play all that psychological work). And does not all this, in its complexity, become a sort of screen? But I don't want to get into mysticism.

To come back to your title, you talk about transparence. Must evil be transparent?

Usually I don't have any trouble with the titles of my books, but for this one I couldn't find a title; nothing, until the last moment. The title really means the transparition of evil; it is not the transparence of evil, to be truthful.

That means you are standing Rousseau's philosophy on its head. He said the good man was transparent. According to you, it's the bad man.

Yes, indeed, things do get turned upside down. One can try to exorcize evil, but its method of apparition is transparition. It is possible that there is a mode of 'apparition' (appearance) and of disparition (disappearance). This idea interests me not as a play on the mode of repression but a play which is of the order of appearance and I haven't yet developed these ideas. I hope to do so.

You have said that we ought to forget about the nineties, because they are useless, and use the time to rewrite the twentieth century.

I was being deliberately provocative. This decade is not a speeded-up film of the whole century. It's a patching-up and at the same time a wiping-out. This reversion, this retroaction of history is a funny kind of process. It isn't only a matter of gathering things together, of stocking them up, of memorizing – we do all that, of course – but also we rehabilitate everything that wasn't good.

You say: 'There is lots of memory and no ideas.'

Unfortunately, I think that's true, and also in the manner in which events are presented, a manner so suspect that it is no longer certain whether any history took place, whether we are talking about events in Eastern Europe or about Carpentras (and there the doubt remains about the facts themselves). I don't want to say that nothing is happening; on the contrary, more and more things are happening, but they make neither sense nor non-sense. It is my impression that we are in the process of restoring and dealing with a situation dominated by the deterrent of – thirty years of the deterrent have brought about this state of indifference to things, and it's an interminable process. Previously there was finality about things, even if it was all mythology or ideology, that's how we experienced them. History always had the dimension of this possible transcendence. But now we are in a state of interminable repetition. What is there now that can happen, what is there that can produce a real event? We are living a pure science fiction existence, and this is interesting. In indifference there is a situation that is not at all ordinary: an original situation in my opinion.

Reading your Cool Memories *I had the feeling that you were writing a chronicle of immediate experience.*

It was an attempt at fragmentation. A fragment implies that it is no longer a question of finding a central point, a point of interpretation. In this book I get near to this simple requirement: phenomena appear, we must grasp them as they appear, hardly giving them time to begin to make sense, then steer them immediately into the director of their disappearance.

You often bring up the idea of a break (coupure)*; there can't be knowledge, the work of thought, without break.*

People are always calling me 'melancholic, despairing, a purveyor of nothingness, a mortician'. I'm tired of it. It is such a misunderstanding, or deliberate distraction; on the contrary, writing has always given me pleasure. It's essential, it's not at all despairing, just the reverse. One recourse seems to me to have been open: never to abandon language but to guide it in the direction where it can still utter without having to signify, without letting go what's at stake, bringing illusion into play. In one sense, in this book, I stroll around in illusion, but not in reference, not in ideology.

And there are truth-facts (faits de vérité)*?*

There are some weak points in *Cool Memories* but I didn't write it to a formula. In certain places, with a bit of luck, I have chanced upon that rare and privileged thing: obviousness (*évidence*) rather than truth.

©1991 *Le Journal des Psychologues*. Interview with Jean Baudrillard, *Le Journal des Psychologues*, 1991. ©1993 Mike Gane and G. Salemohamed this English translation.

18

THIS BEER ISN'T A BEER
Interview with Anne Laurent

AL *Can you recover Brecht in your thought today?*

For me there was a golden age of the theatre: at the end of the fifties, when I used to go with Barthes. There was Brecht, Chinese opera, Piccolo ... Brecht has remained as a theoretician. But Brecht, like Nietzsche, became part of my practice. I will never read them again, but their influence remains with me in other ways. Their effectivity is like a watermark. A short time ago I had occasion to re-read *Dialogues d'Exiles* that I had translated in the sixties. And there I found two or three things that I used in my book on the Gulf War, and there I found Brecht who was not a dialectician in the Marxist, but in the paradoxical, sense. For instance, when Ziffel says: 'This beer isn't a beer, but that is compensated for by the fact that this cigar isn't a cigar either.' If the beer hadn't been beer and the cigar really had been a cigar, then there would have been a problem. That's rather like my book about the war, that the war wasn't a war, but that is compensated for by the fact that the news wasn't news either. If the first had been a war, but the second not news, there would have been a disequilibrium. And then there's the other quotation, later, when Kalle says: 'Where nothing is in its place, there's disorder. Where everything is in its place there's nothing there, and that's order.' And war too is just like that.

AL *And how did you personally get through that war?*

There was a certain vitality. Faced by an event like that war, which I see as a non-event, a product of deflation, you either share that depression, the depression of military violence, or you transform the non-war by writing. And that is how it happened with me during those six weeks. If the war doesn't go to extremes, then writing must be allowed to, one way or another. That is its role. It's a description of a society in a state of undifferentiation, of neutralization, implosion, entropy, etc. But it is obviously a transfiguration brought about by writing. It is writing's 'fatal strategy' to go to extremes. And that strategy is a happy one, vital. That is my vitality, and that is why I will always survive. I'm melancholic, but most certainly not depressive. You never see the form itself of what I write, so you search the content, an ideologized content. So really that produces a negative balance, and that's enough to depress anybody . . .

AL *It is possible to read the first chapter of* Capital *or Mauss's* The Gift *as if they were Zarathustra, as if they were poetry, that is to say, without any possibility of commentary or debate. But it is a marginal reading, and perhaps even a heretical one. After all, these writers were trying to be 'scientific', and were not trying to open the doors of a metaphysical world. But you yourself continue to be identified and interviewed as a sociologist, or at best as a philosopher. Now sociologists are serious people, and as for philosophers, well, they know everything. How should we see you?*

I don't like the word poetry, I don't read any poetry. But it is true that the essential function of the poetic act is to set things alight, to go to extremes. . . .

But my articles in *Libération* on the Gulf War also tried to say that politically that war didn't happen. It is also a statement of impotence in the face of the total political debility on both sides. There remains only that sort of policy one calls deterrence, that is to say a consensual system of mutual terror. And you can be sure I've got my feelings about that! But above all, what is really happening on the ground there, in Iraq, it's so vile. It's enough to drive you either into depression or into a rage! It arouses feelings you can neither describe nor transpose. What can a writer say about this heap of cowardice and stupidity? While the situation presented itself in abstract terms of war or no war, it was an exciting problem. But now we are in the real. If I fall into the real, I experience the same anger as the others, even if they've taken plenty of time to react, all these kind souls.

AL *In this non-real world that you are so fond of, people might nevertheless say that you were shutting yourself off in a writing prison – utopia.*

I suppose that there is an almost neurotic, obsessional mode. It's possible. There is also a system of intellectual self-defence. It must be pretty solid, because people for the most part don't manage to break into it. But they are in a state of fascination, they don't know what to make of it, and it depresses them. So they project; it is a depressive thought. Indeed, writing is the only political act that I am capable of. Barthes said that quite well. I am not a *littérateur*, and I can't get very far with writing considered as a sacralized act. I have always been a bit of a situationist. I am a man of actuality, of actualization.

AL *You have decided that you would not aim to write anything that would endure, that you prefer to write in an off-the-cuff way. You call that being an intellectual of no consequence. Are your resistances to the reification of the intellectual always pataphysical?*

181

Yes, almost biologically so, it's the only way to be immune. It's a symbolic defence. It would be like dying, to feel myself immersed in sentimental ideological pathos. I just can't breathe in this world of petitioning intellectuals. However, amongst them there are some I like quite well. The double page of *Libération* with the pros and cons of the Gulf War was for me a funeral plaque for thought in France. It was a way of trying to 'affect' the world with an affect that doesn't even pose the question of its reality or lack of reality, which continues to look for a 'moral conscience' . . . . As far as that's concerned, I am completely unconscious. The question of the intellectuals, moreover, is a bit of a joke. Obviously, I am one of them as far as life-style is concerned. But I don't feel myself to be an intellectual in the sense that, if there are three of them together, I flee. Moreover, I am no longer an intellectual in the sense that I no longer pretend to that privileged position of a person who has the right to know and to write. I just write for myself. It is true that people take a certain pride in being in that marginal and exceptional situation, therefore in a situation that also confers a privilege. But like the capital of capitalism, there is no more symbolic intellectual capital to manage, there are no more stocks. Radicality can no longer exist in our heads, it has passed into things, and it is in things that one can, at best, try to decode it, decypher it, to force it to appear, but not in terms of a subject of knowledge or as a subject of writing. I no longer take a position as intellectual. My work now is to make things appear or disappear.

AL *Like a conjuror.*

A bit. There is a form of conjuring, in the sense of the word. That is possibly where the break is. All these people, these 'intellectuals' – I say that without contempt – don't grasp the power of the illusion of things. They are all realists/socialists – the two terms are never very far away from each other – concerned with morals, as if all that still existed. They are all in a state of reanimation, rescuing, sending out SOS messages. And that is why I think they are all depressives. There are very few of them who really have a 'vision of the world', rather than merely a sort of defensive strategy for saving what's left.

AL *These intellectuals that you pillory so much, they 'engage in politics'. They imagine that it is possible to have power, to influence things with words and declarations. They are just the kind of people that Brecht laughs at.*

And in that sense there is a strange regression – I'm sorry if the word annoys people – which has been going on for at least ten years. Because that wasn't the atmosphere of the sixties and seventies.

AL *You describe democracy as the 'menopause of societies', and fascism as middle-aged lust* (démon de midi). *If we admit that the moments of highest*

significance in the twentieth century all have virile connotations – wars,
revolutions – and if we agree that, by definition, orgasms can only be achieved
in Dionysian societies, and not in Apollonian ones, then where will we place
the 'great gleam' of the sixties and seventies?

At that time, in terms of rivalry – not rivalry for recognition or prestige,
but theoretical rivalry – things exploded a little bit. Things were no longer
encased in that Marxist sounding-box, in which there was a sort of political
and historical complicity. One was no longer in the dialectic, in the sense
that the dialectic inevitably ends up in dialogue. We were in a 'form' where
the terms of the dialectical apparatus had exploded, each shooting off to an
extreme and forming opposite poles which short-circuited each other. The
dialectical process of synthesis became impossible. And that led to a greater
measure of freedom. Each pole required a sort of freedom, and rushed off
in some random direction. No more debate, no more discussions, no more
of the intellectual dialectic. But there was an increase in power, stemming
from the very disorder itself. But all that was dissipated during the eighties.

AL *That means that you can date the genetic catastrophe of capitalism from*
those years? You think that the coup de grâce *was given in the capitalism*
of the sixties and seventies, and that therefore those years have an impor-
tance which is more than historical, and which has to do with civilization itself?

It became clear that this revolution in the dialectic, in spite of a certain
continuity in utopian idealism, made it possible for each element to follow
its own trajectory, perhaps into the void, but much further. In fact, it was
a period of catastrophic transition. Ever since then we have been in a
depolarized, demagnetized situation. And we can't re-magnetize it. Unfortunately, we are even reversing the process. We are causing recurrence in
rehabilitating the old values. But I consider myself lucky to have participated
in the dialectical, Marxist, political phase, even if I was always somewhat
marginal to it all. I took part in historical events: the Algerian War, and May
1968. I was in the real, with all its affects, even if I adopted a position which
was a little more ironic than that of the others. Moreover, I didn't start to
think about it until afterwards, when things ceased to be tenable, when the
real and its logical organization was no longer viable.

So, is it possible to reinsert oneself into a place in another system? For
a long time I was preoccupied by the question of reversibility. That is something
you will find in my writings. You will find a catastrophism which, in a unilateral
sense, brings about the apocalypse. The end of the social, the end of history.
It's all absurd if one simply means 'There's no more': it's absurd. Whereas
the idea of reversibility, which is precisely the opposite of the dialectic (the
terms interchange, but they no longer produce third term, and thus no longer
give rise to any transcendence, etc.), is in itself, from the point of view of our
continuous, linear sense, an intellectual catastrophe, in a total immanence

183

of things. All my ideas on symbolic exchange, on seduction, have to do with this idea of reversibility. From the moment the two terms are no longer governed by a single given supersession, it is obvious that they can be attracted into another logic. The dialectic was perhaps a specific form. Reversibility is another. There is, in fact, as you say, a genetic mutation. And that game is something infinitely more interesting than the other. We haven't yet discovered the rules of this new game. They are symbolic and unconscious. We can't yet make sense of them and put them forward as a system.

AL *You say in books that the old roles are obsolete just as silent films gave way to the talkies. In* Cool Memories *you imagine new passions which are supposed to emerge: the objective risk, the ellipse, allegory, humour .... But you never get going on this new universe, you refuse to produce anything even if it is the merest embryo of a positive universe.*

I so wish I could cast off this yoke of *simulacres* and simulations which, incidentally, I have never treated as the last word of history, and with which I am truly fed up. I've heard these tunes too many times. I would like to do something on illusion as opposed to simulation, as something that works against simulation.

AL *The theatre against hysteria?*

You have said it. In other words, I would like to go back to the 'principle of evil' as I described it in *La Transparence du Mal*. I would like to go towards a sort of Manichaeism. If you start from the idea that the world is a total illusion, then life, thought, become absolutely unbearable. So you have to make every effort to materialize this world, realize it, in order to escape from this total illusion. And the 'realizing' of the world, through science and technology, is precisely what simulation is – the exorcism of the terror of illusion by the most sophisticated means of 'the realization of the world'. And so it's illusion against *simulacre*, the only system of defence that men have found to avoid confronting this illusion. This total illusion of the world, I don't know exactly where to place it. I am not going to 'recover' it, but I want to jettison this business of the *simulacre*. If there is a destiny, it is illusion, not in the unreal and timeless sense, but illusion as putting into play, as a great game, on which almost all cultures have played, except our own from the time when it adopted the 'making real' solution. The 'realization' of the world is a utopia which has lost in advance.

AL *Would you say that the reifying logic of market societies – and of their most highly developed form, capitalism – must have stemmed originally from a metaphysical terror, which could lead us into an even worse trap?*

The paradox of capitalism in so far as it is no longer a capitalism subject to contradiction, dialectical and therfore capable of revolution is that it swallows up the real more quickly than it manufactures it; and that leads us into completely aleatoric processes. The antibodies work much more quickly than the bodies ... I don't know if we can still call this system capitalism. Let us say it is rather an enormous piece of techno-realist machinery which exacerbates all the non-symbolic means of control over illusion, that is to say, which exacerbates its elimination. We must be frank and brutally honest: we live in extermination, in which physical exterminations are merely episodes. I treated the Gulf War in that way, as a process of the extermination of war, an operational stage set of a fact, war, which in former times, however, was above all a symbolic duel relationship. It was 'realized' by sophisticated technical means, and it doesn't take place, in the sense that there's no event.

AL *Does such a hypothesis imply a totalizing philosophy of the human genre and of its functioning?*

There is such a gigantic undertaking, which does in fact today have all the means of realizing itself at a world level. But at the same time there is a crazy resistance everywhere. Take Islam, for instance, where there are still some strong symbolic processes, but which exact a high price. Their value consists in their being irreducible. What place do they occupy? Are they only 'reactualizations', in which case they would still be part of the same system – or are they really resistances? I don't think I'm in a position to judge yet. Moreover, is this not all played out? Can reversibility seize control of systems? Is there going to be, at some time in the future, such a destabilization of all this undertaking by living elements, by cultures of illusions, by symbolic systems?

One could also imagine that the purpose of this undertaking was disappearance (*disparition*). Through this desperate momentum for realizing the world the human species will reveal itself in its most advanced form of natural selection, and will create the conditions for its own disappearance. This is a thought which doesn't necessarily have anything to do with negative catastrophism. Species are called upon to appear and to [have the power to] disappear. It's destiny, and I continue to believe in it, although not in the religious sense of the term. Who knows, this human species, which claims, in its extreme form of capitalism, to ensure its certain survival at the expense of other species, is perhaps in the process of staging its own disappearance. This isn't science fiction: these are philosophical hypotheses. On the question of Iran, it seemed to me that Foucault had the right idea. He had taken a risk, and he was severely criticized. It is not a question of siding with these movements. We ourselves are not really involved. But there is a challenge, a real antagonism, insoluble, immobilized in a sort of Manichaeism. Challenge and reversibility are non-dialectic forms, and I think I would tend to believe in their efficacity.

185

AL *You also mention, in another way, the notion of the cycle, a spiralling cycle. Do you remove that form from time and from history?*

The spiral is a form of escalation in power but in linear, in terms of accumulation or intensification. It is in fact a modulation, but it has no transcendence. The spiral always occupies the same space. It travels towards some confines of its own, I don't know what they are, and it can invert itself or come back .... We are in a topology that I haven't quite mastered yet, a non-Euclidian space of movement. It is possible that in such a space the forms that we consider the most contradictory can exist at the same time. And there is another thing that has always interested me – the question of inseparability – but for the moment it only exists as a metaphor. It is the fact that there is a separation between the elements of the system, but that there is still a sort of secret affinity between the particles which gives them a common destiny. This non-separability is a form of reversibility. Each particle can always exchange itself with an anti-particle. One is a bit in a dream. I like oriental thought, but I'm wary about using it as a reference point. There is a great danger in trying to link up with a continent that has its own system of rules. There might be a few connections, a few analogies, but no more.

AL *The nostalgia for the great primordial ocean, the viral desire, all that stops somewhere. In spite of appearances, you're not a great adventurer .... But to get back to utopia, in* America *you advance the hypothesis that America is a place where utopia was realized by a geographical displacement conservation of the ideas of the eighteenth century. Do you think that can be done again? Do you think that men are still capable of dreaming up an Elsewhere and an Otherwise and then firmly believing in it? Is a revolution of that kind imaginable? After all, in your mind, philosophy and science fiction aren't far apart ...*

It is no longer clear what sort of utopia is in question. Do people still make these imaginary projections in time and space? Geographical displacement to another planet has happened already, but what could utopia be? There is a caricature of this in the biosphere in southern Arizona. I visited it just before it was finished. Architecturally, it is very fine. Rather like the glass pyramid of the Louvre transported to the great desert of Arizona. It's quite splendid. Inside they have mocked up a synthesis of the planet, with its climates and everything. And there are eight people inside. It is a sort of utopia; they've got together everything you need for extra-terrestrial survival in space. It is all presented in a very optimistic way, as a sort of experimental science, but nevertheless it is placed under the sign of a possible catastrophe. It is completely artificial, there is nothing real in there. There are four men and four women for two years. I asked, 'And if they reproduced?' The contract gives them no right to reproduce. Nobody wants to know what would happen from the sexual point of view. Only the objective conditions have been created, and they are considered interesting. The subjective conditions have to do with supplies: Will they come or won't they: we'll see. There will certainly be accidents, termed experiments. I wouldn't have stayed there for two days. It's the 'exterminating angel', this experimental imprisonment! It's really looking for a catastrophe on the psychological plane .... Oh! They are broken in. They are quite prepared to undergo this neutralized white test. They are dressed in red cosmonaut's outfits. They are all scientists aged from 20 to 60 years old. Everything has been thoroughly expurgated. There are no scorpions in their desert, no germs. It doesn't make sense, even scientifically. It's a nonsense. It's more an ideological experiment. You can see that the way they've done it represents a sort of utopia. Now there is nothing at all of the space world imaginary inside there. When you come out you see that in the American town everything works on the same principle: recycling, prophylaxis, prevention, neutralization. But it really would be funny if they reproduced the usual anthropological schemes. For example, if one of them became the boss and subjugated the others. If things began to go wrong one would stop the experiment. If the real, being dramatic and passionate, intervened, it would cancel the set, which is like a precise and clean psychological organization. There would be nothing audacious. Just the defensive balance sheet of the species. All America is like that. It has changed since I wrote *America*. It now functions only on the mode of protectionism, survival ...

AL *So where are the possible germs of new utopias?*

I have lost my exaltation over America. It's become trivial *(banalisée)*. At first, the model had a strange and enigmatic side to it. Since then it seems to be lacking in inspiration, and it can't function simply on its own dynamic. It doesn't give me the impression of a model in ascendance, in transformation. It finds it is being overtaken by a non-realistic model such as the Japanese model. It's a unique model which escapes the universal, and therein lies its strength and its potential. The Western model wanted to be universal and could have been universal. The Japanese haven't even got words to express the universal. And it's not at the level of economic competition that all this operates. Between Japan and the rational and technicist West, there is an irreducible antagonism, quite unlike our antagonism with Islam. It is not a question of there being an alternative. Confronted with the hegemony of the Western model, which was not in question a few years ago, we now find some erratic models, which have found an aggressive singularity and their own sort of violence.

AL *Do you think that the old elements of magic thought could re-emerge, avoid regressive and obscurantist pitfalls and find new fecundity outside the strictly literary domain? The re-evaluation of the non-verbal (and the*

187

reappearance of the problematics of hypnosis) or the para-religious irrational
– are all these things regressions or possibilities?

In Brazil, for instance, there are some potentials which are certainly not 'developing' in the Western sense of the term. There magic thought takes sustenance from rationalist thought in some extraordinary confusion. It is not necessarily magic thought as we have analysed it that might arise. It's perhaps something totally different. It cannot be the same magic as that which existed before the rationalist surgical operation.

In France we find some signs of this temptation. As for hypnosis, the manner in which we approach it seems to be very much a part of the movement of general regression, which is also political (rehabilitate, reinstall, bring back things that have been forgotten and eliminated by the onward march of rationalism, etc.). We see no possibility of explosion there. If that is the way it is being presented, then I think Freud was right, it would be better to forget all about it. In terms of lost objects, I prefer seduction to hypnosis. Hypnosis seems to be turning back on itself. It only functions as a means of self-defence against psychoanalysis as it functions today, and that greatly limits its validity. I have sometimes had the idea of writing something about this *fin de siècle* as a process of turning back, a dusting-down of everything that had been rejected, not allowed to find its destiny.

AL *You are closer to young scientists than to old witch-doctors, are you?*

Yes, what I write has no scientific relevance, but it does at least venture into unexplored territory. You can of course reawaken and re-examine everything, and everything deserves this treatment. But I am very suspicious of this movement.

AL *Your last book about the Gulf War you laughingly called a 'novel'. What did you mean?*

I couldn't write a novel. Stories I tell all the time, but always in elliptical form I tell them quickly, finish them quickly, in an impatient sort of way. No, I said 'novel' because basically I invent the war for myself. It's the only thing to do. You can't, after all, call it realism! After the first article in *Libéra-tion, Les Presses de la Cité* invited me to go to the Gulf and cover the war. They were going to give me everything: money, documents, flights, etc. I live in the virtual. Send me into the real, and I don't know what to do. And, anyway, what more would I have seen? Those who went there saw nothing, only odds and ends.

AL *You would have done what you did with* America. *You would have gone off with a reading grid à la Godard, incorporated sufficient images, and then come back in fine form before you had even got your return ticket.*

You would have done as Roussel did in the hold of his ship: 'The coast of Africa is in sight? Right, we're off home!' You would have done it like the character did in Evelyn Waugh's Scoop. *You would have written spoof articles and they would have been perfectly accurate.*

That is exactly what I did by staying where I was and writing the book about the war. The ideas of *Presses de la Cité* were very funny. I imagined going there with somebody else, with Virilio. Dupont and Dupond. He would have done it better. He's more of the operational tactician. But he wouldn't have got any new ideas out of it, he had absolutely no need to go there either. No, I couldn't do it. Besides, I can't bear the idea of being a gringo. I no longer travel as a tourist, only when I'm commissioned to go somewhere, with a pretext. And in this case the pretext was really too artificial.

AL *Basically, any strictly sociological or political interpretation of your books over the last fifteen years is a misconception?*

There is a permanent misunderstanding. For instance, *America*, a book I wrote in a flash of inspiration. I loved that country. The book is talked about a lot, but there have been nothing but negative reactions. On the one hand, I've been treated like the last of the Europeans, stuffed with prejudices and self-satisfaction, who had understood nothing about the reality of America. It was impossible to correct that by saying that I was not presuming to judge American reality. My critics were reading the wrong book. On the other hand, some people read it another way. At the time when he was doing a number on America for his revue 'Le Messager Européen', Alain Finkielkraut read *America*, liked the book and asked me to write something. I discussed things with him for a bit, I realized that he too had completely misunderstood my book. He thought I was condemning the dehumanizing influence of America! He was blind to the rest. This didn't surprise me at all. He and I do look upon cultural matters from very different standpoints! But I really can't have anything to do with this sentimentalism, this pathos. In fact, *L'Échange Symbolique et la Mort* is the last book that inspired any confidence .... Everything I write is deemed brilliant, intelligent, but not serious. There has never been any real discussion about it. I don't claim to be tremendously serious, but there are nevertheless some philosophically serious things in my work! In the fine arts milieu I was received fairly well, but with such misunderstanding! I had to decline their reception and show that there was misapprehension.

So gradually desertification sets in. I like the desert, and it doesn't prevent me from continuing on my way. In other respects, I no longer have such need for intellectual debate. So it's not the problem of that strange reception that grieves me. On the other hand I sometimes find myself longing for that lightness of spirit we had in the sixties, when people had more zest for collective interventions and group action, even when they did it anonymously and secretly.

19

SUBLUNAR AND ATONAL LANDSCAPE

Interview with Nicole Czechowski

Today, the orgy is over. The United States, along with everybody else, faces a soft order of things, a soft world situation. It is the impotence of power.

To discover that one can exult in the liquidation of all culture and rejoice in the consecration of in-difference. I speak of the American deserts, and of the cities which are not cities ... no oases, no monuments; infinite panning shots over mineral landscapes and freeways. No desire: the desert.

(Baudrillard 1988a: 123)

Indifference is first of all the indifference of world without quality, of the more and more undifferentiated world which surrounds us, a world where people experience and talk about anything at all; and to talk about anything at all to somebody is to turn him into anybody at all. This indifference is the indifference of the desert in the negative sense. The indifference I'm talking about, the profound indifference of desire, is the desert of the soul, on which the absence of quality confers a strange quality. To make somebody indifferent to himself, to make him lose his own differences, to deprive him of his role as actor, to destabilize him in his position as a responsible subject ... that is a strategy.

NC *You talk of strategy, which would imply that there is a will to be indifferent.*

Yes, it's a strategy which implies certain attitudes .... You become indifferent to yourself in order better to plunge the others into a sort of stupefaction; that way they become vulnerable. Basically, it's a neutral and subtle form of seduction. But that isn't the strategy of a responsible, moral subject, it's the strategy of an object. You make yourself inert like an object, devoid of responses, thus gaining an enigmatic strength. But this absence of response has its consequences.

NC *If you accept the term 'victim', you can then talk of an executioner, or at least of an aggressor.*

'Victim' is a term that you used. As for me, nowhere have I used that word, because there is no victim, there are only things at stake. Everything is reversible. That's what Canetti said: what is the point of vengeance given the order of things, and the fact that everything is implicated and reversible, spontaneously, including the relationship of victim and executioner? So there is no point to bringing in some pretentious moral (ill) will or other.

NC *So you think we are presented with a situation with no victim, no aggressor and no aggression?*

Let us say in an indifferent world. Because it is the world, including our social universe, which has become objectively indifferent. In an indifferent world, the emergence of behaviour without quality, or more indifferent still, constitutes an event. It compels things to redistribute themselves, differently, and sometimes to produce exaggerated responses. Indifference is a game in the dull, serious sense of the term, where everybody occupies positions. I tend to think that indifference is a superior strategy to that of difference, less attached to consciousness and decision, a revenge of the object on the subject. In the world of power, it is those who affirmed their difference who were the masters, the rest being reduced to indifference. It is the revenge of this negative destiny.

NC *At the start my question was about forgiveness in the face of the aggression which, to my mind, constitutes indifference. In the situation that you outline the question of forgiveness and the unforgivable no longer arises.*

Forgiveness and the values of which you speak arise in a well-distributed value system, which is not the case in a system of indifference. The game of indifference is the game of indeterminateness. You can see it even in the sciences, this perversion of the object, of the micro-object.

NC *But once you start talking about perversion then it is no longer a question of indifference.*

Indifference can become a game in which you catch your opponent in the trap of difference, just as in perversion you catch your opponent in the trap of the law.

NC *Someone is caught in a trap and yet cannot be called a victim?*

Yes, it's contradictory, but that's the way it is. Because the trap of indifference, like that of illusion, works the same way for everybody: it is by definition undifferentiated. Thus, the object of science takes vengeance to the extent that, today, it has become totally elusive; it is nothing more than a configuration on the computer screen, so the privilege of the subject likewise becomes completely elusive. Science advances nevertheless, but in a zone of indifference, in an irreversible movement towards the indifferentiation of the subject and the object.

NC *Indifferences from science to law: in legal terms, failure to assist a person who is in danger is punishable by law. In such a case, in the eyes of the law, there is a victim.*

Within the framework of the law, certainly. The law institutionalizes a kind of minimal solidarity, but it's an epiphenomenon because 99 per cent of acts of indifference, even criminal ones, are invisible. The idea of forgiveness, like that of grace, presupposes a dual form, a transcendental reciprocity, which eludes us today. Our society only recognizes a calculus of responsibility, which often turns into a calculus of psychological probability. Why revive this out-worn form, or the word itself, which has become a mere polite expression?

NC *In individual terms, does the question of forgiveness arise?*

No, it is only posed in terms of the dual. Individually it is a question of psychology, there is no more forgiveness, all that is left are pulsations and motivations *ad infinitum*. It is psychology itself that has put an end to values .... Today I no longer have any criteria for judging whether the things people do are good or bad, and therefore possibly no criteria for forgiving them. I can no longer see things in terms of guilt. You have to have legitimacy in order to forgive. You have to have a statute, otherwise forgiveness is a miserabilist prejudice, like pity, compassion, solidarity. These values do not exist, they are hypocritical and pretentious. In the name of what can you claim solidarity with somebody, pardon him, help him? It is a hard thing to say, perhaps at the limit inhumane, but it seems to me to be more con-sistent to the state of things. We have no longer a hinter-world, no transcendence, no collectivity, no source from which to draw legitimacy. Therefore I can no longer forgive anybody. There is no longer any moral authority for that.

NC *So this question of forgiveness would only arise if we sought to reintroduce moral values by force?*

That is what we do when we try to restore them everywhere, to gently rehabilitate them. But these exalted moral values are only a second-hand scenario. In painting, abstract art had one dramatic outcome – the destruc-tion of the figure. Later we saw figurational art return, or the neo-figurational. But we will never again see figurational art as it was before the destruction of the figure. We mustn't confuse the two. If today we recreate so many differences, it simply proves that they were lost. I am trying to take cognizance of this decisive event, the loss of values. And rather than try to fill the gap I put my money on indifference. I do the same with my own life: I preserve the void in the hope of seeing another sort of event emerge from it. I prefer waiting that way to trying impatiently to resuscitate the dead. But although values have disappeared, the same is not true of forms; that is quite another matter. Forms govern, and in the valueless space you can see more clearly how forms work: seduction, challenge (indifference is an atonal form of challenge).

NC *There is something that belongs to the same family as indifference. It is contempt. Do you notice a sliding from one towards the other? There can be a contempt for a social class, even for a whole continent, for instance the attitudes of the West towards the African continent composed of both indifference and contempt?*

But what people don't understand is that it is the Africans who despise us! Their contempt for the way we live and die is much greater than ours for them! From the depths of their state of dispossession, they all know that they have values that we have lost; our Western world is bereft of values, unacceptable (*invivable*), and its objective is to colonize them in its own image, reducing them to zero degree value.

NC *So, according to you, values are incarnated today in those still traditional societies that we call the Third World?*

No, they incarnate nothing. They are the ironic, antithetical mirror of the disincarnation of the West. That is why Iran has been the object of such opprobrium. There we have to deal with the idea of value pushed to its highest degree in terms of total challenge. Whereas we are disappearing in terms of intensity of values, as the Spaniards disappeared in terms of faith and religion before the sacrificial rigour of the Aztecs. And that they couldn't forgive and still haven't. Just as we haven't forgiven Iran. The West will not rest until it has brought to heel all phenomena which, in their contours and their violence, show it up in all its banality, in all its indifferentiation.

NC *What are you expressing now, approval or regret?*

I am a Westerner. But my most cherished desire is to see the West lose face. In fact, I have three desires: to see the political class humiliated, and the West in general, and the Western satellites like Saddam Hussein in particular. I think that a domination exercised through a zero value has no force whatsoever, I can only deny it. I think of the example of Japan: there, one finds such an intensity, such bearing (*tenue*), such symbolic power, that before them one can only feel humiliated to be a Westerner. Those things are infinitely more precious than anything we can pit against them.

NC *But for the Japanese the concepts of forgiveness, vengeance, etc., are very much alive.*

Certainly, because their culture is secure. But they pay a price that we would never find acceptable.

NC *And you say that this is the system of values that you would like to see triumph over the degree zero of the West?*

Yes, a non-psychological, non-moral, non-ideological order. If I must valorize something, that is it. The peoples I've just been talking about are not victims. On the contrary, they enjoy unbelievable luck: they have reasons for living and dying that we no longer have. And that is the only thing that matters nowadays, not the resurgence of our petty provincial values ...

NC *Can you forgive the West for having become what it is?*

No, I do not forgive it! When I see one of our feeble-minded politicians on television I do not forgive him for being so feeble-minded, so cowardly, and above all for taking us for idiots, for saying any old rubbish, and for believing it himself. The only unforgivable thing, as Flaubert thought, is stupidity. Stupidity is unacceptable.

NC *You have slid from the unforgivable to the unacceptable.*

Yes, I see that in terms of an almost biological rejection.

NC *But you can consider forgiveness in biologial terms, in the sense that in order to survive or in order for a society to survive, it is necessary to pass through forgiveness in order to arrive at another stage.*

Yes, but in that case forgiveness becomes a very functional metabolism, just as forgetting, which has regenerative functions. It no longer has any symbolic value. Today forgiveness has turned into tolerance, the democratic virtue par excellence, a sort of ecology that shields all the differences, a sort of psychological demagogy. We tolerate everything, even the most unacceptable.

NC *You are now talking more and more about value.*

Perhaps the only strategy to adopt towards value when you no longer believe in it is to come back on the offensive, against those who claim to represent it, to expose their secret indifference to value. Value exists but I don't believe it, like Andy Warhol for art, like the agnostics for God. It's useless to add belief to all that. I'm not going to play the game of this false difference, these false values – and you who do play it without believing in it, if I can contribute to your disappearance, I will. Indifference is my form of terrorism. In another social context I would be a terrorist, but here we have to stick to talking.

NC *Indifference is a very passive sort of terrorism which does not endanger anything.*

Yes, because the risk I am taking is that of destabilizing myself, of creating a void to set off a chain reaction against the things I want to see fall. It is not a question of positive action of the revolutionary sort. All that I can do is to create this zone of strategic indifference, but it is not without danger because I'm putting my life at risk. It's a non-militant, non-spectacular sacrifice, the opposite of action as it is usually understood. It is more difficult to live it. It mustn't be interpreted as a passive or depressive *parti pris*, because there is not even a pale reflection of the will left. One is in a state of total transparence. The danger of this indifference is taking delight in it in a sort of perverse contemplation: the perverse benefit of indifference to one's own life.

But I have said enough about it. Now I would like to know what you are talking about.

NC *I am talking about the indifference which seems to me to be an attack, an invisible aggression, intangible although active and virulent, against which there is no defence, as opposed to contempt, which is more active. Indifference is a state, a state that kills silently. What I think is missing in what you say is the idea of suffering, of pain inflicted and therefore felt. And I ask myself, who is the indifferent person (somebody so wretched that he defends himself to the point of becoming indifferent?), and what is the position of the one who is the object of indifference, destabilized, reduced to nothing, victim of a negation to which he cannot react? And once you start talking about injuries, individual or collective, then the question of survival arises, but also the question of forgiveness.*

Forgive in order to survive . . . . Personally I prefer to change the world or change the air.

Part V

WHEN REALITY MERGES WITH THE IDEA . . .

20

BAUDRILLARD: THE INTERVIEW
Interview with Monique Arnaud and Mike Gane

MG *For a book of interviews it would be good to consider the question: what is an interview?*

That's a question of confidence!

It's an adventure – but a problematic one. There was a time when I was saturated with interviews and I couldn't even bear the thought of doing one. You had the impression that the people interviewing you either hadn't read your work, or just said anything, or they wanted to see you speak so as to stage-manage you, in fact stage-manage not the ideas but the person.

So I ended up refusing to give interviews except where the person interviewing was also actively involved in the interview as much as I was or where there was something at stake. There needs to be something at stake. Most of the time people want a facsimile; they want to worm information out of you. You feel like a hostage, you feel as if you've been taken hostage. In a sense this is a very modern situation, but not a funny one.

But from time to time it can become a kind of intellectual psycho-drama. Or it can be the kind of interview I had with Sylvere Lotringer, which was a very long, sustained interview. But for the most part interviews are part of an obligation one has. More and more they take the place of true intellectual polemic, that is of real discussion, something that should take place at a different level and which is negotiated bit by bit through the media, for example, or the press. This is how things are now most of the time. But that isn't judgement on all interviews.

It's possible, just the same, that the idea of doing a collection of interviews could make something different emerge, a different perspective. Then there is the fact that other people have had collections of their interviews published – Foucault, for example. But I know that Foucault and Derrida are very exacting in this respect. They re-read everything and sometimes they rewrite their interviews. I have never had the courage to do so, or the patience. There are interviews I gave that I felt went well, but when reading them afterwards I said – oh my God!

Interviews vary, but what is true is that there comes a moment when you feel saturated with them. It's also true that the media have a kind of *droit de cuissage*. Equally, they exercise a kind of blackmail over you. That is to say, if you say: 'No, I don't want to do any more interviews, I have done enough already. If you want to know more, read my books – it's all there and if you like what you find there *you* talk about it. Don't make me talk about what I have already written and which is better expressed in a written form.' If you do that, they get angry. I am referring to journalists. They get angry. It's as if you were betraying them, betraying a cause, as if one had a responsibility, or that they had the *droit de suite*. Here one is like a hostage, hostage to one's own work.

Yes, you are right to ask the question, because at first you think that interviews are a parallel, secondary activity which does not have very much importance, but necessary. Then you find that it is a parasitic activity, which substitutes itself in fact for the other, writing. It gives a superficial image, a screen behind which there is nothing. Therefore, I don't have any exalted view of the function of the interview.

MA *Is it then a form of voyeurism?*

There is a form of interview which forces you yourself to cut up what you have said into slices, into stereotypes. It's the same thing when you find yourself on the radio. On TV it's even worse. If you are in a TV studio in front of the camera, you have the impression of reading a text as newscasters do when they read from a prompter. It is as if you read out your own writing looking at the prompter in your own head! It's very unpleasant, one feels uni-dimensional and there is no real. That's television for you.

Radio can be much more interesting but even then, through all the paraphrases, commentaries, glosses, involved in such interviews, more and more I sense their parasitic aspects and something that's tedious about them. So I have cut back on giving such interviews. But journalists – I am only talking about the average journalist – don't want to over-exert themselves. In any case, they don't have the time to read books in order to form an opinion about them. A journalist is given an official assignment and naturally turns up like a mercenary and changes you into something like a mercenary in relation to your own work . . . well, it's a strange relationship you are made to develop with your own work.

MG *You have made a critique of the idea of pure human communication with its rationalist and humanist assumptions. Is an interview a dialogue?*

How can an interview avoid becoming a humanistic dialogue? Well, an interview is normally not even a dialogue, it's a monologue. You are like an automatic dispensing machine . . . . When you analyse this you are conscious that there isn't much that's human about it. It's a dehumanized type of exercise to the extent that the people involved in it themselves give it only an extremely relative value. They are not involved in it personally and truly. On the one side you have someone who is only doing his job, a more or less skilled professional. On the other, you have, let's say, an image so that the other person addresses himself to an image .... Generally, all they do is repeat. I have had to do interviews where I have had to respond to an article about me, one which appeared in a journal other than the one of the journalist interviewing me. That's how things are. Articles are exchanged and passed round. Journalists come to interview me but, in fact, they repeat what they have read elsewhere, which they then change to suit their own purposes. The result is that one doesn't get the feeling of going anywhere.

But there are exceptions. There are times, for instance, in conferences, when there are happy moments, moments which are new, giving one the impression of taking part in something original. Most of the time it's not like that at all.

Well, strictly speaking, it's true that having made a critique of this form of communication which is vaguely humanist, vaguely dialogic, I should refuse to do that kind of thing. I should refuse every bit of it, naturally. But, then, one cannot but enter into the game. Even then, there is still something human in this to the extent that there is some kind of challenge in it, an altercation, perhaps. You have to defend yourself. People don't come and ask you questions so as to illustrate your thoughts and so forth, they come to save their face. And there is, as far as you are concerned, a kind of aggression towards you. It's like a combat, a sort of duel. So, when you are on the radio, or on TV, it seems clear that the journalist plays his own game: he must win. At any rate, someone needs to win. Here there is at stake something that is perhaps not very humanistic but which can be experienced as a challenge. And in a sense it's better like that than when you are faced with having to give a paraphrase of things. As long as you take an interview in this spirit it's fine, but this is very rare. For the rest it must be said that there is no great human enthusiasm in interviews unless the interview is stage-managed and includes other players: for example, an interview with Lévi-Strauss on TV, which then resembles an oratorio. Here there is a form of spectacle. This is a completely different kind of thing, it's a show.

MG *Let's pass to your work itself. Can you clarify what you mean by the double spiral of the symbol and the sign? Is this idea still the best way to understand your work?*

There is throughout my work something which goes like this: there are always two forms in opposition to each other, the polar opposite of each other ... but there isn't any 'explanation' here. There is a type of development which is more like music or at any rate like a rhythm. There is a polarity, opposition between production and seduction, political economy and death, the fatal and the banal. You can't say, though, that this implies the existence of progress. I have never made any progress; I think everything is already there at the start but an interesting modulation takes place.

What is interesting is that notions and concepts criss-cross each other, slide into each other, melt into each other. There is a change of landscape and the light changes. The 'double spiral' is something of a metaphor *vis-à-vis* DNA, a game. One must not take it too seriously. It means there is no static opposition, no binary system that functions *ad libitum* from beginning to end. It means that polarization is in movement, in a rising upward curve. Just the same, one feels, and this could be an illusion, of course, that this is an upward movement in the sense that one is carried away by something, including the necessity inherent in the concepts themselves to destroy and reproduce themselves, or to regenerate themselves in other ways.

For me, concepts have always been something one can't control and manage. There is no political economy of concepts. It's necessary to destroy concepts, to finish them off. Of course, concepts regenerate themselves, they metamorphose themselves into something different. So there is at the same time a polarity, a polar intensity and a movement which comes from inside this 'machinery' – a machine which causes the appearance and disappearance of concepts. This, moreover, is what makes it different from 'research work', what involves 'thinking' as that word is traditionally understood, i.e. thinking as construction and a process of building up progressively towards an objective, which leads to a discovery. There is nothing to discover, there is a swirling (*tournoiement*) and regeneration. These have nothing to do with intellectual 'production' as such, but with appearance and disappearance. It may sound boastful, but what I try to describe about the content of ideas is also to be found in the same form in relation to the conception of evolution. This too is formulated according to a scenario of the same type.

Things appear, things disappear. You cannot say that there is an accumulation of things. But at the same time, it must be added that there is a relative accumulation and simultaneous disaccumulation. This is another type of game, quite different from the traditional intellectual one. It is probably the reason why there is so much hostility, so much resistance, because people wonder: 'What can we do with this?' They might say: 'Well, that's all very well, but what's it all about?' It's true that this eludes people because it's not a game about being productive or constructive. These concepts are there, but are they still really concepts? I don't know. This is a kind of 'theory-fiction' where things in the end simply fall apart by themselves. There is a kind of auto-destruction. There is not, in any case, a centralization of the arguments, of the referent. We have something less stable, less solid, but serious just the same. It is another kind of play. The culmination of all this is the fragment, and the form where what is most important is not even the content of each fragment but the void and the blank, spatially and temporally, between each fragment and the play of correspondence between such and such fragments.

Here we still have thought but can we still call it 'theory'? It is already something else. It is not 'literature' either. When I am told that I write 'literature' I reply that this isn't the case. Here there are still ideas and thoughts, but they develop in a different way. Their movement is accelerated, they appear and disappear more and more quickly. For a long time my books have contained stories, they were fragments, but they were still 'composed'. But my latest books have a form that can only be described as 'splintered'. Each fragment, each opuscule appears and disappears at the same time. But even then they echo each other. But this is the most extreme form and I am not sure that one can hold onto it. I am therefore tempted to write a 'real' book. But am I still able to do this?

MA *Can we turn to specific influences on these developments? What for you is the importance today of the work of writers like Nietzsche, Marx, Freud, Durkheim, Saussure, Mauss .... With whom do you find the greatest affinity?*

Well, things have changed over the years. Mauss was very important to start with but not a dominating influence. Freud and Marx were important as they were for everybody. Nietzsche, as far as I am concerned, is the one who has continued to be the most important, but not as a point of reference, as someone I would cite, but as a spirit (*esprit*), as a stimulus (*impulsion*), or inspiration. For me Nietzsche is a little exceptional. But there are people I haven't sought inspiration from. Durkheim I read when I used to do sociology. Mauss inspired me much more. Saussure, yes – but only one aspect of Saussure, the anagrams. As far as Saussure's general theory is concerned, I can't say that I am all that familiar with it. In short, most of the authors you mention have had an influence at one time or another.

I think I remain, when all is said and done, not faithful to Marx in so far as content is concerned – I don't believe in the 'death' of Marxist thought, I don't believe in this at all – it's something different, but all that has shifted onto another plane, continues to make a contribution even though it does not have the impact it once had politically.

Nietzsche still has a metaphysical or anti-metaphysical influence on me. This remains highly current and relevant. The problem for me has always been that I see my interlocutor from the perspective of what is current (I don't mean in the journalistic sense), according to the situation. I am always a bit of a situationist and for me Nietzsche is someone who is completely topical. Whereas the others, well, it's different. They retreat a little into the background or they drop out altogether. I have never had a problem with Nietzsche in that respect and, in fact, because there is no problem, I don't even refer to him. He exists and that's that.

There are also others who have influenced me. Sartre at one time, but he has faded out significantly. Roland Barthes is someone to whom I felt very close, such a similarity of position that a number of things he did I might have done myself, well, without wishing to compare my writing with his. Then, more and more, I find myself drawn towards authors like Canetti, etc. They are not necessarily theorists or philosophers.

So there is no regularity to this horizon. But the epicentre, one might say, is Nietzsche, not in the sense of a gravitational pull or as reference point. In a very nebulous sense.

MG *Are there people in the younger generation of French thinkers you admire?*

Oh, I don't really want to talk about that. Well, no, not really, there aren't. I'm afraid of saying this because I sound like an old warrior. The next generation will judge. I have had experience of this myself, from the other side, with Henri Lefebvre. Lefebvre helped me a lot. He taught me at university and so on. He thought I was a disciple and this in the end spoilt our relationship because I was not his disciple. He must have thought: well, fine, this young Baudrillard, he will do, etc. Well, he was wrong. So you see I do not want to make the same mistake with the next generation.

What remains the most interesting thing for me today is the thought of what people of my own generation, or people older than that, can do – Lyotard, Deleuze, etc. In contrast, I find Serres and Morin, for example, have done well what they set out to do but that they have become less interesting.

But all of us generally have to face the same problems, even people like Lyotard: this is the danger of repetition, the problem of entering into an era when there is no strong symbolic nourishment. We continue to do the same, and it's true for everyone, even for me. So the real problem is . . . well, it seems to me that the young intellectuals who have recently arrived on the scene partake a little of the insignificance of the situation in which they find themselves. They are the contemporaries of the situation. Our problem, by contrast, is different. It has to do with a certain nostalgia we have for the 'grande époque', because we find ourselves in an era which is less exalted.

The problem is deciding whether one continues or not. I was tempted to give up, to say: 'Well, I'll stop for a while and then we'll see . . .'. That was the Rimbaud in me. To say: 'That's it, I'm getting out of this. You are not forced to write all that, to write all your life.' I haven't ever felt that I was a writer, a thinker, a *littérateur*, either institutionally or subjectively.

So I must say that it is a tricky period we are living in and this being so it's difficult to judge the value of things, to be able to say this is good or this is bad. All we can do is to engage in simulated judgements. As for knowing what is original and what's not, it's difficult. But you can detect what are *simulacres* in the bad sense of the word, a rewriting, a revival. Nine-tenths of what passes off as belonging to the intellectual world are simply by-products. But then when you say this, you pat yourself on the back, and I don't like that. I won't labour the point.

I would like to add this. The problem with everything that is *simulacre* or simulation is that when one talks about things like that, one says things so one believes them, so one thinks they are true, but at the same time one expects to be contradicted. One hopes that reality will contradict you, and that something will come back and hit you in the face. One does not wait to be truly right either: it's always a kind of challenge to reality to react even violently. So the problem of discovering – because *simulacres* and simulations are everywhere – that everything that's written is *simulacre* or simulation, is something that no longer worries me. What I want to say is that simulations are everywhere, it's completely trivialized. So when what you said becomes true, when it is confirmed by everything around you – then suddenly you find you have nothing more to say. What you've said has become such an ordinary feature of life, it's become part of reality. It's not worth talking about it any more. The too great a pragmatic success of an idea effectively destroys it. Naturally, people talk about it, they will continue to do so, but as far as I am concerned I want to invent another game, to talk about something else.

You see, there is a problem here, and that's the reason why, when talking about interviews, my reply is somewhat pejorative, since interviews lead to the fossilization of ideas by making them appear definitive, whereas this is never my intention. When I say something in writing or otherwise, it's always a hypothesis, always a kind of provocation, a challenge, something given to play with, something that a fundamental opposition, like reality itself, will contest. When reality merges completely with the idea, it's the end, the game is over. This is the situation in which I find myself.

MA *Can we look at a fundamental opposition of this kind? Have you ever believed in a proletarian revolution? To what extent was Marx responsible for what happened in the USSR since 1917?*

I'm not sure you could call it a belief. I don't think it was an ideology. I have never in any case belonged to a party, or adhered to an idea as simple as that. Revolution, yes, but rather in the sense of a myth or utopian or imaginary dream. There is an enormous energy in all this. But as far as its concrete realization is concerned through a concrete class, etc., it's the same paradox as the realization of things. I don't believe in the 'realization' of things, neither where the proletariat is concerned nor for other things. I even think that the fact of passing into reality is a degeneration of things. It's always the end of a utopia. Well, when revolution takes place, naturally, it turns out to be not at all revolutionary. This is precisely what happened in the USSR. So Marx is not responsible. He is not the one who has brought all this about. True, he introduced the idea, which led to a practice, a historical practice, etc. So as a philosopher he is in a less paradoxical position, if I may put it like that, than something more direct and political. But one is not going to blame him for what happened afterwards, neither can one talk of deviation or of perversion. It's like that: there is a logic (*déchaînement*) of things. It is a little like chaos theory, where a very slight cause creates vastly unpredictable consequences, which may even be independent once the causes have disappeared. This is rather what has happened in Eastern Europe. Things have developed the way they have precisely because they were only a sort of special effect, ideological and bureaucratic, and therefore have crumbled so quickly and without any apparent cause either. It's a kind of effect that has just become dissipated. Whether this has anything to do with 'history' or not, I don't know. One could call into question the historical principle itself in these things. So Marx cannot be held responsible. But Marx was always in the 'orthodoxy' and not in the chaos of things.

Since Marx, nevertheless, the world has entered into a period of instability and chaos and, obviously, he couldn't foresee that. I think that looking for someone to blame is the worst thing to happen. It is a way of shifting the blame on to something or somebody else, or to try to find a cause or someone onto whom you can shift and get rid of the whole process, which is infinitely more complex. So it's best to avoid that kind of judgement. One can, in principle, assign responsibility, that goes without saying. But this is only possible in very precise political situations where one can see things clearly. In the field of ideas, and particularly where the connection of theory and practice is concerned, the connections are so uncertain and unresolved that we are perhaps dealing with a false problem. The question of responsibility immediately disappears to the extent that the very manner in which the relationship between theory and practice is formulated has never been precise. Even Althusser and others have never been able to define this field. This is doubtless because, at bottom, the very distinction is problematic and speculative, and serves only to rationalize things. Today one can no longer talk about distinctions of that kind, and this is why the problem of responsibility is difficult to determine, even in legal matters. We all know today the question of responsibility, punishment, is much more complex.

MG *Can we turn to the Gulf War? What do you think of the negotiations taking place now between the Palestinians and the Israelis?*

As far as the recent negotiations are concerned, I haven't followed them that closely. I don't know much about them, but I don't think they will succeed. It's only a vague thought, but I don't think the Israelis, or even the Palestinians or the Arabs, will enter into anything real. I don't know. I don't have a great deal of hope about all this. I don't think anybody has, to tell you the truth. Negotiations are held in much the same spirit. It is a kind of machinery, just as the war was a kind of machinery, with its gigantic montage, special effects, etc. It's so blatant that everybody can see through it. In short, I don't believe any of that. This war is a good example of a synthetic object (*objet de synthèse*). This does not mean that damage and destruction didn't take place. There is violence, but it is not real, it is virtual. There is also violence in the virtual but it's like a simulation model, a parachuted war that does not take place. It is already programmed and takes place as it was programmed. But this one didn't even go as planned because in the end it went completely off the rails. Therefore, there aren't even any consequences. Nothing has been solved. On the contrary, the situation is perhaps even worse than before. So it was a *simulacre* of a war, the only consequence of which is a *simulacre* of negotiation.

All this is part of the same process. But I don't think for a moment that this has elements of a concerted policy on the part of the Americans. There was no policy at all. It's clear that the Americans are all-powerful, militarily and otherwise, but politically they are feeble. Moreover, they understand nothing about the Islamic or the Arab world. Events take them completely by surprise. Then there is this: they talk about a 'new world order'. It's a kind of legislation, a kind of law-making at the world level, by a great power supposed to sort things out. We are all supposed to be going in this direction. Whereas it is more and more the reverse of this that is taking place. People fight each other on the ground (Yugoslavia, etc.). It is therefore obvious: the 'new world order' will come about but only in assemblies and speeches – in real life people will continue fighting each other. There will continue to be factions, splits, and all that, in reality, but there will be an attempt to cover this up under the so-called 'world order'.

But here I am expressing an opinion. I can't say that it's a political opinion. I am not a political analyst. But I do not believe all that much in the political. The so-called politicians do not have a better idea of what is going on than we have. They believe they are putting order into things and controlling them, but one finds that they are uncertain about things as much as anyone else. From time to time they succeed in producing effects, in Madrid, etc. But I am not a prophet, I am not engaged in political analysis. I am only trying to stand at a distance from all that and to refuse to take them seriously. My impression is that it is necessary to fill up (*remplir*) the political scene, the international scene, to weave the illusion that democracy is on the march and making progress. I can't say that I am very hopeful.

This interview is continued in 'Afterword: *Amor Fati*', on the next page.

© 1993 Mike Gane. Interview with M. Arnaud and M. Gane, November 1991. Translated by G. Salemohamed and M. Gane.

AFTERWORD
Amor Fati (a letter from Baudrillard)

Paris, le 11/12/91

Dear Mike Gane,

Thank you again for your visit.

I have really tried to complete our interview all alone in front of my cassette recorder, but I am truly incapable of recording anything in a tête-à-tête with a machine. It's perhaps characteristic. But I have overestimated my capabilities in this respect.

I hope that you can use the best part of our exchange of the other day. In any case I would hardly have been able, or perhaps not even keen, to answer some of the questions ... on Thatcher, Cresson, Le Pen ... on 'political' and 'ideological' questions. I have burnt my fingers over talking about the thoughts at the back of my mind (*arrière-pensées*), most often the secret ones. As for the questions on the East, a response can be extracted from the offprint from *Débat* – the current situation being nothing more than a worsening of the struggle (*accentuer le bras de fer*) between the decomposition of the East and the so-called New World Order.

What do you think of Gorbachov?

I like Gorbachov, he is still a man with a world strategic view, whereas the others are nothing more than provincial separatist dictators.

Have you ever envisaged writing something on Great Britain? How does a French intellectual view British culture?

I do not want to venture into giving my opinions about Great Britain. It strikes me as being a very strange country. Five hundred years after the discovery of America we now have to discover England.

Writers like Mailer and Vidal are very pessimistic about the future of America. Are you less pessimistic?

As far as America is concerned, the question is not one of pessimism. I am not a judge in political or economic matters (the specialists are not either).

208

My opinion does not count any more than that of others here. It is a question of knowing to what rules societies (particularly of the world type like America) will manage to function *beyond* the economic or the political. That is to say, the indistinction of values and in the confusion of genres. Perhaps Brazil, Italy and Japan are in this respect more advanced societies than America. Pessimism itself is something that only afflicts Western values and is itself part of Western values. It may be that the fateful date of the 500th anniversary marks the beginning of a reconquest of the Western world (by submersion, viral infiltration, demographic promiscuity) by all those whom it had subjugated to its law.

Can one really live in a state of amor fati *in the West today?*

Amor fati is not at all a principle of inertia and of passivity. 'Fatal strategies' consist as much in pushing the old world towards its destruction (*à sa perte*), to push that which wants to fall, said Nietzsche.

Nietzsche tried to transcend his ressentiment. *Have you overcome it in your life?*

One can never be sure to have gone beyond *ressentiment* (which is opposed correctly to fatality, to *amor fati*). What is certain is that the spectacle of generalized repenting in our societies, of their *ressentiment* in relation to their own liberation, to their own revolutions and conquests of modernity, of all this movement of reversal of history, is enough to put you off it for ever.

Has feminism influenced your thought in any way?

Feminism has never influenced me a great deal (except in an abreactive sense). It is truly one of the most advanced forms of *ressentiment*, which consists precisely in falling back on a demand for rights, 'legitimate' and legal recrimination, whereas what is really at stake is symbolic power. And women have never lacked symbolic power.

I stop my replies there. Perhaps we will have the opportunity of picking this all up again. I hope to discuss all this in person (but, as you are so right in saying, it's in the written form that I express most radically what I think) ... I wish you ... *de bonnes fêtes et un 'pessimism lucide'*!

Cordialement

JB

© 1993 Mike Gane. Translated by G. Salemohamed and M. Gane.

SUGGESTED FURTHER READING

Mike Gane, *Baudrillard: Critical and Fatal Theory*, London: Routledge, 1991.

Mike Gane, *Baudrillard's Bestiary. Baudrillard and Culture*, London: Routledge, 1991.

Douglas Kellner, *Jean Baudrillard. From Marxism to Post-Modernism and Beyond*, Cambridge: Polity, 1989.

Julian Pefanis, *Heterology and the Postmodern. Bataille, Baudrillard and Lyotard*, Durham and London: Duke University Press, 1991.

BIBLIOGRAPHY

This is a bibliography of Baudrillard's works in French and English only. It does not include other language translations or interviews.

1962–3a 'Uwe Johnson: La Frontière', in *Les Temps Modernes*, 1094–1107.
1962–3b 'Les Romans d'Italo Calvino', in *Les Temps Modernes*, 1728–34.
1962–3c 'La Proie des Flammes', in *Les Temps Modernes*, 1928–37.
1967a 'Compte rendu de Marshall McLuhan: Understanding Media', in *L'Homme et la Société*, No. 5, 227–30.
1967b L'Ephémère est sans Doubte', in *Utopie*, 1, May, 95–7.
1968 *Le Système des Objets*, Paris: Denoel.
1969a 'Le Ludique et le Policier', in *Utopie*, nos 2–3, 3–15.
1969b 'Le Practique Sociale de la Technique', in *Utopie*, nos 2–3, 147–55.
1969c 'La Morale des Objets. Fonction-Signe et Logique de Class', in *Communications*, 13, 23–50 (in 1972 and 1981b).
1969d 'La Genèse Idéologique des Besoins', in *Cahiers Internationaux de Sociologie*, July–Dec., 45–68 (in 1972 and 1981b).
1970 *La Société de Consommation*, Paris: Gallimard.
1972 *Pour une Critique de l'Economie Politique du Signe*, Paris: Gallimard (in translation 1981b).
1973 *Le Miroir de la Production*, Tournail: Casterman (in translation 1975a).
1975a *The Mirror of Production*, St Louis: Telos.
1975b 'Langages de Masse', in *Encyclopaedia Universalis*, Vol. 17, Organum, 394–7, Paris.
1976a *L'Echange Symbolique et la Mort*, Paris: Gallimard.
1976b 'Conversations à batons (in-) interrompus avec Jean Baudrillard', in *Dérive*, 5–6, 70–97.
1976c 'La Réalité dépasse l'Hyperrealism', in *Revue d'Esthétique*, 1, 139–48.
1976d 'L'Economie Politique des Signes', in *Traverses*, 1.
1976e 'Le Crépuscule des Signes', in *Traverses*, 2.
1976f 'La Mode ou la Feerie du Code', in *Traverses*, 3.
1976g 'Crash', in *Traverses*, 4, May, 24–9.
1977a *L'Effet Beaubourg: Implosion et Dissuasion*, Paris: Galilee (in translation 1982c).
1977b *Oublier Foucault*, Paris: Galilee (in translation 1987c).
1978a 'Territoire et Métamorphoses', in *Traverses*, 8.
1978b 'La Précession des Simulacres', in *Traverses*, 10, 3–37.
1978c 'Quand on Enlève Tout, Il ne Reste Rien', in *Traverses*, 11, 12–15.
1978d *L'Ange de Stuc*, Paris: Galilee.

1978e *A l'Ombre des Majorités silencieuses, ou la fin du Social*, Fontenay-sous-Bois: Cahiers d'Utopie (in translation 1983a).

1979a *De la Séduction*, Paris: Denoel-Gonthier (in translation 1990a).

1979b 'Rituel – Loi – Code', in M. Maffesoli and A. Bruston (eds) *Violence et Transgression*, Paris: Anthropos.

1979c 'Clone Story ou L'Enfant Prothèse', in *Traverses*, Nos 14/15, April 1979, 143–8.

1979d 'Holocaust', in *Cahiers du Cinéma*, No. 302, July–August, 72.

1979e 'L'Ecliptique du Sexe', in *Traverses*, 17, Nov., 2–30.

1980a 'La Fin de la Modernité ou L'Ere de la Simulation', in *Encyclopaedia Universalis*, 1980 Supplement, 8–17.

1980b 'Desert for Ever', in *Traverses*, No. 19, 54–8.

1980c *La Séduction* (with C. Ackerman, J.-Y. Bosseur and S. Collin), Paris: Aubier.

1981a *Simulacres et Simulation*, Paris: Galilee.

1981b *For a Critique of the Political Economy of the Sign*, St Louis: Telos (translation of 1972).

1981c 'Beyond the Unconscious: The Symbolic', in *Discourse*, 3, 60–87 (part translation of 1976a).

1981d 'La Cérémonie du Monde', in *Traverses*, 21–2, May, 27–36.

1981e 'Le Fatal ou L'Imminence Réversible', in *Traverses*, 23, Nov., 24–40.

1981f 'Fatality or Reversible Imminence: Beyond the Uncertainty Principle', in *Social Research*, 49, 2, 272–93 (translation of 1981e).

1982a 'Histoires de Voir: Jean Baudrillard' (interview), in *Cinématographe*, July–August, 39–46.

1982b 'Otage et Terreur: L'Echange Impossible', in *Traverses*, 25, June, 2–13.

1982c 'The Beaubourg Effect: Implosion and Deterrence', in *October*, 20, Spring, 3–13 (translation of 1977a).

1983a *In the Shadow of the Silent Majorities*, New York: Semiotext(e) (translation of 1978e).

1983b *Les Stratégies Fatales*, Paris: Grasset.

1983c 'What are you doing after the orgy?', in *Traverses*, 29, October, 2–15.

1983d 'Les Séductions de Baudrillard' (interview), in *Magazine Littéraire*, 193, March, 80–5.

1983e *Please Follow Me* (with Sophie Calle: Suite Venitienne), Paris: Editions de l'Etoile.

1983f *Simulations*, New York: Semiotext(e) (part translation of 1981a).

1983g 'De la Croissance à l'Excroissance', in *Débat*, 23, January.

1983h 'What are you doing after the orgy?', in *Artforum*, October, 42–6.

1983i 'Is Pop an Art of Consumption?', in *Tension*, 2, 33–5.

1983j 'The Ecstasy of Communication', in H. Foster (ed.) *The Anti-Aesthetic*, Port Townsend: Bay Press.

1983k 'Le crystal se venge: une interview avec Jean Baudrillard', in *Parachute*, June–August, 126–33.

1983l 'Nuclear Implosion', in *Impulse*, Spring–Summer, 9–13.

1983m 'Sur le "Look Generation "' (interview), in *Nouvel Observateur*, February, 18, 50.

1983n Interview, in *Psychologie*, May, 65–8.

1984a Interview, in *Cinéma 84*, January, 16–18.

1984b 'Astral America', in *Artforum*, September, 70–4.

1984c Interview: 'Game with Vestiges', in *On the Beach*, 5, Winter, 19–25.

1984d 'L'Enfant-Bulle', in *Traverses*, 32, Sept., 15–17.

1984–5a 'Intellectuals, Commitment, and Political Power', in *Thesis Eleven*, 10–11, 166–73.

1984–5b 'Une conversation avec Jean Baudrillard', in *UCLA French Studies*, 2–3, 1–22.

1985a *La Gauche Divine*, Paris: Grasset.

1985b 'The Masses: The Implosion of the Social in the Media', in *New Literary History*, 16, 3, 577–89.

1985c 'The Child in the Bubble', in *Impulse*, 11, 4, 13.

1985d 'L'an 2000 ne passera pas', in *Traverses*, 33–4, 8–16.

1985e 'Modernité', in *Encyclopaedia Universalis*, Vol. 10, 139–41.

1986a *Amérique*, Paris: Grasset (in translation 1988a).

1986b *Passage, Marite Bonnal: photos JB*, Paris: Galilee.

1986c 'Clone Boy', in *Z/G*, No. 11, 12–13.

1986d 'The realised utopia, America', in *French Review*, 60, 2–6.

1986e 'Le Puissance du Dégoût', in *Traverses*, 37, April, 4–13.

1986f 'L'Amérique comme Fiction', interview with J. Heric and Guy Scarpetta, in *Art Press*, 103, May, 40–2.

1986g 'Interview with Jean Baudrillard', by Catherine Francbin (translation by Nancy Blacke), in *Art Flash*, October–November.

1987a *L'Autre par lui-même*, Paris: Galilee (translation 1988c).

1987b *Cool Memories*, Paris: Galilee.

1987c *Forget Foucault*, New York: Semiotext(e) (translation of 1977b and includes interview 'Forget Baudrillard').

1987d *The Evil Demon of Images*, Annandale: Power Institute.

1987e 'When Bataille attacked the Metaphysical Principle of Economy', in *Canadian Journal of Political and Social Theory*, 11, 3, 57–62.

1987f 'Modernity', in *Canadian Journal of Political and Social Theory*, 11, 3, 63–73.

1987g 'The Year 2000 Has Already Happened', in *Body Invaders*, A. and M. Kroker (eds), London: Macmillan, 35–44.

1987h 'Le Xerox et l'Infinie', in *Traverses*, 44–5, 18–22.

1987i 'Nous sommes tous des Transsexuals', in *Libération*, 14 October, 4.

1987j 'Au-dela du Vrai et du Faux, ou le Malin génie de l'image', in *Cahiers Internationaux de Sociologie*, Vol. 82, 139–45.

1987k 'A perverse logic and drugs as exorcism', in *UNESCO Courier*, 7, 7–9.

1987l 'Amérique', in *Literary Review*, 30, 3, 475–82.

1987m 'Softly, Softly', in *New Statesman*, 113, 6 March, 44.

1987n 'USA 80s, and Desert Forever', in *Semiotexte USA*. New York: Autonomedia, pp. 47–60 and 135–7.

1988a *America*, London: Verso (translation of 1986a).

1988b *Jean Baudrillard. Selected Writings*, Cambridge: Polity.

1988c *The Ecstasy of Communication*, New York: Semiotext(e) (translation of 1987a).

1988d Interview 'Jean Baudrillard', in *Block*, 14, 8–10.

1988e *Please Follow Me* (with Sophie Calle: Suite Venitienne), Seattle: Bay Press (translation of 1983e).

1988f *Xerox to Infinity*, London: Touchepas (translation of 1987h).

1988g 'Necrospective autour de Martin Heidegger', in *Libération*, 27 January, 2.

1988h 'Eloge d'un Krach virtuel', in *Libération*, 2 March, 6.

1988i 'L'économie virale', in *Libération*, 9 November, 6.

1988j 'Hunting Nazis and Losing Reality', in *New Statesman*, 19 February, 16–17.

1988k Interview: 'America as Fiction', in *Eyeline*, 5, June, 24–5 (translation of 1986f).

1989a 'The Anorexic Ruins', in D. Kamper and C. Wulf (eds) *Looking Back on the*

End of the World, New York: Semiotext(e), 29–45.

1989b 'The End of Production', in *Polygraph*, 2/3, 5–29 (part translation of 1976a).

1989c 'Politics of Seduction', interview with Baudrillard, in *Marxism Today*, January, 54–5.

1989d 'Panic Crash!' In A. Kroker, M. Kroker and D. Cook (eds) *Panic Encyclopaedia*, London: Macmillan, 64–7.

1989e 'An Interview with Jean Baudrillard' (Judith Williamson), in *Block*, 15, 16–19.

1989f 'La Dépressurisation de l'Occident', in *Libération*, 14 March, 10.

1989g 'Décongelation de l'Est et fin de l'Histoire', in *Libération*, 15 December, 5.

1989h Interview with John Johnston, in *Art Papers*, Jan.–Feb., 4–7.

1990a *Seduction*, London: Macmillan (translation of 1979a).

1990b *La Transparence du Mal. Essai sur les Phénomènes Extrêmes*, Paris: Galilee.

1990c *Cool Memories*, London: Verso (translation of 1987b).

1990d *Cool Memories II*, Paris: Galilee.

1990e *Revenge of the Crystal. Selected Writings on the Modern Object and its Destiny, 1968–1983*, London: Pluto.

1990f 'Le Snobisme Machinal', in *Les Cahiers du Musée National d'Art Moderne*, Winter, 1990, 35–43.

1990g 'L'Hystéresie du Millénium', in *Débat*, No. 60, May–August, 65–73.

1990h *Andy Warhol: Silk Screens from the Sixties* (translated from English, P. Bauthinon). Schmirer-Mosel.

1990i *Fatal Strategies*, London: Pluto.

1990j 'L'Ere de Facticité', in L. Sfez and G. Coutlee (eds) *Technologies et Symboliques de la Communication*, Grenoble: Presses Univ. de Grenoble.

1990k 'Fractal Theory: Baudrillard and the Contemporary Arts', interview with N. Zurbrugg, in *Eyeline*, 11, August, 4–7.

1991a 'La Guerre du Golfe n'aura pas lieu', in *Libération*, 4 January, 5.

1991b 'The Reality Gulf', in the *Guardian*, 11 January, 25.

1991c 'La Guerre du Golfe a-t-elle vraiment lieu?' In *Libération*, 6 February, 10.

1991d 'La Guerre du Golfe n'a pas eu lieu', in *Libération*, 29 March, 6.

1991e *La Guerre du Golfe n'as pas eu Lieu*, Paris: Galilee.

1991f Interview with Brigitte Lievre, in *Le Journal des Psychologues*.

1991g Interview with Anne Laurent: 'Cette bière n'est pas une bière', in *Théâtre/Publique, Revue du Théâtre de Gennevilliers*, No. 100, July–August, 56–61.

1991h Interview with Nicole Czechowski: 'Paysage sublunaire et atonal', in *Le Pardon*, Editions Autrement, Paris.

1992a 'Transpolitics, Transsexuality, Transaesthetics', in *Jean Baudrillard*, W. Stearns and W. Chaloupka (eds), London: Macmillan, 9–26.

1992b 'Revolution and the End of Utopia', in *Jean Baudrillard*, W. Stearns and W. Chaloupka (eds), London: Macmillan, 233–42.

1992c 'Baudrillard Shrugs: a Seminar on Terrorism and the Media with Sylvere Lotringer and Jean Baudrillard' (edited by E. Johnson) in *Jean Baudrillard*, W. Stearns and W. Chaloupka (eds), London: Macmillan, 283–302.

(in press) 'Conversation with Jean Baudrillard', in *Conversations with French Philosophers*, by Florian Rotzer, Atlantic Highlands: Humanities Press International.

Translations from German into French

Weiss, P. (1964) *Pointe de Fuite*, Paris: Seuil.
Brecht, B. (1965) *Dialogues d'Exiles*, Paris: L'Arche.

BIBLIOGRAPHY

Weiss, P. (1965) *Marat/Sade*, Paris: Seuil.

Weiss, P. (1966) *L'Instruction*, Paris: Seuil.

Weiss, P. (1968) *Chante du Fantoche Lusitanien*, Paris: Seuil.

Weiss, P. (1968) *Discours sur la genèse et le déroulement de la très longue guerre de libération du Vietnam*, Paris: Ains.

Muhlmann, W. (1968) *Messianismes révolutionnaires du tiers monde*, Paris: Gallimard.

Marx, K. and Engels, F. (1971) *L'Idéologie Allemande* (translated with H. Auger, G. Badia and R. Cartelle), Paris: Editions Sociales.

NAME INDEX

SUBJECT INDEX

221